Monstrous Women and Ecofeminism in the Victorian Gothic, 1837–1871

ECOCRITICAL THEORY AND PRACTICE

Series Editor: Douglas A. Vakoch, METI

Advisory Board

Sinan Akilli, Cappadocia University, Turkey; Bruce Allen, Seisen University, Japan; Zélia Bora, Federal University of Paraíba, Brazil; Izabel Brandão, Federal University of Alagoas, Brazil; Byron Caminero-Santangelo, University of Kansas, USA; Chia-ju Chang, Brooklyn College, The City College of New York, USA; H. Louise Davis, Miami University, USA; Simão Farias Almeida, Federal University of Roraima, Brazil; George Handley, Brigham Young University, USA; Steven Hartman, Mälardalen University, Sweden; Isabel Hoving, Leiden University, The Netherlands; Idom Thomas Inyabri, University of Calabar, Nigeria; Serenella Iovino, University of Turin, Italy; Daniela Kato, Kyoto Institute of Technology, Japan; Petr Kopecký, University of Ostrava, Czech Republic; Julia Kuznetski, Tallinn University, Estonia; Bei Liu, Shandong Normal University, People's Republic of China; Serpil Oppermann, Cappadocia University, Turkey; John Ryan, University of New England, Australia; Christian Schmitt-Kilb, University of Rostock, Germany; Joshua Schuster, Western University, Canada; Heike Schwarz, University of Augsburg, Germany; Murali Sivaramakrishnan, Pondicherry University, India; Scott Slovic, University of Idaho, USA; Heather Sullivan, Trinity University, USA; David Taylor, Stony Brook University, USA; J. Etienne Terblanche, North-West University, South Africa; Cheng Xiangzhan, Shandong University, China; Hubert Zapf, University of Augsburg, Germany

Ecocritical Theory and Practice highlights innovative scholarship at the interface of literary/cultural studies and the environment, seeking to foster an ongoing dialogue between academics and environmental activists.

Recent Titles

Monstrous Women and Ecofeminism in the Victorian Gothic, 1837–1871, by Nicole C. Dittmer
Thomas Pynchon's Animal Tales: Fables for Ecocriticism, by Keita Hatooka
Ecopoetics of Reenchantment: Liminal Realism and Poetic Echoes of the Earth, by Bénédicte Meillon
Indian Feminist Ecocriticism, edited by Douglas A. Vakoch and Nicole Anae

Monstrous Women and Ecofeminism in the Victorian Gothic, 1837–1871

Nicole C. Dittmer

LEXINGTON BOOKS
Lanham • Boulder • New York • London

Published by Lexington Books
An imprint of The Rowman & Littlefield Publishing Group, Inc.
4501 Forbes Boulevard, Suite 200, Lanham, Maryland 20706
www.rowman.com

86-90 Paul Street, London EC2A 4NE

Copyright © 2023 by The Rowman & Littlefield Publishing Group, Inc.

All rights reserved. No part of this book may be reproduced in any form or by any electronic or mechanical means, including information storage and retrieval systems, without written permission from the publisher, except by a reviewer who may quote passages in a review.

British Library Cataloguing in Publication Information Available

Library of Congress Cataloging-in-Publication Data Available

ISBN: 978-1-66690-079-8 (cloth)
ISBN: 978-1-66690-080-4 (electronic)
ISBN: 978-1-66690-081-1 (pbk.)

This is dedicated to all my fellow "monsters" who overcame their conflicts, and for those who will.

Contents

Acknowledgments ix

Introduction 1

Chapter One: Social Behavior and "Domesticated" Women 23

Chapter Two: Forbidden Desire, Mental Degradation, and Nature: Repression of Gothic Madwomen 55

Chapter Three: Neglect, Rage, and Reaction: Female Criminality and the Victorian Gothic 99

Chapter Four: Monstrous Transformations and Victorian She-Wolves 141

Conclusion 183

Appendix 187

References 207

Index 217

About the Author 227

Acknowledgments

I would like to express my deepest gratitude to Dr. Chloé Germaine and Dr. Emma Liggins, who offered never-ending support and advice throughout this journey. Their extensive knowledge in both theoretical material and Victorian content has been invaluable. Without their unwavering belief in my work, especially at those times when I had none, this monograph may have ended up in the trash bin instead of at Lexington Books.

This book would not have been possible without the support of my best friend and husband, Rob. I extend a special thank-you for your enduring emotional and mental support throughout this extensive journey. Thank you for the time spent invested in me and my work. Without your patience and encouragement, this would not have been successful. Words cannot express my true gratitude.

Introduction

> Rarely is a woman wicked, but when she is, she surpasses the man.
> —Cesare Lombroso and William Ferrero 1895, 124

THE MONSTROUS JOURNEY OF VICTORIAN GOTHIC WOMEN

When you think of the term "monstrosity," where do your thoughts take you? What images appear in your mind? Are these pictures of specific monsters? What time period are they from? Are these figures gendered? What are the reasons for their monstrous status? Reflect on these questions, or don't and continue your exploration into the causation of Victorian Gothic monsters.

Offering a new perspective on female monstrosity in the nineteenth century, this journey will explore a domain of the Victorian Gothic unfrequented by popular scholarship. Engaging with behavioral, medical, and cultural texts from the period, I explore the ongoing discourses that perpetuate dichotomies of women's identities in the early-to-mid-Victorian period. Female instability and degenerative biological functions became a notable source for discursive conversation as a result of evolutionary theory and reproductivity. Propagating the fear that women were capable of corrupting society, such gender-specific rhetoric warned of their destructive tendencies due to their inherent connection to nature. Thereby, nature became a female phenomenon for patriarchal institutions to redefine and control. Bound by the biased beliefs of an authoritative society, women, and their instincts, were quarantined within boundaries of repression and gender ideologies. Without the possibility for agency or independence, women's rejection of conformity resulted in depictions of what society designated as monstrous. Consequently, labeled as transgressive she-monsters, these immured women presented in gothic fiction as madwomen, criminals, and she-wolves, seek to destroy or escape patriarchal confines, suggesting that madness, death, and exile are better than repression.

Women and nature, both historically supposed as intertwined, were considered wild, uncontrollable, and dominated by excess passions, emotions, and desires. This excess of emotions, and what was identified as contradictions, "emanated from within" and presented a monstrous female figuration that society was "powerless to control" (Botting 2014, 8). Regarding the treatment of women during the early-to-mid Victorian period, truer words could not be spoken. Regulated by institutional discourses that aligned female nature as inherent and chaotic, as Fred Botting's above quote dictates, women were faced with the forced prescription as man's helpmeet to ensure authoritative control. Faced with a rigid moral structure of forces as essentialism and biological reductionism, women were confined within a constructed role of domesticator and procreator dictated by institutional rhetoric. Those who failed to restrain themselves and behave according to social stipulations, or refused such confinement of these boundaries, found their situation as one of "monstrous" status that necessitated force and control. These "rare" women, as suggested by criminologists Cesare Lombroso and William Ferrero (1895, 124), were considered "wicked" and proclaimed as corruptive by Victorian society. These rare and wicked women who struggled to gain agency, although rejected by early-to-mid-Victorian society as problematic, were celebrated in literature of the period. Exhibited as hysterics, criminals, and in the obscure occurrence, she-wolves, these transgressive women found homes within the pages of nineteenth-century publications such as those from popular gothic novels to the more ephemeral penny bloods and dreadfuls.[1]

While there is an array of scholarship about the many facets of monstrosities, this work offers a new perspective for these unfortunate figures, one that has not been previously examined. The following content highlights unexplored perspectives of female monstrosity within the Gothic during the early-to-mid-Victorian period. Focusing on uncelebrated penny bloods and dreadfuls alongside canonical literature, there is an intricate exchange about transgressive ontologies and psychosomatic exhibitions between these commonly disassociated narratives. Juxtaposing ephemeral texts by such writers as George W. M. Reynolds, George MacDonald, and James Rymer, with high literary works by Mary Elizabeth Braddon, Charlotte Brontë, and Emily Brontë through a monistic lens, a previously ignored intertextual dialogue about monstrous women as unfragmented entities is exposed. Engaging with the philosophical and scientific theories of monism, new materialism, psychoanalysis, ecocriticism, and neurology, these intersectional concepts call attention to material-semiotic figurations of monstrosities that oppose dualistic conceptions of subjectivity. Since such transgressive she-monsters in the Gothic are material *and* semiotic figurations, they are informed by the entanglement of both material conditions and immaterial rhetoric, culture and nature, human and nonhuman. These women, then, maintain an informative relationship to nature and demonstrate how they are not fragmented pieces of the space, but substantial partners attempting to reclaim their inherent instincts and agency.

NEW MONSTROSITIES: AN OVERVIEW

While the concepts of repression and monstrosity proliferate through gothic scholarship, nothing in this way has been done before. Joining together all-but-forgotten texts with established canonical literature between the years 1837 and 1871, this work evaluates monstrous women as monistic figurations of ambiguity and agency. When analyzing psychosomatic behavior of these women, Western thought often adopts a Cartesian Dualist perspective, conceived of two independently interacting factors: immaterial mind and material body. Disrupting this dualistic approach and aligning with the sixteenth-century philosopher Benedict de Spinoza's (1667/2014, n.p.) theory that "nothing can take place in the body without being perceived by the mind," the following content emphasizes the unified effects of the mind and the body. By integrating monism into studies of the Victorian Gothic, the discussion of transgressive ontologies and monstrosity bridges a necessary void that traditionally defragments women into independent minds *and* bodies. The first chapter, then, begins with the historical medical and cultural literature that positions women into sublimated roles of femininity, creating a foundation for subsequent chapters. Interjecting such theoretical approaches as psychoanalysis, neurology, and ecocriticism, forced repression of natural instincts and transgressions into conscious psychosomatic rejections of confining boundaries is exposed.

In the Gothic, transgression occurs between the binaries of mind *and* body, and nature *and* culture, thereby underpinning an adoption of monism for female monstrosity. By tasking she-monsters as monistic material-semiotic figurations, they are exposed embodiments of Nature's *conatus*, or drive, thus prioritizing natural desires and instinctual traits over cultural identities. Therefore, it takes a new materialist approach and locates these women at the center of both culture *and* nature by arguing that all things have agency and that humans are derived from, not masters of, nature. Likening ambiguous she-monsters to Eugenia DeLamotte's (1990, 22) spatial model, these figurations embody identity transgressions where "the physical and metaphorical boundaries that one ordinarily depends on prove unstable, elusive, ineffective, nonexistent." Contrasting the hysterical behavior of Catherine Earnshaw, Bertha Mason, and Agatha Jeffreys, with the criminality of Mrs. Lovett, Linda Mowbray, and "Lucy" Audley, alongside the wildness of Christina, Nisida of Riverola, and the young woman, a previously ignored connection is created between the transgressive boundaries of nature, wildness, and monstrosity in gothic literature. Intertwining material feminisms complicates the figurations of these women by suggesting that the psychosomatic exhibitions are merely bodily mapped expressions of their desires to return to nature. All of these monstrous women, inextricably bound to nature by their instincts, reject social repression and present stages of mind-body reactions through such exhibitions of hysteria, criminality, and lycanthropy. Demonstrating that the Gothic is in conversation with early-to-mid-Victorian medical institutions and discourses, these novels respond to social fears of women's connection to the natural self. Perceived as both icons of morality and sources of feral reproductivity, these women embody this binary conflict between culture and nature. These characters, then, maneuver within the Gothic to expose the repressive consequences of Victorian ideals on inherent connections to nature.

All of the chosen narratives are in conversation with early-to-mid-Victorian medical discourses and are connected to the restriction and social concerns about female nature. Such texts about aggressive female behavior, as Elaine Showalter (1993, 31) insists, invert "a potent symbolism of gothic spaces and images." In the Gothic, women typically find themselves filled with emotional distress, stripped of agency, and facing a life-or-death decision. While heroines occasionally find positive resolution to their tumultuous experiences, the unfortunate individuals in the texts discussed herein, do not. These women struggle with the restriction of prescribed roles, repression of their sexual instincts, and a desire to return to their natural selves. Despite the quantity of criticisms available for the selected canonical novels, there has been little research into the individual psychosomatic agencies of these characters in relation to nature. Further investigating the ecoGothic in terms of ecophobia and the instability of the environment (i.e., weather), a connection between these gothic figurations and fear of catastrophic weather events are established. Therefore, women face psychological imprisonment within social confines and use their connections with nature to express repressed emotions. These canonical and ephemeral narratives of the early-to-mid-Victorian period demonstrate mind-body figurations of female monstrosity as a result of psychological repression, biological reductionism, and a forced disassociation from nature.

The common theme, then, for the following project focuses on the repression of women's primal instincts, conscious psychological, and physiological conflicts in Victorian Gothic fiction. Psychoanalysis, as Juliet Mitchell (1974,

231) argues, functions as a method for "understanding and challenging the repression of women." It is from this perspective that constricting behavioral boundaries of patriarchal society and the repercussions involved is explored. Furthermore, it is this psychosomatic monism that demonstrates the relationship between psychology and neurobiology through figurations of female monstrosity as affectations that influence neurochemical processes and promote conscious responses that create reactive psychosomatic disjunctions in the women of gothic fiction. The development of the consciousness is a result of biological processes located in the brain and the neurological system. Informed by environmental and internal influences, neurons create a mapping structure appropriate for survival, thus resulting in a conscious reconstruction of both behavior and identity. Without ceding to a reductionist interpretation that would emphasize mechanistic causality, I propose a unified substance that is both mind and body, whereas a reductionist would say there is nothing but the material form. The mind is only neurons firing and subjective consciousness, or any mental causation, is not permitted. Thereby, utilizing a Spinozian approach to analyze women in the Gothic, the gap is bridged between mind and body because monism allows for both mental causation (desire/*conatus*) embedded within the body, or instantiated within the body, since both are one substance.

The selected novels, for example, feature women who struggle with the dominating binds of gendered restriction. Female characters within these texts succumb to overwhelming innate desires and fall into what has been institutionally categorized as hysteria, criminality, or general monstrosity. Since the individual's identity is contingent on the communication between its segments, not solely on the independent parts, each of these figurations function as monistic ailments. These illnesses unify the immaterial mind with the material body and contradict the Cartesian dualism often inscribed in Victorian Gothic literature. For example, hysterical disorders, or mind-body rejections of behavioral constructs, as they were categorized by medical institutions are a result of instinctual and self-repression. That is to say, the sublimation of natural instincts forced upon women by social systems which divide the mind from body and self from nature. Indeed, nature is, then, a necessary aspect of women's monistic agency. Exploited by cultural, medical, and social discourses, nature is treated as a malignancy that corrupts female ontologies. Both current and early-to-mid-Victorian contemporaneous medical theories, provide recognition of female sexuality and discuss how its suppression through institutional intervention arises from biological fears. Originating as innate inclinations, female affections are diagnosed as psychological aberrations resulting in material corruptions and psychosomatic exhibitions. It is through this exposition of Victorian medicine and modern sciences that sexuality became defined as a pathologically inherent illness that affects both the mind and body.

The Monster Within the Woman: Gothic Sexuality

Female ontologies and the presentation of conventional behavior were essential for social assimilation. This period emphasized the restriction of female moral behaviors and strictly repressed sexual, or aggressive, tendencies in middle-and upper-class women.[2] Driven by an institutional context, fixated on the biological reduction of female identities to reproductivity and sexual miscreance, the Victorian Gothic engages with gender issues that explore the enigmatic and supposed dangerous side of individuals. Indeed, social concerns were brought about by behaviors outside of the normative, therefore rigid restrictions were imposed. Utilizing this popular mode since the mid-eighteenth century, the Gothic, according to Carol Margaret Davison (2012, 124), has been used to "interrogate" the cultural, legal, and scientific roles about gender identities and relationships. Whereas the Gothic is used to explore deviations from the Victorian traditions in a safe space, it also serves as a metric for social tensions and is an appropriate form to navigate the repression of female identity. Any rejection of conventional gender ideologies created unrest and anxiety in the fragile middle-class and aristocratic social and domestic structures. While aiming to construct ideologies and rehabilitate women into epitomes of morality, antithetical ontologies were constructed for those who refused to conform. As an ongoing source of unease, female sexuality impacted the stability of the conventional societal structure. This ability to construct authentic identities is difficult because female sexuality and form is enigmatic and complex. Therefore, women in the early-to-mid-Victorian period were aligned with the gendered designation of femininity as a form of social identity and behavioral restriction.

The ideology of womanhood that prescribed roles of domestic wives and mothers led to the social vilification and regulation of their carnal nature. It is through this pathologization and psychology of the period that essentialism typically operated as a reductive materialism that paradoxically positioned women in a dualist logic. By which is meant that Victorian discourses maintained that women were merely procreative beings, thereby minimizing their identities to non-agentic forms driven by their reproductive biology. Visiting such medical texts and theories of evolution from the period, in relation to notions of the material/immaterial, gives a different perspective on female wildness. Indeed, to psychiatrists, physicians, and pseudo-scientists, women necessitated restriction under guidelines to limit their expression of natural instincts. Identified as disparate from men, women were segregated as "angels" or "whores" to alleviate concerns over social authority. These dichotomous identities of fragile subjects and monstrous women both inform and are informed by gothic fiction. From a Bakhtinian approach, Jaqueline Howard (1994, 16) claims that the Gothic, as a genre, constructs its novels from the "literary and non-literary." It utilizes and recontextualizes information from popular discourses and reimagines it into novelizations about the fragmentation of beings. The heteroglossia of the genre occurs through its incorporation of discourses and institutional content derived from medical, cultural, and theological, therefore the Gothic is an amalgamation of institutional languages. In its array of intermingled rhetoric, it creates a conversation used to traverse the negative contradictions that separate Victorian women's identities into binaries of mind *and* body and exhibits consequences of female repression through monstrous figurations.

These boundaries are reflective of socially derived stereotypes with women classified as sexual predators or vulnerable victims. Gothic literature not only perpetuates these two models for transcendence of stereotypical boundaries but uses them to blur definitive lines and create new identities. Women are figured as mothers, objects of passion, and monsters all defined by their dichotomous biology as either a villain or a victim. Whereas the villain is a figuration of danger, ensconced by beauty and desire, the victim is often portrayed as the fragile and incapable woman. These dual identities of women possess characteristics necessary to act as either socially acceptable damsels in distress, or as sinfully deviant creatures who reject the boundaries of civilized society. Thereby, female attributes were not founded upon the anxieties of women's sexuality but upon the fragile male ego and their waning control over a degenerating social structure. Victorian literature, medicine, and social theory, as Sally Shuttleworth (1994, 16) notes, used a "shared vocabulary" between medical and scientific rhetoric that dynamically shifted as beliefs changed. Therefore, female promiscuity was targeted as a scapegoat that threatened to contaminate the fragile class structure, and also jeopardized the safety and security of men's power and authority. Purposefully correlating women's behavior into the angel/whore dichotomy, these discourses promoted the ideals of self-regulation through fears of degeneration and ostracization. As it will be explained in chapter 1, institutional rhetoric promoted the ideal virtuous womanhood while denouncing the unwanted, and dangerous, aspect of women's behavior.

Women's sexuality, and their reproductive functions, became the foundation for many afflictions and abnormal behaviors, resulting in such behaviors as criminality or hysteria, as it is explained further in chapters 2 and 3. Although the seminal works by Josef Breuer and Sigmund Freud (1895, 3) on hysteria were not published until the *fin-de-siècle* period, this disorder was under investigation during the early-to-mid-Victorian period. Feeding into Breuer and Freud's later theory that sexuality has a significant role in the pathology of hysteria as a psychosomatic element, earlier theorists such as Thomas Laycock (1812–1876) and Robert Brudenell Carter (1828–1918) also recognize female sexuality as a key concept in women's ailments. Uncontrollable sexuality linked to excess, or repression, created psychological reactions determined by physiological irritants of female reproductive systems. Sexual repression, as postulated by these medical experts of the period, informed the central argument of hysteria, by which Breuer and Freud (1895) suggest that the hysteric demonstrates such an exhibition due to the excess of sexual instinct and the individual's repression to achieve social normalization. Building on research from the early-to-mid-Victorian period, later theories centralized female sexuality and repression of instincts as the genesis of hysteria. Through this implication of unstable sexuality, women's minds and bodies were transformed into objects for medical observation and cultural discourse. Concentrating on cultural texts from the earlier period, the ground for Freudianism and its subsequent incorporation into the Gothic is revealed both as a theme and a critical approach. This denaturalizes, then, Freudian readings of the Gothic, and gothic women, by exposing the social, medical contexts of the preceding period and the way these contexts were already mediated by material-semiotic gothic figurations that both inscribe and call into question ideas about female sexuality that are crystalized and become normative in later theories.

Female proclivities and their natural instincts were causes for concern in the patriarchal social structure during the early-to-mid-Victorian era. Women were treated as erratic creatures motivated by carnal instincts and were suspected as threatening to the prosperity of society. Authoritative males demonstrated enmity toward female sexuality therefore popular discourse professed it as a socially threatening, abnormal, and an uncivilized characteristic of women. For example, John Ruskin (1865, 13) insists that the "best" women are those that are submissive and only gain attention or recognition through the satisfaction of their husbands and education of their children. This fear of female instincts and their potential for corruption exhibited itself in the figuration of monstrosities in the Gothic. These threats of nineteenth-century degeneration, as Botting posits, were not primarily centered on familial or city constructs per se, but on the threat of sexual or criminal tendencies that arose from these areas. The Gothic, then, as paralleled with gender-specific discourses of the Victorian era, offers social perspectives and a scientific rationale that focus on female nature and identifies it as the origin of the threat. Institutional discourses about human nature and inherent sexuality promoted dangerous assumptions about the corruptive, and corrupting, nature of women and their impact on a fragile social structure. In this case, the threat of the degeneration of an androcentric social structure was perceived as a potential outcome of the natural inclinations of women, therefore society necessitated categorization for behavioral regulation. It is through this fearful institutional rhetoric that gothic literature responds to the reductive discourse of the period and identifies how transgressive female identities and repression of natural instincts, and their figurations are both informed by, and a response to, social institutions.

Ontological Transgressions and Monstrous Expressions

The Gothic is, put simply, a literary mode of comprised contradictions based upon the discursive reality of the period in which it was created. Gothic fiction, a space commonly constructed from oppositions and ambiguity, allows the reflection of cultural anxieties through the expression of non-narrative female ontologies. Ellen Moers's (1976) seminal study on the Female Gothic establishes that this subgenre allows expression of the deepest and darkest fears confined within the structure of the female form. In the early-to-mid-Victorian period, Victorian Gothic magnifies society's perspective of gender identities. It joins the cultural discourse to reflect and exaggerate patriarchal fears by projecting women as beings of materiality, chaos, and irrationality. Expanding upon Moers's theory, Sandra Gilbert and Susan Gubar (1979, 3) argue that monstrous, or mad, figures are representations of the female author's anxiety—"a double" and an escape. Women are viewed as objects of danger and lust therefore the Gothic provides a space that allows female characters freedom from obstructive boundaries enforced by patriarchal principles and discourses. These polarities elaborate such distinctions between male and female roles, emphasize the repression of women's socially prescribed roles, and promote the concepts of morality and immorality that men project onto women. Indeed, while the Gothic is a space for female expression, it is also used to highlight, contradict, and destroy immuring borders. Therefore, the Gothic is not used as a mode of escapism but as a form of protest presented through boundary and behavioral transgressions.

Transgression is then utilized as a method to reinforce the virtue, social conventions, and values. Therefore, by crossing, ignoring, or blurring limits, it reinstates the necessity for policing and redefinition of these boundaries. This common motif, while acting as a reminder to restrict behaviors, also signifies the "excess and ambivalence" of gothic figurations (Botting 2014, 4). These boundary transgressions form the basis for, what DeLamotte ascribes as her spatial model. Drawn from Eve Kosofsky Sedgwick's (1986) theory that that the self is restricted access to a necessity or a personal right, the source of gothic terror is placed anxiety, not as a cause of entrapment, but from the transgression of personal boundaries. With this spatial model in mind, the Gothic provides a "symbolic language" about the "boundaries of the self" (DeLamotte 1990, 13–14). There is language that identifies clear and definitive barriers concerning those of the individual that both enforces restriction and entices defiance. These transgressions are problematic because they demonstrate the ability for behavioral and ontological transformation. Simply put, this transformation, or transgression of the self, is defined by DeLamotte (1990, 21) as: "[w]hat was x becomes y, the line dividing them dissolving." By rejecting behavior characteristics that defy social restrictions, in this case expression of sexuality, this mode emphasizes repression and conflict in Victorian women. While the origins of the Female Gothic highlight the struggles of dichotomous identities through constructivist immaterial interpretations, later works continue this legacy through a discussion of fractured ontologies. Female self-expression and transgressive identities are essential to gothic form, as they deviate from the constructivist dualism that characterizes early accounts of the Female Gothic. Accentuating the internal conflict of each gothic anti-heroine, it is clear that the suppression of human instincts, and separation from nature results in transgressive psychosomatic monstrosities.

These monstrosities are case studies of ontological transgressions in gothic fiction. Tearing and clawing their way through the pages of Victorian Gothic narratives, these fragmented and volatile women refract the fragility of a patriarchal system. Typical of modern scholarship regarding monstrosity, such monsters function as societal scapegoats for all social and cultural tensions. As embodiments of anxieties, repressed emotions, and instability, they mirror the vulnerability of society. Disturbing figurations of autonomy, monsters are the epitome of contradictions embodied within a material figuration. Antagonistic to a strict social structure, they are liminal beings whose transformative and ontological transgressions reject fixed positions and disrupt the social order. In the context of the early-to-mid-Victorian period, female monsters push the discursive boundaries of limits constructed for gender ideologies. These Victorian monstrosities destabilize the rhetoric of medical beliefs. Monstrous women, then, are responses to social constructs created by institutions for the confinement of female nature. By the early Victorian era, questions of evolutionary theory became tantamount to discourses about this relative female sexuality and reproductivity. Pre-dating Charles Darwin (1809–1882), Jean-Baptiste Lamarck (1744–1829) introduced the nineteenth century to the human evolution theory, species' environmental adaptation, and generational inheritance of traits. Informed by environmental factors, reduced to their biological functions and procreative abilities by medical, pseudo-scientific, and cultural discourses, nineteenth-century women were promoted as, what Val Plumwood (1993, 4) argues, "closer to the animal and the body" than men. Therefore, the use of the term "monstrous" or "monster" then, refers to women who challenge these beliefs and reject the parameters of the subjective, phallogocentric immaterial discourses of societal confinement.

The oppression of early-to-mid-Victorian women intertwines with female (re)presentations of monstrosity in gothic narratives. Acting out crises, contradictions, and subjectivity, the Gothic operates as a genre of unstable development, a method of reflecting and providing agency to society's repressed women. The influence of Victorian gender ideologies in gothic narratives are pervasive. The alignment of female physiology with primitivity in Western theological, psychological, and philosophical traditions allows for their social categorization. While within the narrative of the patriarchy, monstrosity, as Marie Mulvey-Roberts (2016, 106) suggests, is the classic model for the "construction of femininity." Therefore, women have been rendered unnatural and vilified because of their reproductive and sexualized bodies. These comments are germane to the mid-Victorian period, which saw a proliferation of discourses and narratives evoking fear of the sexualized nature of women and its effect on a delicate patriarchal social structure. This is most emphatic in the incumbent categorization of women into dichotomized socially prescribed roles of moral paragons or prurient beasts. These duplicitous identities created acrimonious and apprehensive sentiments toward women in society. The Gothic, which celebrates concepts of Others and identity fragmentation, is a productive space when analyzing the discourses of early-to-mid-Victorian women because it typically reveals perspectives of female abjection by a society that restricts expression. These anxieties are categorized in the Gothic as conceptual and corporeal representations of antagonistic polarities, conflict, and resolution, embodied within a singular structure. In recognition of this embodiment, mid-Victorian discourse, as Andrew Smith (2013, 4) postulates, has "internalized" such trepidations and monsters began to emerge with psychological issues. Monstrosities, once viewed as external villains, became inextricably concealed within the repressed identity of early-to-mid-Victorian women.[3]

Going beyond Smith's claim about the emergence of psychological monstrosity, the corporeal and incorporeal results of antagonistic ontologies condensed within figurations of gothic women seeking to destroy the contradictory boundaries and figurative constructs. A fear of women's assumed instability caused Victorian society to quarantine both the psychological and physiological hazards of female sexuality. Beyond this notion of the monstrous as only discursively constructed figures, the material bodies of women, fictional and otherwise, have causal power. This contrasts with the cultural or constructivist belief that gives weight to discourses, language, and social structures in determining female ontology. This unique approach eschews dichotomous and dualistic readings of the Gothic which have tended to dominate criticism to date. While women from this period, and their representations in fiction, are often dissected as either fragmentations of affected minds *or* sexualized bodies, there is a unification of female ontologies through the lens of philosophical monism, an appeal to nature, and a sympathetic reading of the gothic monstrosity.

Approaching the Female Mind-Body

Generally, Cartesian dualism results in a segregation of consciousness from the material and a bifurcation of the natural sciences from other disciplines and modes of study. While the natural sciences focus on theories of physical causation, cultural and linguistic constructivism has dominated sociological study and the humanities.[4] Scholarship of monstrosity in gothic fiction tends to perpetuate this dualism, focusing on mind *or* body, reading monsters as figures produced by nature *or* culture, whereby the latter dominates, resulting in female fragmentation. For example, Mary Russo (1994) articulates monstrous bodies as cultural, or social, creations and promotes the notion that the grotesque form is a social figuration.[5] The monstrous body, then, is argued as a visual projection of inner conflicts informed by its deviation from traditions and its abject treatment by society. Similarly, in his "Seven Theses" of monstrosity, Jeffrey Jerome Cohen (1996, 20) suggests that the monster embodies a specific cultural event, therefore it is a formation of "pure culture." In both arguments, monstrosity is assigned as physical projections of social, or cultural, influences negating the monistic interrelation of mind-body and nature-culture. This separation results in a philosophical reductionism which fragments the whole being into fragmented parts. This division of self, also known as reductionism, is defined by the principles of René Descartes (1596–1650) who suggests that the only way to fully understand something is to break it down into individual properties and analyze each part. As a bias of philosophy, this reductionism is used as a popular model for rational thought. Although this dualism allows the analysis of individual properties, it removes the importance of the whole being. By exploring the dichotomous approaches which speculates on the gothic mind *or* body, these dualisms offer a chasm of unexplored terrain. In recognition of the importance of the mind, the monstrous figuration does not reject dualism for the eliminative materialism that dominates in the natural sciences, nonetheless, it also does not repeat the long-standing patriarchal technique of reducing women solely to their bodies. It, however, does necessitate the unification of the mind *and* body arguing for a retention and reconfiguration of the female connection to nature that has been the ground of their subjugation in societal and fictional discourses. Though Victorian Gothic and Female Gothic often remain entangled in dualistic assumptions, a new monistic reading of their fragmented and monstrous women will reconcile culture and nature alongside the material and immaterial.

Monism is the primary lens that promotes the unification of the mind with the body under Nature. Monism is a philosophical theory that posits the unification of immaterial-material elements and rejects dualist ontologies that propose two distinct components of reality: mind and body. Monism also offers alternatives to reductive materialisms and to idealisms, which would reduce reality to either body or mind stuff, respectively. The mind and body attributes, then, determine how material beings and immaterial ideas are relational. Whereas all material beings present ideas, these ideas are not just contemplative thoughts of the individual but notions that exist either in God or Nature. Offering an antithetical solution to Descartes's mind-body dualism, this monistic belief, then, argues for the mind-body as a singular figuration as indelibly interlocked and affectively informed, thereby proving that all immateriality is inextricably linked to materiality under a single substance: either God or Nature. While suggesting that there is an exclusive substance with derivative modes and attributes, this presents the idea that substance could have "infinite attributes" or limitless ways in which the being (inclusive of material transformations and immaterial actions) are expressed. Attribution of substance to God, or in this particular case, Nature, suggests that all things are pieces, or modes, of a singular being's essence.

Spinoza's monism proposes that the mind and body are intertwined through the extension of substance in space. Humans are singular entities comprised of the infinite attributes of extension and thinking; therefore mind-body is a single unit conveyed in different methods. Human intellect, will, and physical being are finite modes of the infinite substance, or Nature. Derived from this substance, as Spinoza so succinctly alleges, all humans are finite modes thereby all actions and behaviors are derivative of the unified source. Finite modes are extended expressions of Nature's being. The body is a mode of Nature's extension confirming its essence in human physical form. Whereas an idea, which Spinoza considers as subsequent to the finite mind, or determinate mode for thought is Nature's essence extending into the human mind. Body and mind are conducive of the infinite substances' attributes of extension and thinking, therefore every material condition is immaterial, while immaterial is also material, not two separate attributes. The mind-body is a singular element expressed through two attributes of Nature's unified essence. Therein, according to Spinoza's monism, the human mind and body are not dual constructs, but derivative from a single cause. The mind, as a finite mode from an infinite substance, is the "idea of the body; the body is the object of the mind," therefore every occurrence within the body simultaneously happens in the mind (Lord 2010, 58). This perfect correspondence of mind-body suggests that all physical events are fully comprehensible mental events, thereby marking human experiences as both physical and psychical. Therein, events classified as either psychological or physiological induce simultaneous reactions in the mind-body. Restoring fragmented female identities as a unified structure and reclamation of natural agency, it exposes how immaterial discursive social practices of reductionism created a disjunction in the ontologies of women, resulting in material responses of monstrosity.

Material-Semiotic Figurations of Female Monstrosity

Scholarship of the Victorian Female Gothic generally cleaves to the immateriality of the genre.[6] Critics read this mode as a vehicle to navigate socio-cultural anxieties and explore subjective and/or fragmented identities in a manner that Diana Coole and Samantha Frost (2010, 3) classify as "radical constructivism," thereby reinforcing culture over nature. Through this approach, materiality is dismissed, and power is attributed to the immaterial language and discourse about the material. For Coole and Frost (2010, 3), such perpetuation of constructivist thought "privileges language, discourse, culture, and values"; however, it also encourages the dismissal or ignorance of the material form and its elaborate functions. The avoidance of matter in this dominant perspective in the humanities circumscribes the material world and negates both the symbolized being and the environment in which they live. This popular literary approach maintains the dualist perspective and sequesters the immaterial from the material, thus restricting early-to-mid-Victorian women to discourses informed by institutional constructs. This approach to the exploration of early-to-mid-Victorian women is inadequate. With this dichotomous constructivist model, Victorian discursive practices perpetuated the duality of women, creating binaries of angel/whore, mind/body, and nature/culture. This role imprinted upon social language and the demonstration of these immaterial practices of ideology define cultural womanhood while removing women's agency. The dichotomization of the immaterial and material segregates women into these fragmented conceptualizations, void of complexity, agency, or authority—as beings controlled by cultural discourses and expectations. In negation of this constructivism, which centralizes humans over nature, the she-monster is a material-semiotic being of both nature and culture, caught in a complex web of subjectivity.

Moving beyond a constructivist approach to literature this works reorients Victorian Gothic women as material-semiotic figurations, informed by immaterial affects and material conditions, that blur the distinction between culture and nature. In reference to Donna Haraway's (1991) material-semiotic actor theory, the term "material-semiotics" is a method that explores how social practices are intertwined as semiotic and material "weaves." In this sense, since the weave contains meaning about the corporeal form, and the form itself, the actor may be machine or nonmachine, human or nonhuman, thereby inclusive of such monstrosities. In either case, the actor is an active contributor, or possessor of information, participating in production or meaning. As a concept that also refuses reductionism of a single-sided construct, material-semiotics explores how meanings are influenced by material and social elements which create performative weaves, webs, and patterns of meaning. In this weave of materiality and meaning, as Haraway claims, within their interaction, they are interlocked and unable to be separated. The term "intra-action" is defined by Karen Barad (2003, 33) as a concept that *"signifies the mutual constitution of entangled agencies."* Through this entanglement, agencies are not independently distinct and only identifiable through their enmeshed relationship. This indivisibly promotes a distinct relationship of the immaterial to the material, the symbolic to the embodied. The refusal of dualism is not the reduction of the former to the latter, but an assertion that the latter emerges from the former. In this material-semiotic entanglement, life creates form.

Evoking material-semiotic entanglements, figurations of female monstrosity are reflective of cultural and ideological forces affecting, and imposing limitations on, women's repressed mind-body. In their subjective figurations as, what Rosi Braidotti (2003, 2) refers to, "a materialist mapping of situated, or embedded and embodied, positions," monsters such as madwomen, criminals, and she-wolves are symbolic exhibitions of internal and external affectations. Deviating from the immaterial of poststructuralism, this complicates theories of meaning, by thinking about the intricacies and formation of the body and its behaviors, while recognizing and transgressing such borders and limitations. Since poststructuralism concentrates on the fluidity of language and the structure of meaning to explain the social world, Braidotti interjects a material mapping as the source of meaning. Utilizing these figurations of embodied subjectivity, the unpredictable form is substituted in place of immaterial discourse. As mappings of embodied and embedded subjectivities, these depictions of monstrosity figure the violence enacted on women, thus presenting a transformative exhibition of repression. As beings of what Braidotti (2003, 5) labels "enfleshed or embodied materialism," these figurations caught in an entanglement have to deal with institutional discourses that define immaterial constructs of regulations that ultimately force the removal of agency. Indeed, it is this sense of embodiment and corporeality that the important issue of material bodies rejects the immaterial restrictions enforced by social rhetoric. Similar to Michel Foucault's (1976, 83) argument that bodies are the "inscribed surface of events (traced by language and dissolved by ideas)," this notion postulates that bodies are not just organisms, but material formations of indetermination informed by other systems. Although these malleable bodies are influenced by their relations with nature, culture, society, and biology, they lack control over their own abilities or agency. This postulation of uncontrollable bodies informed by institutional discourses demonstrates how subjective figurations of monstrosity are embodiments of social and cultural expectations embodied within a metamorphic material form. Analyzing women in the Gothic as entangled within the material-semiotic web of early-to-mid-Victorian discourses, it is clear how the transformations into figurations of madwomen, criminals, and she-wolves are all symbolic rejections of phallogocentric dominance.

Nature, Women, and the EcoGothic

There is an historically implied connection between women and the natural environment. While the natural space is argued as feminine, as Stacy Alaimo (2010, 5) suggests, most feminist scholarship, especially those of the second wave, has attempted to "disentangle *woman* from *nature*" and struggles with the negative implications attached to the connection. It is from this belief that many feminist scholars claim female devaluation or biological reductionism. For example, Sherry Ortner (1974, 73) argues that studies of the female body identify women solely with nature while separating them from culture and it is through this connection with nature that culture identifies women as "participants," however, their connection to nature is more authentic and inherent, thus dominant. This incomplete transcendence from nature allows humanity (i.e., culture) to assert dominance, thus resulting in female devaluation. Sharing a similar perspective, Carolyn Merchant (1980) identifies how the separation of women's minds and bodies promotes constructive binaries which undermine agency. Due to the biological functionality of women's reproductivity and metamorphic physiology, they have been connected to nature by patriarchal discourses, such that their role in society is secondary to men. Similarly, Anja Höing (2018, 35) posits how women, as reproductive constructs, are shrouded by men in nature narratives. Indeed, female inferiority within nature faces deprivation of agency and materiality with an ontological reduction to mere animals or unthinking slaves of their instincts, as will be discussed further in chapter one. Women are confined by a constructivist discourse which promotes males as authority figures and females as clandestine beings of reproductivity. This figuration promotes female biological functions while simultaneously removing women from the narrative, leaving a genealogical legacy. These theorists determine nature as an uncivilized and oppressive space antagonistic to civilized culture, thus their desire for disentanglement. Ortner, Merchant, and Höing agree that while women are sanctioned within the confines of nature, their agency is weakened by reference to their natural biological functions. Cleaving to a dualist perspective, then, they argue that both women and nature "need to be liberated from the anthropomorphic and stereotypic labels" that cause degradation and inferiority (Merchant 1980, xxi). Typical of second wave constructionist feminism, these theorists argue for the necessity of women's liberation from biological identification. Purposefully negating the connection between women and nature, such scholars further remove women's potential for wholeness. This dichotomization casts women solely within the cultural sphere and denounces any affiliation to natural tendencies, leaving nature on the subordinate half of a binary still very much intact. While these theorists negatively assert the concept that women are assumed as "closer to nature than men," therefore must embody its essence, it is actually this embodiment of Nature's characteristics that shape and define female identities and promote agency (Merchant 1980, 73).

In contrast to these constructivist accounts, modern scholarship on women's materiality and nature promotes a reclamation of the natural identity. Embedded within a social construct, women are promoted by cultural discourses as inferior in their association to nature. This derogatory removal of female agency is the basis for what feminists identify as the foundation and purpose for misogynistic applications, thereby advocating a release from this association. While feminists argue that women viewed as connected to, or controlled by, nature is a negative aspect, reframing this notion can be used as a position of power. Contrary to these beliefs, Alaimo (2000, 22) demands a reclamation of nature as an "undomesticated space." From this so-called material feminist approach, nature is not removed from a relationship with women, but is redefined or transvalued as agential and a signifier for independence. Nature, in this sense, is approached as an agentic nonhuman space of knowledge and freedom, inseparable from humanity, that allows for influential interconnectivity. Through this affective relationship, nature is removed from the domestic construct and serves as a "model for female insurgency" where women could be untamed and unruly (Alaimo 2000, 16). Drawing from this notion of nature revision, the interconnectivity of nature and women is highlighted by an ecoGothic lens and allows for a revivification of female ontology and a transgressive role for gothic monsters.

Nature, or the environment, in the ecoGothic, as Lisa Kröger (2013, 19) submits, functions as a "conduit of emotions" and a free space of expression. In consonance with this approach, the figuration of the female monstrosity and the affective impact on and from, environments illustrate how the contradictory Victorian perspectives of women's nature, as moral spirits, biological functionaries, and illicit promoters of carnal passions, expose the repressive confinements of social stereotypes. Reflecting on Dawn Keetley and Matthew Sivils's (2017, 5) claim that the monstrous subject is a central figure to the Gothic, the ecoGothic then provides the domain, or space, that reflects how the form is never solely human "but always a blend of the human and the nonhuman," therefore allowing the environment to exhibit how the human mind-body is a monistic entity under nonhuman nature. From this perspective, monism sees mind and bodies as different expressions of the one substance, with the added implication that this approach rejects the anthropomorphism detected in some forms of monism, since human minds and cultures are instantiations of the same substance as animal minds. They operate as unified material under the singular substance of Nature, which reconfigures traditional human behavior and visual aesthetics of femininity. This singularity results in a range of monstrous abnormalities reflected by women in the Gothic as madwomen, criminals, and shapeshifting she-wolves. Since women's mind-bodies are unified with Nature, they can be affected and influenced by external stimuli (i.e., physical/mental abuse, neglect, and ignorance). When impacted by such stimuli, the monistic mind-body reacts and presents retaliatory behaviors and monstrous visages. Indeed, as an affect to monstrosity in gothic narratives, nature functions as a domain of repressed female expression, personal freedom, and an affective environment that informs behavior.

There is an interrelation between women and nature that evokes a monistic response which joins the psychological to the physiological. Modern scholars of affective ecocriticism investigate, for example, how human behavior is a response related to environments. Arguing that humans are prominent points in which affect theory and ecology conjoin, Kyle Bladow and Jennifer Ladino's (2018, 3) theories offer how nature impacts the mind-body and explore how human and non-human beings are the location where affectation and the environment coalesce. This perspective incorporates the interdisciplinary information of affect theory to examine how ecology and neurobiology synonymously affect human and non-human biological processes through emotional responses brought on by environmental influences. Similarly, Diane Mitten and Chiana D'Amore (2018) investigate how the juxtaposition of women/nature inform the monistic mind-body causing dysmorphic exhibitions by demonstrating how society's unrealistic expectations interfere with the natural body. They suggest that women's negative emotional impact from failing to achieve social goals leads to a disjunction in bodily responses, resulting in such issues as dysmorphia. It is only through the relationship with, and acceptance of, nature that women have the potential to heal and/or reject patriarchal standards.

Likewise, Elizabeth Grosz (1999, 2) emphasizes this concept of nature, arguing that "[t]he natural world preconfigures, contains, and opens up social and cultural existence to endless becoming; in turn, cultural transformation provides further impetus for biological becoming." Following this argument, the natural world, and the transformations it prompts, are foundational for the study of female monstrosities in the Gothic. Valuing nature in this way counters the impoverished sense of nature as half of a duality in which women's bodies are routinely reduced to nature as a mutable substance. The term "nature" is also used in the reclaimed sense that Alaimo expounds, where it designates a space beyond mind-body and culture-nature identities. Nature, as a space for female expression and freedom, a connection to access authentic identities, and an omnipotent substance that unifies the mind-body finds purchase differently in each chapter of this text. While it is the overarching theme, the concept of nature is approached variously. Foremost, it is a necessity in this project, providing what Alaimo claims as a space where women can express unrestrained emotions and behavior and reject the restrictive boundaries of cultural expectations. For women to find the symbiosis between nature and culture, as Alaimo (2000, 10) points out, "nature itself" must be redefined. Nature, then, must be reconceptualized as a space of feminine purpose that reaffirms agency and removes polarization. Furthermore, it is necessary to retain the connection of women to nature and reconstruct the meaning into a space of power, freedom, and female expression within gothic narratives. This dynamic of nature can be seen through instincts that inhere in humanity, or in drives that perpetuate desires. This notion of nature, then, proliferates throughout each chapter as the rationale for women's rejection of social boundaries and confinement.

As figurations who possess instinctual connections to nature, women in these gothic narratives project their innate passions and wildness into the environment producing, for example, storms and fires and displays of atmospheric events and weather patterns. As well as reading such natural events as representations of women's vociferous rejections of their oppression, nature is also read as an external influence on their mind-bodies and affectation, demonstrates how the natural, and artificial, environments inform women's behavior in the Gothic. These environmental affectations influence female figurations and shape their ontology to navigate through society and the natural world. Lastly, the concept of Nature as defined by Spinoza's monism is implemented to identify the woman-nature relationship as an integrated mode. Classified as a singular substance, Nature unifies the mind and body and amends the popular dualistic approach into a monistic one. Utilizing nature as an environment that informs female behavior and reflects internal conflict, it is evoked as the ground for material-semiotic gothic figurations of madwomen, criminals, and she-wolves.

Monstrous women, then, are not monsters but material-semiotic figurations of female repression and social influences. Monstrosity is a sign that communicates a meaning of female subjugation and a concomitant desire for free expression. Created from a semiotic web of Victorian institutions, social expectations, and popular literature, women in the Gothic embody the overlapping influences of material and social behavior. Forced into a state of confinement, monstrous women signify a mind-body rejection of social boundaries and attempt a return to nature, not in the sense that it manifests in the Victorian dualities of angel/whore, but as a space of possibility free of ideological gendered constructs. Therefore, subject to biological and psychological reductionism, Victorian women faced inferiority within a patriarchal system. This conflict is portrayed through the material-semiotic figures of monstrous women and their connections to nature.

NOTES

1. For more information on penny publications (i.e., bloods, dreadfuls, and awfuls), refer to the forthcoming edited collection: Nicole C. Dittmer and Sophie Raine. *Penny Dreadfuls and the Gothic: Investigations of Pernicious Tales of Terror*. Cardiff: University of Wales Press, 2023.

2. Albeit located within varied class structures, all the women in these stories either perform within the boundaries of the middle- and upper-classes or replicate the necessary behavior and appearance to allow their infiltration. In the Victorian social hierarchy, lower-working-class citizens were subjected to unsanitary urban conditions, had sparse education and medical attention, and limited access to nourishment. These environmental conditions, of course, render lower-working-class women prime candidates for fears of degeneration and monstrosity. On the contrary, middle- and upper-class women, resided in cleaner conditions, had access to healthcare, education, and limited access to political or public events. Women of these classes were subjected to a sanitized environment informed by morals and forced ignorance. While middle- and upper-class women were not influenced by the same daily stressors of lower- and working-class citizens, their relatively easier existence forcefully repressed their instincts and held them to a higher standard. This is not to say that there is not an intense class-based critique available for the texts I will discuss, of course. I am mindful of this context, though it lays beyond the scope of what I consider in the main body of my analysis. It is, however, from the middle- and upper-class ideologies of "womanhood" that the monstrous female emerges for the sake of this research.

3. See Horace Walpole's *The Castle of Otranto* (1764), Ann Radcliffe's *The Mysteries of Udolpho* (1794), and Matthew Lewis's *The Monk* (1796).

4. Donald Favareau asserts that Cartesian Dualism renders the truth claims made by science independent of the humanities and vice versa, therefore arguing that the subjective experiences of mind was ruled unfit as an object of science.

5. Mary Russo compares the grotesque body to the language of the classical political theory of aesthetics. While the classical body is associated with the public, the grotesque, in its uncanny form, moves toward a fantastical interior area, it moves away from social spaces. Throughout her analysis, Russo refers to Michel Bakhtin's material body principle and discusses how the grotesque is not enclosed within the singular material body but within the collective of people.

6. See Sandra M. Gilbert and Susan Gubar, *The Madwoman in the Attic: The Woman Writer and the Nineteenth-Century Literary Imagination* (Boston: Yale University Press, 1979/2000); Diane Wallace and Andrew Smith, *The Female Gothic: New Directions* (Hampshire/New York: Palgrave Macmillan, 2009); Angela Wright, *Gothic Fiction: A Reader's Guide to Essential Criticism* (Hampshire/New York: Palgrave Macmillan, 2007).

Chapter One

Social Behavior and "Domesticated" Women

[F]rom the dawn of human society every woman was in a state of bondage to some man, because she was of value to him and she had less muscular strength than he did.

—J. S. Mill 1869, 3

The early-to-mid-Victorian period (1837–1871) was fraught with sexual repression and the ontological restriction of middle- and upper-class women. This was an era that inculcated virtuous ideals into female behavior, forcefully shifting natural instincts, or innate traits from birth without learned experiences, from expressive passions to docile morality. These repressed instincts, as associated with female sexuality, were often feared by authorities as a source of volatility that would endanger marriage and familial lineage, thereby impacting social stability. Driven by this fear of excess passions, Victorian society perpetuated feminine ideologies through institutional rhetoric that categorized women into prescribed gender roles to promote self-regulation, submission, and virtue. Thereby, such discourses stemming from powerful institutions, shaped and encouraged these normative behaviors. In an attempt to construct socially appropriate principles of morality, medical, cultural, and educational institutions subjugated women and restricted their inherent desires. By means of discursive controls involving politics of female biology, these institutions constructed conflicting specifications that regulated what Michel Foucault (1976, 139) refers to as the "performances of the body." Where women, whether real or imagined, refused to conform to traditional roles as domesticated wives and mothers, there emerged an antithetical ideology to identify their uncontrolled carnality and social opposition. Therein, the creation of the categories and labels "angel" and "whore," were cultivated for early-to-mid-Victorian women. These duplicitous binaries allowed patriarchal institutions to create a regulatory space for behavioral restrictions and self-discipline. Throughout this period, unrestrained female sexuality was detrimental to societal functionality, threatened familial lineage, and successful perpetuation of "civilized" society. From this perspective, constructs of female identities were structured to identify and define specific behaviors for Victorian women.

This chapter focuses on these particular ontologies of early-to-mid-Victorian women and their concomitant subjugation. Examining the lesser studied period 1837 through 1871, it illustrates the popular perspective about women in the middle- and upper-classes and exposes how the dichotomy of either the angel or fallen woman figurations are determined by ideological roles constructed from biological capacities and the negation of human instincts. While this section does not explicitly discuss theories of the Gothic, it does explore the historical content of subjective womanhood that creates a foundation for future chapters and the discussion of gothic narratives. Illustrating a thematic topic of morality and instinctual repression, the following institutional literature that spans from early-to-mid-Victorian medical sciences, to culture, to law, to theology perpetuates the rigid construct of femininity as outlines for "proper" women and sanitized sexuality. Therefore, it is this examination of Victorian rhetoric that exposes the immaterial popular opinion informed by institutional discourses and how it was enforced upon material bodies, thus manifesting roles for gendered performance, while simultaneously creating a new literary perspective of the female gothic monster for later chapters.

POPULAR (NON)SEXUALITY

Classified as "angel[s] in the house," an ideal adopted from Coventry Patmore's (1858, 39–40) narrative poem, middle- and upper-class Victorian women faced a life of behavioral restriction, free of independent expression and confinement within the domestic domain.[1] Whereas women were expected to restrain natural sexual pleasures, popular discourses contradicted this belief by claiming that female sexuality was based on reproduction, hence it was shrouded by uterine functions. Unable to indulge in carnal urges, women, albeit suspected as "more broadly and continuously erotic than men" were, as Michael Mason (1994, 199) argues, restricted to male pleasure and reproduction, therefore the existence of "female genital pleasure" was "often elided." Targeted by the belief that they were products of external pleasure and productivity, women were reduced into constructed roles based on female materiality as embodiments of nature and unstable biological functions.

Contextual material from this period promoted these ideologies of essentialist femininity, including those of popular theology, conduct books, medical journals, and treatises that draw upon aseptic influences. Contemporaneous texts from such authorities as Thomas Laycock (1840), Sarah Stickney Ellis (1839–1842), Forbes Winslow (1851), Robert Brudenell Carter (1853), William Acton (1862), John Ruskin (1865), and John Stuart Mill (1869), among other notable voices, present a unified approach about women that institutions utilized to create the dichotomous virgin/whore paradigm. This early-to-mid-Victorian discursivity of "medicine, psychiatry, psychology, ethics, pedagogy, and political criticism" created ideologies based on women's biology (Foucault 1976, 33–34). These mechanisms of sexual discourse were constructed around themes of flesh, morality, and penance; however, in relatively recent centuries, this singular uniformity fragmented into identifiable rhetoric. This initial theological formulation of temptation and the obligation of confession splintered into institutional language of sexuality that stemmed from social anxiety and tensions. Thereby in an attempt to adjust, or re-transcribe the conversation of sexuality, nineteenth-century discourses objectified sex and sexuality through "rational" discourse and analysis. Negation, and redefinition, of female instincts according to these strict social necessities, permitted society to remove agency and confine women into repressive roles. Precipitated in stereotypes driven by institutional provocation, women's sexual potency was sanitized and metamorphosed into affectionate desires for familial gratification. Moreover, this popular opinion of reductionism and immateriality informed by institutional discourses exerted its force over material bodies, thereby creating roles for female performances.

Medical rhetoric helped shape the negative perspective, social attitude, and popular literature toward expressive female sexuality. The development of the advanced medical science and the organization of "experts" into professional and influential figures, created a crucial influence on the social beliefs of what women are supposed to be. These roles as authoritative doctors, surgeons, and alienists qualified them as gatekeepers of privileged ideas, therefore since most professionals were men, women were subjugated to the biased male perspective. Arguably then, the practice of British sexuality was restricted within the boundaries of the home. As a subject of taboo and silence, sexuality was transformed into a moral structure and the Victorian woman was metamorphosed into a construct of domesticity and reproductivity. As authorities of the household, the male half of this so-called model defined the gendered expectations of sexual practices. This familial intervention and discursive sanction classified and confined women to solely biological roles of impossible womanhood that resulted in the dichotomized roles of either saint or sinner. Women's behavior was thus situated with opposing identities: one that aligned with the practicality of society and the other, instinctual. Sexuality, then, as determined by Foucault (1976, 4) was identified and associated with behavior in a "social space"; as one that "avoided contact with other bodies" and maintained sanitized speech for "verbal decency"; therefore, those who insisted on making sexuality "too visible" were designated with "behavior [that] carried the taint of abnormality." Regarding this behavioral admonition, medical institutions linked women's health and characteristics to domestication to avoid and subdue the so-called abnormalities of women and promote virtuosity. Therefore, the subject of women's sexuality was silenced in behavioral practice through structures of femininity and domestication.

As a popular and intriguing theme, the discursive context of conventional Victorian femininity circulated in middle-class conduct guides informed by medical guides and popular literature. The stigma against female sexuality was encouraged by the rhetorical posture of patriarchal institutions. A significant problem centered on the influx of literature published by institutions about the absence, or peculiarity, of female sexuality. Throughout the early-to-mid period, women's inherent passions were promoted as unconceivable, or atypical, in popular discourse. Viewed as abnormal by Victorian medical men, female sexuality proliferated throughout society as an irregularity. Stemming from the pages of medical treatises and journals, this negligence of, and negative perspective about, women's overt sexuality infiltrated the pages of popular household manuals, and fiction as a source of female "monstrosity"—a trait to repress or destroy. Informative publications such as conduct books, poems, and tracts presented women as virtuous paragons, free of impulses and sexual desires. Much of this early-to-mid-Victorian literature idealized women as nonsexual reproductive objects. This method of control was used by patriarchal institutions to repress social interactions and define womanhood as innocent and pure. Through these sanctioned depictions of feminized conduct, women were viewed as susceptible and in need of control and guidance. Therefore, medical experts neglected legitimate studies to scrutinize female sexuality but in fact, used fiction, such as depictions of extreme femininity in romance literature to create what Susan Kingsley Kent (1987, 32) refers to as "practical prescriptions" founded on "stereotypes and metaphors." Drawing from this notion about prescriptive discourses, both nonfiction and fiction narratives demonstrate how ideologies of femininity were created and compelled throughout the early-to-mid-Victorian period.

Throughout the nineteenth century, authoritative institutions informed gendered expectations of women. In Western society, concepts about female sexuality were formulated by varied institutions: cultural, medical, scientific, and religious. Indeed, all social practices, sexual codification, and behaviors are a result of these discourses. In Victorian England, then, regarding the discourse of sex, "silence became the rule" (Foucault 1976, 3). Therefore, female sexuality, as perpetuated by prominent institutions, became repressed in such a way that this subject was often silenced or discussed only when promoting the ideologies of sexless virtue and morality. In his seminal theory, the "Repressive Hypothesis," Foucault suggests that while the tangible activities of public pleasure were socially prohibited and taboo, the theme of prurience was prominent. Furthermore, in the nineteenth century, theories of sexuality were categorized into two categories of knowledge: "a biology of reproduction," that continued to develop based on the standards of scientific norms and "a medicine of sex" constructed from institutional beliefs about methods of control and behavioral expectations (Foucault 1976, 54). It is through these two distinctions of sexuality that popular rhetoric informed social practices about female behavior. The constraint on physicality determined that sex was intended as a private involvement between husband and wife. However, through theological, cultural, and medical literature, another space for sexual discourse was offered. This discussion of sexuality provided society with authoritative power over individuals and restricted or controlled their behavior. Informed by these biases, women were confined within the strict boundaries of artificial, socially prescribed roles. With the creation of these gendered restrictions, the objective was to reinforce constructed roles for Victorians to behave accordingly, therefore women were responsible for their own actions and behavioral regulation. Furthermore, due to the promotion of science and sexuality, medical institutions converted roles of metaphorical and literary pure women into reductive beings of flesh and blood. This concept of the pure woman was utilized as a form of control in the nineteenth century to regulate the prescribed behaviors between men and women. Moreover, the transformation of bringing fictional women to life allowed society to establish and impose a new identity for women constructed from their sexuality. Under a scope of idealistic and reductionistic medical experts, women were scrutinized and reduced to their biological functions through discursive means.

It was during this period that the sexuality of middle- and upper-class women became defined as pathological, manifesting in the form of various illnesses that affected both the mind and body. Foucault, in his influential study, *The History of Sexuality*, explores the progressive knowledge of this sexual segregation in what he defines as *ars erotica* and *scientia sexualis*. *Ars erotica*, most notably discussed in Eastern societies, draws information about sexuality directly in relation to pleasure. Intimacy is explored as an unrestricted pleasurable experience that is analyzed based on its "intensity" and the impact it has on the "body and the soul" (Foucault 1976, 57). The purpose for its secrecy is not to repress sexuality, but to preserve the effectiveness and virtue of the intimate event. Contrary to this belief, Western societies propagated the practice of *scientia sexualis*, or confession of sex, to explore and shape the context of sex and sexuality. Promoted as a process of knowledge-power, *scientia sexualis,* in the nineteenth century, emerged at the intersection of science and confession to produce truth about sexuality. This form of knowledge-power kept the process of confession at its nucleus for production of truth relevant to sexuality. Institutions used this discursive method about psychology and physiology to shape ideals and approaches to female sexuality. Thereby, treated as procreative beings, women were aligned solely with their reproductive functions. Viewed as necessary for genealogical continuation, women's biology caused concerns for early-to-mid-Victorian society.

WOMEN'S BIOLOGY AND MEDICAL DISCOURSES OF SEXUALITY

Much of the nineteenth-century discourses paradoxically treated women according to a materialist or biological reductionism but, at the same time, promoted an antithetical dualism that separated their spirituality from their physical form. John Gideon Millingen (1848, 157), a British Army surgeon, claims that women, with their "exalted spiritualism," were "more forcibly under the control of matter." Promoting the idea that women were more influenced by the uterus than the brain, he argued that this led to wild sensations and uncontrolled passions. Entering this conversation of uterine affectations, William Tyler Smith (1858), a medical writer and obstetrician, proposes that women's uteri are the hearts of society, and their functionalities are essential for the progress of humanity. Smith argues that the uterus is the most significant organ in a woman's body and claims it is as if God had constructed the female form around the uterus as a nexus. This determination of the uterus as central for female functions contributed to the argument that women are a "necessary evil" (Poovey 1988, 35). Governed by reproductive processes for species propagation, women possessed the ability to destroy sacred patriarchal institutions. This differentiation between women and men was a postulation promoted to restrict female behavior and encourage their subjugation. Since Smith's research on obstetrics was standard in early-to-mid-Victorian medical discourse, it helped shape society's perspective of women as inherently wild and governed by reproductive functions.

This eroticization of reproductive organs led to social beliefs that female functions were a source of instability. Victorian medical experts promoted the "doctrine of 'uterine physiology,'" therefore encouraging the belief that women's sexuality was disseminated through their material form, thus controlling their immaterial events (Mason 1994, 198). According to this uterine theory, the uterus, the ovaries, and their conditions influence women's psychological and physiological being. Whereas men's reproductive functionalities emerge from their testes, women's biology and procreativity, as associated with the uterus, were suspected as having a greater impact. The womb was viewed as the source to influence women's psychological and physical structures. Thus, the condition of the uterus and its varied reproductive phases was believed to impact women's disposition. As a result of this belief, Victorian medical institutions amplified this logic of uterine theory to incorporate the potential of women's venereal proclivities thereby making sexuality a dominant issue of female physiology and mental maladies.

While some theorists catenate psychosomatic hysteria to women's uterine processes, Thomas Laycock (1840), a prominent neural physiologist, correlates this disorder to the ovaria and nervous system. The ovaries and uterus were argued as responsible for changes such as puberty, menstruation, and menopause, however, Laycock, while compelling speech about corporeal and incorporeal abnormalities of women, argues that they are not the only factors for the supposed peculiarities. Correlating the generative organs to neurological functions, Laycock ascertains that while in any one of these stages, the female nervous system as more susceptible than that of the male, is in a vulnerable state and "affected by all stimuli, whether corporeal or mental." Unresolved stimulation to the reproductive organs causes behavioral disruption. The belief that a husband's inability to sexually satisfy his wife resulted in theories that highlighted psychosomatic breaks and unstable behaviors. Any such influential stimuli inflicted upon the organs, affects the hemispherical ganglia, the central source for the nervous system, thereby impacting the mind through reflex reaction. This practice that typifies overt sexuality in women suggests the destructive impact of female psychosomatic, and hence, social functions. Furthermore, Laycock defines sensation as having a direct correlation into the consciousness through nervous reflexivity. Thus, affects transition into both physical and psychical reactions. This potential for sexual capacity challenged social constructions of traditional ideologies. Assumed as primarily material forms with problematic reproductive functions, women were classified by the medical institution as unstable and potentially destructive.

Contrary to Laycock's diagnoses, other medical experts contend that sexuality induces afflictions on the reproductive system. Arguing against the theory that psychological disorders emerge from ovarian dysfunction, medical and social discourses suggested that women's passions and aggressive sexual proclivities informed and encouraged changes in the reproductive organs. Medical experts promoted the notion that certain disorders affecting the uterus or internal ganglia were the result of excessive sexual influence and stimulation. For example, Robert Brudenell Carter (1853, 2) theorizes that hysteria, a psychogenic disease that commences in "convulsive paroxysm," or psychically induced spasm, results in "uterine complications." As influenced by sensations, women's reproductive organs, as Carter asserts, are impacted by the indeterminate frequency of changing blood levels more than other body parts, thereby maintaining perpetual instability. When subjected to continued stimulus and activity, the uterus is declared as vulnerable to changes and is thus responsible for the output of strong emotions. Following the popular Victorian stereotype, reinforced by experts including Charles Darwin, that women were more susceptible to emotions than men, Carter (1853, 4) also argues that they "endeavour[ed] to conceal them." This repression of emotions and sexuality consequently disturbs the uterine functions, therefore resulting in psychosomatic functions and irregularities.

While this medical rhetoric correlated psychological dysfunction to inherent sexual passions, some promoted women's libidinous expressions. Not all physicians, alienists, and psychiatrists denied or demonized female sexuality, some theorists claimed that women's passions, when directed toward a spouse, were natural. In particular, British social theorist George R. Drysdale (1854, 38–39) submits that the prescriptive role of women is artificialized as "pure." Offering a secular approach to popular theological beliefs, Drysdale argues in favor of female sexuality and suggests that molding women into figures of virtue is in opposition to their inherent nature. Contrary to Laycock and Carter's ideas of female sexual excision, Drysdale refutes the distinctive characteristics that differentiate women's desires from those of men, therefore rejecting social stereotypes of conventional femininity. Claiming that society promoted sexual morality or the monogamy of marriage, he asserts that sexual relationships outside of marriage was taboo and forbidden. This purpose for female chastity was deliberated by the male perspective as well as "erroneous views of man," and "The Christian Church" (Drysdale 1854, 187). Moreover, men faced exemption from the restrictions and negative attitudes about active sexual expression, however, as social roles were constructed by the biased views of man, women's overt sexuality was consequentially limited. With this proclamation of the consequences about the nature of female sexuality, copulation between married couples was encouraged, hence sexual abstinence was discouraged. Without this expulsion of energy, the repression of carnal gratification could result in a "morbid growth of sexual passions" (Drysdale 1854, 187). Drysdale also promotes healthy sexual relationships between spouses claiming that prostitution will be unnecessary and, as a result, mental health issues and the spread of venereal diseases are preventable. Although there are those that encouraged female sexuality, there are many who feared the repercussions of passionate vocations. Social anxieties of women's carnality were promoted through these types of popular medical discourses that perpetuated the stereotype of inherent inability and uncontrollability. Reinforced by scientific research that defined and connected female characteristics to nature, early-to-mid-Victorian discourses further perpetuated women's biology and psychology as fragile.

Furthering differentiating traits between men and women, evolutionary theory contributed to the reductionist discourses of female biology. For instance, Darwin (1871, 317) examines biological adaptation and sexual selection between the sexes, arguing that women assume characteristics and physical formations of the skull and brain somewhere "between the child and the man." His theory reinforced the popularized notion that women differ from men both mentally and physically primarily in their tenderness and selflessness. Attributing these dispositions to women's "maternal instincts," which they extend toward their "fellow-creatures," Darwin (1871, 326) differentiates female traits from men, whom he classifies as rivals to other men that delight "in competition" and lead to ambition, thus resulting in selfishness. This assessment of women's inherent morality and compassion, as presented as "hold[ing] good even with savages," perpetuated feminine stereotypes by claiming that men with "natural and unfortunate birth right[s]" are ambitious and competitive while women possess "powers of intuition, of rapid perception, and perhaps imitation" (Darwin 1871, 326–327). It is this proclamation of qualities that made men superior while exposing women's supposed inferiority. Indeed, this stipulation promotes the notion that women are less powerful in mind and body than men. In their subjugation, even in the so-called savage state, women are declared as vulnerable, unstable, and derivative of the so-called lower species. Propagating this rhetoric of Victorian womanhood and tribal behavior, Darwin's research advocates the characteristics of fragility and instability as women's natural state.

In Darwin's investigations, his language promotes the idea that supposed lower races and women are closer to nature than culture men. As Gillian Beer (2009) notes, Darwin's extensive use of metaphors and decorative language surpasses their textual status and propagates additional beliefs and ideologies. Restricted by the language of the period, Darwin was limited in accessible scientific vocabulary, therefore he drew on available words from varied fields. Referring to biological, ethological, and zoological sources, Darwin offers generatively charged discourse "rich in intensivities, expostulation[s], and case histories ransacked for implications" (Beer 2009, 43). It is Darwin's limitation to nineteenth-century language and attitudes that was crucial for his expressions to terms as savagery, primitivity, and supposedly lower races. Drawing from the implications of Edward Burnett Tylor (1871, 11) that Darwin exhibits a "brutal ignorance" of the assumed "advanced races" allowed both him, and Victorian society "to mythologize indigenous peoples back into apes." Demonstrating an authoritative voice that categorizes all living things from human and nonhuman, Darwin's usage of disparaging terms implies the Victorian patriarchal authority of civilized, or cultured, men over all others. The perpetuation of this scientific perspective and derogatory language embedding women in nature as uncontrollable "savages," resounded through literature of the early-to-mid-Victorian period. Both Charles Darwin and, criminologist Cesare Lombroso, two influential theorists promoting discourse of biology in the nineteenth century, speculated that women, as products of their own biological functions were "valued almost exclusively as slaves or beasts of burden" (Darwin 1871, 421). Infusing their language with an imperial perspective that correlated the properties of women to compare with animals and race, they shifted the influence and meaning of common words. Thereby, the discursivity of female nature was promoted through medical discourses as an unsanctioned function necessary for regulation. Institutional discourses such as those proliferated by Darwin, and later Lombroso, promoted these ideals of female behavior and contributed to their treatment and experiences. Since most Victorian institutions were constructs of patriarchal ideals, women faced this subjugation as frangible, easily influenced, and potentially volatile beings.

Subjugated in roles correlative to these scientifically assumed characteristics, women were responsible for the health and vitality of the family lineage. Women's assignment to the domestic sphere was a result of their biological makeup, frailty, and limited energy. Victorian medical experts believed that women's instincts and capabilities were solely purposed for reproduction, not for such activities that include intellect or creativity, thus limiting ontological development. These derogatory assumptions deprived women of agency while also encouraging their dependency on men. Women were prescribed roles exclusively based on their reproductive obligations. On the contrary, men were contenders in abundant sexual adventures and not specifically identified by their reproductive functions. As the progenitors of societal perpetuation, women's identities were shaped according to their materiality, therefore they were designated as either void of sexuality or "helplessly nymphomaniacal" (Kingsley Kent 1987, 31). Since nymphomania was identified as a socially corruptive "mental affection" and, according to Jean-Étienne Dominique Esquirol (1838, 335), was responsible for "obscene" and "most shameful and humiliating" behaviors, institutions limited women's sexual purpose to reproductivity to avoid such monstrous ailments. Creating a role that limited women to submissive procreation, popular discourses subsequently formed a sterile female identity based solely on their material functions and maternal traits. This ideal was the primary reason for women's placement within the domestic not the public sphere. These progenitive abilities, not only established women's positions in the private and social spheres, but also demarcated their values and expectations therein. This social construction of a woman's identity as the "weaker sex" presented a notion of vulnerability and/or corruptibility. While women performed within the boundaries of traditional womanhood, they were treated as respectable and arbiters of morality. However, women who avoided this restriction and rejected socially prescribed behaviors, were perceived as devious monsters and lascivious antagonists.

Demons and Angels: Polarization of Ideologies

Conventional roles of early-to-mid-Victorian femininity enforced by institutional discourses forced women to repress their primal instincts through moral obligations while society exploited their reproductive functions. Objectified as divine beings, English women were defined as pleasing displays who were "remarkable for their chastity," and spiritually created to produce offspring (Winslow 1851, 39). An example can be seen in the writings of Forbes Winslow, a prominent psychologist in the mid-Victorian period, who recognizes the construct of womanhood as both a spiritual and material model. Identifying the ideal female figuration as the epitome of beauty driven by moral love and spiritual grace, Winslow suggests that these aspects are most agreeable and stunning when affected by the activity of the reproductive organs. It is assumed that during these stages the excitation is from the "instinct of love" also referred to as "the sexual passion," which centers women as pleasing in the eyes of men (Winslow 1851, 21). Deriving his logic from Laycock's neurological theory, this suggests that sexual passion is an instinctive reflex for protection and duty. Arguing that sexuality is a psychosomatic function for species' perpetuation, Winslow rejects female self-indulgence and enjoyment. This personal intimacy and pleasure induce a reactive metamorphosis in the nerves, emotions, and behavior, thus resulting in women's transition to *"virago*[s]," or figures of masculine strength and mind (Winslow 1851, 35). It is during this transition that women are assumed to become strong-minded, pursue masculine goals, develop short and severe tempers, and deviate from femininity by demonstrating a boldness that repulses men. At the stages of puberty, when women transition from girlish intentions to "womanly" desires "to be married and bear children," Winslow (1851, 30) suggests, all "instinctive stimuli of desire" should be redirected to domestication. These passions for intimacy are temporary urges of female immaturity and development. Through reproductive maturation, women's inclinations were assumed to shift from carnal indulgence to affectionate familial aspirations.

Outlining the expectations for ideal womanhood, Winslow realigns female passions toward marriage and motherhood. Amorous women unable to comply with Winslow's "two excellencies" of perfect body and divine mind, were noted as suffering from "morbid appetites" (Winslow 1851, 30). This circulation of medical rhetoric about female abnormalities and degeneration proliferated and promoted women's desires as unnatural. Designated as immoral and unstable, passionate women were labeled with the ability to corrupt a frail society. To avoid these conditions, the constructs of womanhood confined women within the boundaries of the domestic sphere. Encapsulated within their homes and distracted by housekeeping and hospitality, women were suppressed and denied access to their natural instincts. A method of control deployed by patriarchal institutions, labels of the angel/whore dichotomy functioned to promote subjective self-regulatory female ontologies. Founded in Western theology through Christian depictions of Eve and Mary, these origins of conflicting female behaviors informed early-to-mid-Victorian stereotypes.

The objective for a patriarchal-dominated society was to restrict sexuality through reinforced ideals of chastity and moral domesticity. Mirroring the two original female figurations in Christianity, early-to-mid-Victorian society perpetuated dichotomies of Eve and Mary. These two women from Western religion represent female duality of two stereotypical ontologies that have been historically constructed for women. On the one hand, Eve as a figuration of the temptress who rejected rules, was epitomized through her carnality, seduced by the Devil, and responsible for the downfall of man. Mary, on the other hand, was the sacrificial pure Virgin, who embodied purity and goodness. Using these two stereotypes as foundations for the binaries of female behavior, early-to-mid-Victorian institutions dichotomized women into antithetical roles. Partly informed by the narrative of wicked and rebellious Eve, Victorian society was conflicted whether women were easily manipulated, or as Mary Poovey (1988, ix) points out, "devilishly wild and uncontrollable." Moreover, women's identities could not be constructed into an identity within a singular maternal role, resulting in the material division of women. Society polarized women into opposing identities: one of morality and the other of wickedness, which perpetuated a dichotomy of "sexless, moralized angel[s]" and "aggressive carnal magdalen[s]" (Poovey 1988, 11). In fear of this deviation and sexual instability, middle- and upper-class expectations of femininity were sublimated into virtuous ideologies.

While society viewed women as sexually contaminative, the illusion of modesty and virtue was instilled into expected roles to enforce sexual neutering. Women who desired social acceptance chose to subdue their urges, repressed their instincts, and submitted to the code of middle-class morality. Adopting these designated expectations of femininity, subjugated women complied with behavioral restrictions and became angels of the private sphere. Subjected to the role of domestic caregivers, these women repressed their personal desires to function within the boundaries of the early-to-mid-Victorian moral codes of conduct. Furthermore, women were assumed as natural companions, individuals to make men's life more enjoyable and comfortable. Echoing the rhetoric of Christian theology, women, as derived from Eve, were "made" as "helpers" (Coogan 2010, 14). Reinforcing the Western religious belief that women were created as helpmeets for men, Victorian society perpetuated this biblical ideal that their only desire should be for their husbands, and that men should rule over them. Therefore, women's behavior was regulated and shaped to be compatible with, and complement, men's personalities without indulging in their own desires. For fear of social ostracization or psychological institutionalization, some women, convinced society of their falsified virtue and moral characteristics to maintain the illusion of sexual restraint.

Whereas some women appropriated institutional identities encouraging aseptic sexuality, other women rejected social confinement. Single, sexually motivated women were perceived as significant issues in early-to-mid-Victorian society. From one aspect, single, or unmarried women were viewed as significant sources of mockery and contempt. It was commonplace for these women, living outside of prescribed societal boundaries, to be ridiculed and treated abhorrently. This occurred because they either rejected, or were refused, the sole purpose of marriage; therefore, those who repudiated, or failed to obtain, this Victorian ideal were ridiculed. However, from another aspect, these women were also the embodiments of patriarchal fears of unhindered female sexuality and social corruption. "Unsexed" spinsters, as Rita S. Kranidis (1999, 174) argues, not only lacked a proper space in the hegemony of society but were considered "problematic and dangerous." As marginalized and uncontrolled, unmarried women were corruptive and superfluous in Victorian terms and deemed as a social concern. "Stigmatized by terms like 'redundant,' 'superfluous,' and 'odd,'" according to Elaine Showalter (1985, 61), such women were cautioned as vulnerable to mental maladies. These women were troublesome because of their abilities to transgress the boundaries of the social spheres. Doing so, they functioned within the private environment of domesticity while simultaneously operating within the public, or social, domain. Albeit single and capable of navigation through both the social and domestic spheres, single women were declared as ignorant of, but nonetheless motivated by, sexual instincts. They were unaware of potential social hazards that led to loss of virtue. For example, W. R. Greg (1850, 456) claims that "women's desires scarcely ever lead to their fall" because prior to the fall, they rarely have such desires, let alone the conscious process to differentiate it from other passions until they "have already fallen," therefore women succumbed to their passions in error. Furthermore, Greg claims that in women, passions are dormant (and sometimes non-existent), until they are excited by their own nature, or by unfamiliar situations. Only realizing afterward that there was a transition from single Victorian lady to corrupt[ible] fallen woman. In opposition to the desires of a patriarchal structure, independent women who indulged in intimacy, consciously or subconsciously, were considered corrupt and toxic to society.

Independent and nonconforming women, as antithetical to virtuous angels, lacked respect and were characterized as "whores" or monsters. This stereotypical "polarisation" of female "patterns of antithesis" as virgin/whore, Avril

Horner and Sue Zlosnik (2016, 1) suggest, challenges conformity to such traditional Victorian expectations of womanhood and leads to the stipulation of monstrosity. Those who obtained this mark were regarded as fallen and ostracized from respectable society. Therefore, these women were labeled as disreputable and classified as part of this disrespectful sphere. These particular women were perpetuated in varied discourses as wicked and monstrously violent, possessed by, and unable to control, their primal instincts. Whereas socially appropriate women abided by strict behavioral prescriptions and identified as uninhabited by desires, albeit voluntarily repressed, indulgent women disregarded moral obligations and succumbed to intimate pleasures. As embodiments of both femininity and natural passions, these women reclaimed their abilities for self-expression and agency through the rejection of traditional behavioral discourse. Female acceptance of sexual aberrance encouraged noncompliance to societal ideologies and moral repression. The rejection of artificial boundaries allowed these women to gain agency and reclaim their sexuality. Therein, women who refused the institutional (scientific, cultural, and medical) confines of morality, were considered dangerous and subjugated to rehabilitative procedures.

PATHOLOGIZATION OF FEMALE SEXUALITY

The popular perspective of early-to-mid-Victorian society designated women's sexuality as pathological and potentially corruptive, therefore a fearful stance was maintained and promoted through medical discourses. While many experts designated female sexuality as an uncontrollable abnormality, some psychologists and physiologists argued that carnal desires were natural, and sometimes beneficial, for women. Forcibly subjected to repression, women's instincts were inculpated as causes for irrationality and destruction, not just in the individual but in society as a whole. Whereas some women embraced the moralistic role and conformed to societal standards, others refused behavioral guidelines and faced ostracization and mistreatment. These women who indulged in passions and neglected the traditional role of mother/wife were regarded as socially antagonistic. Institutions, predominantly those in the medical field, feared that women's sexuality had the potential to cause psychosomatic illnesses. For example, Laycock investigates women's nervous disorders, and suggests that hysteria occurs as a result of inflamed passions. Offering a medical guide about female instability and methods of control, he argues that young women, of equal age to young men, are encouraged by the same inclinations toward the opposing sex. Because of these shared passions, it was recommended that young women and men refrain from association in public settings to avoid the "serious risk of exciting the passions"

(Laycock 1840, 141). These popular medical treatises, similar to theological and conduct literature of the time, suggest that such interactions would lead to injurious practices of both mind and body. While interactivity with men was dangerous for young women's passions, exercise was also a likely culprit. A daily routine that is "little more than a lounging walk in two and two file," was suspected to charge the female sensory system extreme excitability (Laycock 1840, 141). This excitement, or excess energy influences the destabilization of the system, consequently resulting in hysterics. Therefore, this notion of hysteria, as a result of the excesses of energetic women, disseminates through Victorian narratives and is concurrently found in such literature that highlights female wildness. A significant cause for concern, this abundant energy in young girls affected by sensory overload, threatened to become "imbecile in mind, habits, and pursuits," thereby marking them as susceptible for such ailments as hysteria or mania when informed by atypical activities that induce excitement (Laycock 1840, 42). Furthermore, it is assumed that such hysteria is caused by the promotion of sexual excitement as affective influences of the reproductive system. Reinforcing pathologies of sexuality based on external influences, such medical experts as Laycock advise strict behavioral restrictions on social interactions.

While arguing against female precociousness, Laycock's discourse promotes the ideals of Christian morality and position for middle-and upper-class femininity. After young women are introduced into society, interactivity with the opposite sex and indulgences in decadent behaviors act in an injurious manner on the nervous system. Any exposure to the "excitement and competition" of social life, the "excited love, ungratified desire, disappointed vanity" and affections, indulgent activities such as sleep, "late hours," or the excessive consumption of "stimulants, as wines, liqueurs, coffee, tea," result in detrimental consequences on young women (Laycock 1840, 142). All of these external environmental effects were assumed to impede and act upon the uterus and ovaries. Influenced by emotions on the reflexes and nervous system, women were, then, susceptible to hysteria. Though impulsive single young women succumb to their passions and direction by young men, "robust, unmarried female[s], in easy circumstances" have the potential to "escape many of these evils" (Laycock 1840, 142). Laycock reinforces the notion that grown women, mostly those after the age of eighteen, possess fully developed reproductive organs, with accompanying indolence and luxury therefore, similar to the discourse in Sarah Stickney Ellis's conduct manuals for women (discussed in the following section), marriage is recommended to avoid unregulated passions and affections. Perpetuating the theory that aligns untainted femininity toward roles in marital confines, Laycock's expertise in the medical industry promotes the language and ideals of female domestication.

Following Laycock's implications of sexuality and mental afflictions, other Victorian medical professionals entered the conversation to expand upon these relationships. Winslow (1851, 19), as one of these experts, promoted the ideology that women are moral beings when controlled but nothing less than "female animal[s]" when influenced, thereby submitting that their instability is due to latent sexuality. As supposed embodiments of compassion and emotion, women were subconsciously subdued by prioritization. For example, Winslow (1851, 19) claims that women's emotions are centered on their offspring, desires are typically focused on husbands, and their "whole nature is imbued with love," not sexual impulses. Women, then, were considered as primarily moral beings when their passions are focused and directed to spiritual life. When devoted to religion and family, their souls fill with an emotional and spiritual fervor, however, this virtue has potential for interruption when their repressed "nature" surfaces. Claiming that devoted women are both mentally and physically perfect, Winslow argues that these devotions fail when affected by morbidity of the nervous system. Similar to Laycock, Winslow (1851, 32) theorizes that women who suffer "from irregular action of the ovaria on the system," succumb to the degeneration of self into such deceptive and "monomaniacal cunning" beings. Therefore, sexual passion, and the suppression of natural instincts to "fulfil the prescribed conditions," leads to dangerous influences on women's reproductive organs (Carter 1853, 22). Entering the conversation of latent passions by Laycock and Winslow, Carter links this female sexuality to violent feelings in women.

Hysteria, then, is the result of carnal desires in relation to the reproductive organs. Parroting the discourse of preceding medical experts, Carter (1853, 31) emphasizes that "natural manifestations" of strong emotions are continuously repressed to comply with the expectations of a strict society, therefore the resulting abnormalities become prominent. As a result of social subjugation and repression of sexual instincts, women who rejected conventional Victorian behaviors were penalized through medical treatments and confinement. Carter (1853, 35) continues the discourse of degenerative and unstable functions by arguing that "sexual propensities of women" result in the "derangement of . . . sexual organs," thereby leading to hysteria. With the advancing discussion about the degeneration of female reproductivity, social anxieties over sexuality circulated through popular literature, thus patriarchal institutions necessitated treatments for disorderly women. For those women who succumbed to their passions, they were either ostracized by society or faced repercussions by medical treatment.

Carter's theory of repression echoes in Josef Breuer and Sigmund Freud's (1895, 844) later work on hysteria, of which they argue that sexual repression "transpositions" from the lower to the upper quadrant of the body. Drawing from these earlier medical texts, later theories of hysteria reflect how repression of emotions and instincts result in sensations that encourage psychosomatic ailments "in relation to the genitals" (Breuer and Freud 1895, 844). Some women, Carter asserts, were driven to replicate hysteria by purposefully affecting their reproductive systems for sexual attention. These women knowingly produced the illness, thereby creating a somatogenically induced hysteria generating psychogenic madness. Led to believe that suppression of sexuality results in actions that "would make modest women blush," Carter (1853, 26) suggests that uterine complications were responsible for such behavior. It is through these early-to-mid-Victorian theories that ailments such as hysteria and nervous abnormalities were linked to reproductive functions. This connection of psyche to soma informed future research about disorders and perpetuated speculative discourse about female sexuality.

Women who deviated from orthodox middle-class behaviors were treated as mentally corrupt and faced repercussions of medical intervention and realignment of character. As a result, medical intervention occurred from such experts as Isaac Baker Brown (1866), a prominent gynecological-obstetrician who theorizes that excessive sexual desire and personal stimulation is cause for physical and mental deterioration in women. An advocate of maintaining the status quo, he suggests that female masturbation is a threat to society and results in an unnatural sexual role of misused reproductivity, not unlike that of prostitutes. Arguing that these women experience frequent nerve irritation, Baker Brown (1866, 7) posits that excess stimulation results in "paroxysms of abnormal excitement," increased excitability of the nerves, and hysteria. For women to submit to the role as complacent wife and mother, Baker Brown (1866, 9) formulated a "radical cure" of "unsexing the female," which results in clitoridectomy, or the removal of the clitoris with scissors. While maintaining the ability for procreation, women exposed to this mutilation were dispossessed of libidinous passions. It was Baker Brown's purpose to remove women's sexual independence, render them carnally void, and reinstate them as virtuous objects to benefit Victorian men.

While some specialists believed that sexuality was a viable drive in men, it was inherently absent in average women. A British gynecological doctor and medical author known for his expertise on reproductive functions, William Acton (1862, 212) argued that sexuality was presented in males but not typically found in females because "the majority of women (happily for them) are not very troubled with sexual feeling of any kind." He suggests that while sexual impulses are habitual responses in men, in women they are rare exceptions. These exceptions of sexual impulsivity emerge only in women afflicted by nymphomania, thus distinguishing them as abnormal. This prominent medical text that echoes the Christian creation of Eve as helpmeet concentrates on the reproductivity of men while ultimately neglecting women's sexuality. Arguing against sexual relevancy in women, Acton (1862,

213) claims that in general, women of such modesty rarely long for personal "sexual gratification" and only "submit" to their husbands's passions. While Acton claims that sexual urges in most women are irrelevant, unless driven by the necessity to satisfy their spouses, he also argues that were it not for their maternal instincts, women would avoid sexual intimacy altogether. As a popular voice in the mid-Victorian period Acton promoted female subjugation and assisted in the removal of agency and the reduction of women to biological necessities.

Acton, as an influential surgeon and advocate of morality, Emma Liggins (1997, 28) notes, brought attention to social issues such as prostitution and was perceived as an "authoritative" voice. A prominent figure of medicine, Acton promoted discourse that suggests women were free of passions and desire for self-satisfaction. It was this popular belief, founded in Christian theology, that women's involvement in sexual relations was based solely around the desires of men. Using this stance to negate female passions, Acton refers to women's desires as circumstantial or practically non-existent. Surmising that there are many women who "never feel any sexual excitement whatever," Acton (1862, 213), similar to Winslow, also acknowledges that there are some who are "capable of experiencing it." Only experiencing these passions at each menstrual period, these women were temporarily affected. Furthermore, according to his assumptions, many women care, or know little, about sexuality because their passions are focused on family and household. Classifying women as inherently void and incapable of sexual desires, married and/or medical men, Acton (1862, 213) argues, provide a different narrative about "vindictive female nature" that causes such "vile aspersions" or unpleasant attacks on their integrity. It was assumed, primarily by these prominent medical experts, that if women experienced perpetual carnal inclinations, it was a result of mental instability or issues emanating from the reproductive organs. To avoid such ailments that associated sexuality and mental degradation, medical institutions entered the debate to warn of resulting pathologies.

This controversial demeanor of sexually provocative women opposed societal standards and was considered objectionable for women to function according to their passions as Victorian society required female submission. The inimical disjunction between inherent carnal nature versus intrinsic morality positioned women within the space between binary identities, thus removing self-expression and agency. Uninhibited female promiscuity threatened the fragile patriarchal system therefore regulations promoted through popular discourses restricted undesired behavior and repressed sexually devious women. Society viewed these women as insatiable sinners who were "forced to recognize their sins" during which they could become less "carnal" through the acceptance of spirituality (Cott 1978, 36). An idea founded in Western theology and promoted by society, absolution was provided if women repented and repressed their vices. Therefore, early-to-mid-Victorian women were encouraged to reject their inherent nature and submit to social standards and performances as virtuous beings. As a result, society passively silenced women's sexuality by designating it solely for procreation, while negating the pleasurable effects as unnecessary or taboo.

Social institutions advocated for this presumption of passionless identities to construct ideologies that promoted morality as the only acceptable route for compliant femininity. Women were encouraged to evoke the moral traits of chastity and reticence for social acceptance and appeasement of men. This restriction informed female behavior and etiquette that instructed women to be reserved and compliant. In recognition of these expectations, Nancy Cott (1978, 219) coined the term "passionlessness" to explain how Victorian society created a metaphorical understanding about the significance of women's "carnal and moral nature." Epitomized as a concept promoting purified femininity, passionlessness, presents a newly envisioned hypothesis that early-to-mid-Victorian women were not driven by sexual instincts. Society based female behaviors on this supposition that women lacked passion therefore any sexual aggressions and lascivious behaviors were uncharacteristic. While these popular ideas were informed by discourses of inherently sexless women, it was purposefully promoted to minimize sexual characteristics and conventionalize strong morals and dutiful ethics. This construction of virtue as the archetype of female ideology was instituted by the self-declared moral authoritative voices who elected to canonize restraint and place chastity as the objective of feminine achievement. Utilized as a "positive contribution," the core idea of passionlessness substituted female sexuality with spirituality to allow women's faculties to align with societal standards (Cott 1978, 233). This advancement of passionless vapidity separated women from their own sexual proclivities, elevated them above the threatening animal nature that Victorian medical men associated them with, and informed discourses that they were created solely for their purity and reproductive value. Following the discursive trends of neutralized female sexuality, early-to-mid-Victorian medical discourses enforced self-regulated behavior under the guise of middle- and upper-class femininity. While women were expected to maintain sexual passivity in the role of moral domesticity, men were permitted to indulge their natural carnal tendencies. These double standards promoted dichotomous behaviors and expectations for Victorian men and women.

Double Standards of Victorian Sexuality

The early-to-mid-Victorian era period sequestered women's sexual behavior while neglecting regulations for male desires and sexual activities. This purpose of double standards was a result of the social regulation of sexual bodies. A significant concern for Victorian society, female passions were controlled by the institutional "deployment of sexuality"; therefore, discursive regulation was established to regulate pleasure (Foucault 1976, 122). As a method of surveillance and control, perpetuated by institutions, regulations of sexuality and the body were instated not just against the exploited classes but against women of the upper- and middle-classes. Whereas men, as dominant authorities of these classes, were not defined and constructed according to their corporeal forms and biological functions, women were, therefore they were subjected to double standards of sexuality.

Although women were expected to perform within these restrictive boundaries, men possessed the ability to traverse social expectations and partake in sexual activities. Men were assigned the role of master, as individuals who exhibited responsibility and self-control, while women had limited responsibility and were socially designed to be controlled by others. Society thus promoted characteristics that men were reasonable, independent, and self-sufficient; however, women were solely suited for the private sphere. Viewed as submissive, emotional, and dependent, these prescribed feminine qualities were argued as derivative of female reproduction. In this popular opinion, whereas men were complex beings of logic, respect, and independence, women were inferior and lacked agency. These ideals of gendered characteristics were promoted by the theological figures of Mary and Christ. Correlating the relationship of the corporeal form to the incorporeal spirit, Victorian society posited women as vessels for spirituality and men as embodiments of suffering and feeling. It is through this creation of dichotomous identities that institutions promoted the belief that women, as filled with the spirit of God, had no carnal knowledge and that they were naturally virtuous. Men, on the other hand, were representations of God's humanity, therefore filled with his desires, pains, and motivations. It is through this distinct separation that society aligned women with "passivity, expectancy, receptivity" and motherhood was designated "as the supreme fulfilment" (Dyer 1997, 17). On the other hand, men were created as beings with internal conflicts and suffering and were made to suffer under the public social weight. As instruments of God's humanity, forced to experience pain, men, then, were granted the authority to also indulge in pleasure, while women as immaterial representations of divinity, were burdened with chastity.

As their bodies were responsible for the continuation of humanity, women's sexuality, and their natural identities, were sanitized and modified for societal obligations. Thus, Victorian women's desires were assumed as dormant while men's were active. Victorian men categorized their desires and interests into affections and passions, which demonstrate two behaviors: one of married asexuality and the other, independent overt sexuality. Likewise,

Pamela K. Gilbert (2004, 5) argues that these two categorical structures were created because both attitudes were antagonistic, which men found difficult and "projected them" onto vulnerable and unknowing women. Through this compartmentalization of love from sex, men distinguished variations between "good" women, who were asexual (or for reproductive use only) and idealized as domestic partners, and "bad" women who epitomized sexuality and were used for carnal ventures. These double standards informed women that their sexual functions were for procreation, whereas men's sexuality was inherently natural and necessary. If women offered their desires to courting men and refused to resist seduction, they faced ostracism from presumptions of forwardness and ignorance of social regulations. As men were free to satisfy their sexual appetites through such avenues as prostitution, they escaped consequences of sexual promiscuity. Therefore, women were responsible to resist temptation, preserve moral superiority, and function as objects for male pleasure. As beings restricted to chastity and reproductivity, women were preserved in conventional roles of homogenized Victorian femininity as domestic angels.

ANGELS AND DEMONS: PROMOTION OF VICTORIAN FEMININITY

The stereotypical identity of the Victorian angel was socially prescribed to preserve the patriarchal institutions of authority. This ideology of self-sacrificial and agreeable women was promoted through discourses of law, medicine/science, culture, and theology, that continued the conversation and contributed to the stereotypical formula of women and reductive essentialism. This polarity of feminization was used to disguise male anxieties of female equality; therefore, the angel trope was instilled as a means of control. The orthodox image of femininity served as a standard for women's behavior. In this role of domestication and morality, women's actions and behaviors are observed, decided on, and recorded, as Jane Wood (2001, 9) asserts, "in the range of writing across the period." This confluence of discourses on women's moral and social functions created templated constructs about prescribed womanhood. Mirroring and reiterating language about female nature the discursive perpetuation of sexual sanitation forced women into roles of domesticity. Social opinions about such femininity were drawn from popular literary works about how women should perform. Negligent of personal female experiences, early-to-mid-Victorian literature shaped ideologies of women based on social expectations of biological reproduction and behavioral submission.

The role of ideal womanly purity was expressed through sentimental language in popular literature. For instance, Coventry Patmore's (1858) figuration of middle-class perfection in his poem, "Angel in the House," promotes attributes of perfected femininity. In this long semi-autobiographical poem, Patmore linked expectations of women with moral characteristics, which became the ideal stereotype of spiritual Victorian womanhood. In this infatuated exposition about his marriage, Patmore hyperbolizes expectations of middle-class femininity. Written at a time when prescribed womanhood characterized middle- and upper-class women as, what Lydia Murdoch (2013, 134) calls, "chaste, pure, innocent, and uncorrupted by worldly and material desires," Patmore epitomizes Emily as an ideal Victorian woman who embodies all socially desired traits. Presenting the necessary qualities of domestication and morality, Patmore promotes an idealistic figuration of womanhood as:

> Her disposition is devout
> Her countenance angelical;
> The best things that the best believe
> Are in her face so kindly writ
> The faithless, seeing her, conceive
> Not only heaven, but hope of it (*AitH* 1858, 39–40).

Patmore's representation of Emily is an angelic ideal whose overall ontology denotes virtue and purity. As a material embodiment of faith and moral disposition, Patmore's angel possesses the power of positive influence and promotion of theological ideals. As a member of the Anglican faith, but a believer in Roman Catholicism, Patmore promoted this ideology of moral divinity and proliferation of femininity.[2] According to the expectations of Victorian society, moral women are identified and affiliated with their domestic sphere. This virtuous domesticity and subjective compliance presented a significant necessity for middle- and upper-class marriage of which Patmore professes:

> Man must be pleased; but him to please
> Is woman's pleasure; down the gulf
> Of his condoled necessities
> She casts her best, she flings herself.
> How often flings for nought! and yokes
> Her heart to an icicle or whim,
> Whose each impatient word provokes
> Another, not from her, but him;
> While she, too gentle even to force
> His penitence by kind replies,
> Waits by, expecting his remorse,
> With pardon in her pitying eyes (*AitH* 1858, 74–75).

Patmore not only depicts women as responsible for household maintenance and hospitality, but also suggests that it is their obligation to demonstrate gentility and penitence. According to Patmore, it was the *"pleasure"* of women to please their husbands and pardon their wrongdoings (*AitH* 1858, 74–75). Therefore, he structures feminine ideology as a figuration of a meek and modest woman who submits to her husband without objection. Perfect women, as suggested in Patmore's idyllic poem, were expected to present characteristics of modesty, charm, grace, submission, and powerlessness. As epitomes of high morality, women were also responsible for guiding children, caring for husbands, and regenerating society through displays of Christianity. If successful in these actions, then husbands and sons would remain home and not seek their desires and "(morally suspect) entertainment elsewhere" (Mitchell 2009, 266). Patmore's poem, albeit dedicated to his wife, affixes the entirety of Victorian women into traditional stereotypes of femininity.

While popular social discourses aligned women's nature with domestication, some advocates argued its artificiality. British philosopher and civil servant, John Stuart Mill (1806–1873) and activist, Barbara Leigh Bodichon (1827–1891) were outspoken proponents of women rights and freedoms.[3] Commenting on the social appropriation of women's supposed "nature," Bodichon (1866, 5) argues that women operate under the "what is out of sight is out of mind" principle while Mill claims that social institutions all inevitably revoked female agency and instilled a sense of dependency and subordination through this mutability. In Mill's argument against behavioral containment of women, he illustrates how the immateriality of institutional discourses exerts its force upon female bodies. The socially applied postulation of female nature forcefully disassociated women from their inherent instincts and redefined them as artificial figures for domestication. As a method for their confinement into roles as mothers and wives, women were informed that "it is their *duty*" and "that it is their *nature*" to prioritize others, disregard their own interests, and "have no life but in their affections" (Mill 1869, 9). Mill explicitly argues against these forced parameters of feminine ideologies and states that the so-called nature of women is an artificial construct. The purpose for this artificiality of prescribed behavior was to ensure that women possessed limited power, were occupied "but little with anything beyond their own family circle," and were legally subordinate to their husbands (Bodichon 1866, 7). Victorian men, then, feared the social equality of women because of the potential to lose their own dominancy. Hence, female subordination through matrimony was used to create a method of control to restrict privileges and opportunities. As a voice beyond his years, Mill recognizes the immaterial/material figuration of women even during the period. Arguing against the authoritative discourse responsible for creating female constructs, Mill exposes the social subjugation of women's mind-bodies.

Mill targets the social stigma of female sexuality and proposes that institutional repression of women's desire constructed this popular illusion of women as sexually apathetic. Arguing that society's beliefs about female nature are merely "empirical generalizations" formed on assumptions and popular discourses without further analysis, Mill (1869, 39) suggests that the construction of women's nature is formed from opinion and shaped for social standards. From this perspective, in England rule was the social standard, therefore "rule has largely *replaced* nature" (Mill 1869, 40). Indeed, rule may have been strong enough to repress nature, however, nature still resides in the individual. Ergo, rule does not fully replace nature, but it does attempt to distort it. These social rules, as promoted through popular rhetoric, centered on morals and chastity, and were used to manipulate women into the subjugated role of matrimony. By convincing women that they were passionless, it allowed a method for female subjugation by explaining that the "essential part of sexual attractiveness is meekness, submissiveness" (Mill 1869, 10). Surmising that female docility is a desired trait, this persuasive language signified women as vulnerable and incapable, therefore allowing men to take control and create behavior guidelines. Suggesting that the moral definition of female nature was used as a method of repression, Mill (1869, 13, 17) ascertains that it makes women "instruments" of "animal functions," thereby leading medical experts, such as Darwin and Lombroso, to link women to nonhuman figures. In this argument, Mill notably observes how institutional discourse, based on popular opinion, constructed artificial identities for women that subjugated them to their bodily functions, a significant issue in the early-to-mid-Victorian period. As an advocate for the authenticity of women's nature, Mill was a lone voice in the Victorian period. His exploration and vociferous dismissal of social constructs provided a unique materialist perspective that illustrated how the immateriality of institutional discourses impacted and altered the materiality of women through conventional roles with theological origins.

Origins of the Victorian "Angel"

Expectations of demure Victorian women were formulated from Christian theology, based upon the creation, and fall of man. Women, in reference to Eve, were destined for subordination as individuals who offered compassion and companionship without independent thought or free action. Eve, as the original temptress, was easily influenced by nature (as demonstrated through her interaction with the serpent). Based on her ungovernable curiosity and supposed susceptibility to external influences, Eve was punished for her sin. Consequently, subsequent women were destined as inherently destructive and prophesized to corrupt patriarchal society. It is through this conviction of the first woman's desire for knowledge, not carnal passion, that early-to-mid-Victorian institutions assumed that all women were "personified by Eve" (Kramer and Sprenger 1978, 142). Therefore, uncontrollable women were designated as intrinsically licentious, manipulative, and driven by instincts. Based on this assumption and the correlation to reproductive functions, women were considered weak and easily influenced individuals. Promoting this discourse of female instability, the angel ideology was endorsed for moral guidance and self-control.

In the nineteenth century, Christianity maintained an influence on the behaviors and ideologies of Victorian women. Middle-class femininity was established in the early-Victorian era and based on theological movements centered on morality. The Church of England, as Jenny Daggers (2001, 653) argues, "both epitomised and reinforced this social norm" and endorsed subversion of women's domestic confinement. The influential theological perspective of the Church established middle-class respectability by way of gendered constructs rooted in morality. An ideal behavior encouraged by Christian religion, the expectations of female morality circulated through discourses of each faction. In the early-to-mid-Victorian period, the Church of England's distinct factions differentiated in theological and social approaches but reinforced similar ideologies of femininity and morality. The evangelical movement, also identified as the low church, "stressed personal piety, conversion, individual Bible reading, and the serious Christian life" (Mitchell 2009, 245). This sect of Christianity emphasized morality, philanthropy, and reform. Therefore, by the mid-Victorian period, evangelicals from the middle-class had a reputation as rigid and repressed. These evangelicals, then, had a reputation for immutable morality and disapproved excitable activities such as reading non-theological literature, intimate socialization, and social entertainment. As purveyors for personal restriction, evangelicalism aggressively promoted female morality and domestication. The evangelical movement was one of the first movements to align women with the home and to encourage Christian behaviors in all daily actions. Emphasizing the notion that its members were "true Christians," the Evangelicals promoted the ideal that families promote purity, positivity, and "good relations" within their own household and amongst society itself (Flanders 2003, 6). This dichotomy further aligned men with the public domain and business, while solidifying women's roles as socially hospitable helpmeets within the domestic sphere.

Whereas men maintained the difficult social interactions and stressors of life, sheltered women would promote morals through charity and domestic hospitality. Middle-class ideals emphasized the home as the center of feminine morality and a space of renewal. As a son of an evangelical mother, John Ruskin (1819–1900) counseled nineteenth-century women to act as moral pillars in the domestic sphere. In 1865 he published his lectures under the titles *Sesames and Lilies,* and the appropriately named *Of Queens' Gardens.* These lectures offered moral guidance on the treatment, and expectations, of middle-class Victorian women. Ruskin suggests that it is the purpose of women to act supportive to their husbands and to educate their daughters with similar virtues, thereby *Lilies* takes up the stereotype of the angel, and representation of the spiritual female. Ruskin's use in the title strictly refers to women's purity therefore the flowers, lilies and sesames, are symbolized for their own purity and beauty. In the lecture about the dedication of women, Ruskin (1865, 60) references angels who provide men with "a haven in a heartless world," which is a play on words, substituting haven for heaven. Establishing women as angels, Ruskin (1865, 60) suggests that women's natural character can be achieved through the establishment of home, or "heaven." In Ruskin's popular lecture, home was not only a residence but a representation of the feminine ideal, a space of hospitality and protection from the influences of the public world. For instance, Ruskin (1865, 60) writes that the duty of womanhood lies in the practices of comfort, beauty, and assistance, therefore he implies that their "proper" place was within the home. Within these boundaries, women created a hospitable and sanctified environment for their husbands. As arbitrators of housework and hospitality, women were confined within the invisible role of domesticity. As designated caregivers and amiable companions, middle- and upper-class women eschewed authoritative responsibility.

While expected to act as arbiters of order and structure over household servants, women were remiss of other notable authority. Perpetuating this discourse of feminine domestication, Ruskin (1865, 51) posits that "wom[e]n's power is for rule" over their private domain. Claiming that women lacked intelligence for creativity or invention, he proposes that they are capable of "sweet ordering, arrangement, and decision" (Ruskin 1865, 51). This promotes the stereotype that women only possess qualities that further established comforts of the home for their husbands. Echoing Patmore's language of the angel, Ruskin (1865, 51–52) implies that women's greatest function is "Praise," and in return they are "protected from all danger and temptation" of external influences. His language implies that if women follow the conventional Victorian guidelines of middle-class femininity, then they could comfortably live and avoid negative affectations. In their domestic fulfillment, women, as Ruskin (1865, 52) suggests, unless seeking it, "need enter into no danger, no temptation, no cause of error or offence," because the "nature" of the home is "Peace" and "shelter," protected by men. Drawing from the language of Laycock's medical treatise, Ruskin avoids the promotion of mixed company to deter female passions. Perpetuating the ideology of women in the private sphere, Ruskin suggest that protection from patriarchal rulers is located within the home. In women's subjugated roles and confinement to household domestication, Ruskin asserts that they are sheltered from external affectations and excess of stimulation.

Similar to Ruskin's logic, The Church of England viewed any type of excess stimulation or influences as dangerous for women. Similar to indulgence in sexual activity, reading was also considered as detrimental to female morality. According to the *Church of England Quarterly Review* (1842) the primary readership of novels were women who were influenced by the "peculiarly mischievous" content within popular fiction (Ward 2010, 17). Owing to the belief that women were more vulnerable to influences and are more indulgent in certain harmful activities, such past-times as excess reading was targeted as a threat to female morality. Overindulgence in reading was feared by both medical and theological establishments. With the belief that women were vulnerable and open to influential suggestions, patriarchal institutions felt that literature would erode middle- and upper-class morality. Suggesting that female maladies were a result of desire for intimacy and literature, society feared an addiction of reading. An anxiety that compulsion, or indulges, would lead to sexual disgrace became prominent in conservative and evangelical journals and tracts. Both the Evangelicals and Tractarians tried to improve personal behavior and gender expectations through written publications. The Evangelicals, in their works of charity and moral encouragement created *The Religious Tract Society*, which later published weekly magazines called the *Girls Own Paper* and the *Boys Own Paper* from 1879 to 1967. These publications contained fiction with suggestions to encourage morality in girls and chivalry in boys. However, during the early-to-mid-Victorian period, the Church promoted moral discourse through tracts and popular cultural literature.

A second faction, known as the high church, or Anglo-Catholicism, started as the Oxford Movement in the 1830s. Referred to as Tractarianism, this sect took an authoritative approach that highlighted family traditions and self-abnegation. Prominent authors of the Oxford Movement used their literary talents to spread the influence of Christian morality through their writings.[4] For instance, Charlotte Mary Yonge (1823–1901), a novelist and magazine editor, was a proponent of the Oxford Movement and used her influence as a popular English novelist to promote their beliefs and inform middle- and upper-class women's behavior by writing novels of morality and domesticity. In her influential narrative, *The Daisy Chain* (1856), Yonge promotes a sense of duty and feminine morality through discipline and self-sacrifice of two sisters, Margaret and Ethel. As the impulsive younger sister, Ethel competes with her brother, Norman, in studies of classical languages, while negating domestic duties. Margaret, in her desire to see Ethel as "perfectly content and happy," convinces her to reject all intellectual curiosity (Yonge 1856,

633). In a deteriorating state, Margaret persuades Ethel to revoke her studies for domestication and femininity. Acknowledging Margaret's request, Ethel learns self-discipline and devotes her energy to domestic duties and missions for the church. Yonge takes the social concern of impressionable and immoral fiction and creates narratives that teach feminine structure aligned with the beliefs of the high church. As a prominent figure of the Oxford Movement, Yonge used her influence as a popular author to promote ideologies of virtue and morality throughout society. Similar to these theological expectations, conduct books were utilized to encourage prescribed roles of femininity in both middle-and upper-class society.

Cultural and Medical Guides for Feminine Behavior

Women's biological functions and independent thought were problematic to a patriarchal society, therefore behavioral guides enforced regulation. To ensure that they adhered to prescribed behaviors, women of the middle-classes were provided with popular conduct manuals. Presenting overarching themes that specifically addressed ideals of modesty and virtue, these conduct manuals acted as guides for proper feminine behavior and attraction. Women were treated as objects for male pleasure and satisfaction, thereby necessitating morality training to ensure that standards for subjugation were met. Promoting this ideal of the perfect girl, who becomes the perfect woman, wife, and mother was the social objective of early-to-mid-Victorian femininity. The way for women to achieve this respectability was to suppress sexual desires through domestication and motherhood. With this assumption and negative connotations against female intimacy, manuals for behavioral regulation and expectations circulated through Victorian literature.

Used to reinforce the conservative middle- and upper-class social structure, conduct books offered guidance to the behaviors that women should, and should not perform to remain virtuous. Promoting the idea of women's religious and social duties, such influential authors as Sarah Stickney Ellis (1842, 1) argue that there are "many valuable dissertations upon female character, as exhibited on the broad scale of virtue; but no direct definition of those minor parts of domestic and social intercourse, which strengthen into habit, and consequently form the basis of moral character." Seeking to inspire women and young girls through domestic instruction, Ellis promotes morality and female acquiescence for the improvement of society. She approaches the ideals of morality with a specific declaration creating a distinct binary between concepts of good and evil. Women are possessed with "peculiar faculties" as "a quickness of perception, facility of adaptation, and acuteness of feeling," all of which Ellis (1842, 3) claims are "for the part [they] have to act in life." This endowment of characteristics renders women "in a higher degree than men" therefore marking them as "susceptible both of pleasure and pain" (Ellis 1842, 3). Antagonistic to the opinion that women were solely immaterial spiritual representations of a godly figure, Ellis promotes female vulnerability as a fragile crux of women that determines behavioral choice.

While several of Ellis's popular conduct books elaborate on the expected behaviors of women's pivotal positions in life, all emphatically structure the purpose of womanhood as subordinate helpmeets to men. In her persuasive texts, Ellis adopts "A Woman's Mission," which promotes the idea that women's "strength" is through influence (Ellis 1842, 13). According to this missionary statement, women are responsible for leading by example and encouraging righteousness and virtue in others. With this discourse of conduct, Ellis (1842, 3) offers guidance to structure middle-class women as paragons of morality by suggesting that "the first thing of importance is to be content to be inferior to men." Promoting the popular opinion that women are the "weaker sex," Ellis (1842, 3) argues that women, while "inferior in bodily strength" are similarly "inferior in mental power." As a guide for women's personal improvement and self-guidance, Ellis's conduct manuals advocate for this derogatory opinion of inferiority by shrouding it in advantages over men. Arguing that the female frame, aptitude, and movement are more graceful than those characteristics found in men, this discourse creates an angelic image of Victorian femininity similar to Patmore's Emily. In addition to this image, Ellis (1842, 3) informs middle-class women that, although they are "inferior to men," they should be "content" with this position. She claims that this secondary role is a blessing because, while women are limited in intelligence and strength, they possess "softer touches and spiritual beauty" (Ellis 1842, 3). Aligning women with the aesthetic of angelic grace and aptitude, these characteristics are reflective of "Christian meekness" (Ellis 1842, 10). Promoting this ideology of feminine charm and influence, she suggests that these traits establish the necessary behaviors for middle-class functionality. Establishing the belief that it was not just the religious duty of women, but also the moral obligation, Ellis hoped to ensure a supportive and positive influence for men. It was propagated that women's conformation to this subordinate behavior would inadvertently improve social practices and strengthen Victorian traditions.

Aimed at stifling independent female behavior, Ellis's conduct manuals acted as guides for middle-class women. In *The Women of England, Their Social Duties, and Domestic Habits*, she persuades her readers by claiming "it is necessary" for women to cast aside their "natural caprice[s]" (Ellis 1842, 45). To succeed in their roles as wives, mothers, and daughters in the domestic sphere, unwanted characteristics of "love of self-indulgence," "vanity," "indolence," and the "very *self*" must be repressed (Ellis 1842, 45). Disregarding their natural instincts, women were encouraged to assume "a new nature" that is learned and developed through silent observation and prayer (Ellis 1842, 45). Motivated to dismiss personal desires and passions, women found satisfaction in "promoting the happiness of others" while making their own "remote and secondary" (Ellis 1842, 45). If middle-class women rejected these behaviors and responsibilities, or failed "in these roles," they were viewed as "repulsive" (Ellis 1842, 16). Taking this a step further, if their homes were inhospitable, then husbands were expected to disappear, thus rejecting their failed attempts of womanhood. Indeed, Ellis explains that "the extent of ruin and of wretchedness" of impetuous women are "appalling to contemplate" (Ellis 1842, 16). Giving into "impetuous and unregulated feelings" women that "renounce principles" and "act as mere creature[s] of impulse," possess no hope of maintaining a middle-class household or marriage (Ellis 1842, 16). Identifying marriage as a key objective for all middle- and upper-class Victorian women, Ellis's formulation of femininity not only creates a guide for women's conduct but informs medical discourse how to treat troublesome behaviors.

Perpetuating these traits of Christian morality and conduct, Winslow's medical text similarly promotes the institutional discourse of marriage to align women's behavior to the expectations of middle- and upper-class femininity. Claiming that the "women of Great Britain are remarkable for their chastity," Winslow (1851, 39) drives the ideology of the middle-class angel. Idealizing women as "beautiful object[s]," he argues that no matter the "*rights*" of women, it is their "*duty* to marry and bear children" (Winslow 1851, 42). Advancing Ellis's conversation, Winslow states that marriage and motherhood are not only the *duty* but the *privilege* of women. Promoting the theological discourse of middle-class conduct manuals, Winslow claims that it is women's destiny to fulfill their duties. Feeding into this popular early-to-mid-Victorian conversation, he suggests that God has bestowed "the most attractive traits" to women such as "*moral and physical fitness*" for the purpose of their duties (Winslow 1851, 41). Reducing women to their "fitness," Winslow (1851, 41) argues that this "perfect capacity" presented in such physical traits as "brilliant lips [and a] transparent clear complexion indicate[s] health." It is through these physiological features he claims that women are identifiable for their "fully developed form[s] and function[s]," which signifies their capacity to "reproduce the species" as a "healthy race" (Winslow 1851, 41). Winslow's argument for the fitness of women's bodies not only perpetuates the immaterial discourse of reducing women's forms to sole material purposes but echoes the Darwinian stance of genealogical success. Darwin indicates that fitness, relative to reproductivity, "deals with an individual's total genetic input into the next generation" inclusive of the mating system, "for example, monogamy, polygamy, promiscuity," age, and environment (Darwin 1871, xxvii). Winslow echoes this sentiment by suggesting that "sum total of these external indices of sexual fitness," women, "with the *physical capacity*, the requisite *moral feelings* and *sentiments*," present an image of "health and perfect corporeal development" that is "always the most attractive" for men (Winslow 1851, 41). Winslow joins the conversation at the junction between Ellis and Darwin to promote the objectification of women's mind-bodies through reproduction and marriage. Women, then, according to this prolific standard, were created by God as paragons of fitness and health to attract husbands and produce viable offspring. It is through this declaration of moral and physical fitness that Winslow identifies women as enticing and charming to the opposite sex.

While confined to the materiality of their reproductive functions, early-to-mid-Victorian women were objectified and deprived of their agency as functional and capable beings. Women who disregarded the traditional roles were overlooked or rejected. Classified as "sexual anomalies," only open for interpretation by physicians, these women were passed over in "marriage markets" (Wood 2001, 24). Such women were then confined within situations relevant to their bodies. Assigned to perform in roles determined by their biological characteristics, women were unable to escape the feminine construct and faced quarantine in bodies shaped by reproductivity and domesticity. Popular discourses designated the domestic sphere as a safe, ideal space that marginalized and provided new, artificial identities for women founded on family and subordination. Marriage, allocated as a pivotal milestone when girls transition into womanhood, also provided the stigma of dependency on either father or husband and was used to avoid social conflict or accusations of behavioral instability (i.e., hysteria, mania), which is discussed further in the following chapter. Realistically, women's role as objects transferred from fathers to husbands demonstrated a "loss of control over [their] own being," further implying a lack of possession over mind and body (Murdoch 2013, 163). With this consideration, there were no conjugal activities of force or violence inflicted on women by her husband that would hold men liable by law.

Women were denied agency and trapped within the stages that transitioned them from fathers and brothers to husbands and male offspring. Once transferred from their fathers to their husbands, women were objectified and confined within domestic boundaries. With the acceptance of marriage, women lessened the stipulation of negative categorization as whores, spinsters, or madwomen. The sublimation of sexuality forced women to transform their sexual energy into focus on complacency and domestic pleasure. Since women maintained sexual ignorance and passivity in personal satisfaction, an illusion of domestic satisfaction was created to face conformity into a Victorian dichotomous, and one-sided gendered society. Treated as objects of patriarchal possession, early-to-mid-Victorian women were exposed to the ideologies of social institutions, which removed their agency and subjugated them to their corporeal forms. This method of legitimizing immaterial discourse as the authority over female materiality reduced women to their biological functions and established artificial behaviors for control.

Through the navigation of popular texts and a common discursive theme spanning many institutions: cultural, educational, and medical, this perspective of popular literature provided insight into society's presumptions of womanhood. This examination of female confinement provides a foundation for expectations of middle- and upper-class femininity and their origins as well as the guides to perform as conventional Victorian women, which were foregrounded as the motivation or drive for the rejection of female essentialism and reductionalism. These primarily constructivist texts demonstrate how immaterial discourse about women's bodies informed popular literature and created artificial performative expectations for female materiality. With the dichotomous labels of virgin/whore, social institutions constructed ontologies that promoted women's nature as subordinate, inferior, and docile with the repression of instinctual and carnal behavioral traits, thereby encouraging an emergence of the figuration of the female gothic monstrosity.

NOTES

1. While I am aware that lower- and working-class women were subjected to similar expectations of femininity, I choose to look at the relatively sheltered social contexts of middle- and upper-class women, which was not complicated by poverty, working conditions, and other environmental factors particular to the situation of working-class women.

2. Although not strictly devout, Patmore in his early life was an Anglican with tendencies toward the Roman Catholic religion. During their marriage, Emily Patmore, a strict Protestant, converted to the High Anglican Church and Coventry Patmore eased his Roman Catholicism. However, upon Emily's death, Patmore converted to Roman Catholicism.

3. Both Mill and Bodichon petitioned in Parliament for women's suffrage in 1866 and acted as sponsors of the Married Women's Property Bill in 1868. The Married Women's Property Act was presented to Parliament in 1868 that allowed women to keep earned wages independent of their spouses, maintain small inheritances, hold property, and possess liability for children. After two years of reviews and revisions, this law was passed in 1870.

4. Other notable advocates of the high church are Christina Rosetti and Elizabeth Sewell.

Chapter Two

Forbidden Desire, Mental Degradation, and Nature

Repression of Gothic Madwomen

> Mind, they say, rules the world. But what rules the mind? The body.
>
> —Wilkie Collins 1861, 269

Victorian England saw an increase in newly defined mental disorders throughout the period. "The English Malady," termed in 1733 by George Cheyne, pertained to a gender-neutral evaluation of nervous diseases. At the onset of the nineteenth century, however, concepts of the mental malady shifted to focus explicitly on female madness. This realignment of an assumed illness that solely centers on women identifies the dichotomization of their supposed insanity: one side that demonstrates madness as behavioral misconduct, and the other as an exposition of irrational female nature, both of which oppose male rationality and logical structure. These dual notions of madness are founded upon a patriarchal perception of women's disorders. The first image of female maladies coincides with madness as representative of women's wrongdoings. In other words, insanity is a result of a poor choice or negation of traditional behavior. The second is drawn from the male interpretation and exploitation of feminine nature. These images of madness were established via a variety of Victorian pseudo-sciences, which suggested that women's rationality is contingent on their reproductive functions. Beliefs of this instability were then circulated by an informative exchange of literary and medical texts which, through their promotion, created a feedback loop that modified meanings of female experiences. It was during the early-Victorian period, then, that psychiatry began to emerge as a scientific practice. Its immersion in literature, however, presented ideologies subtly integrated with gender specified, and divisive, language within popular discourse. While women exhibited similar behavioral symptoms as men, gender differentiation occurred through psychic diagnosis and the proliferation of discursive literature which spoke to this separation. Madness, then, as it pertained to men, was referred to as the English malady, whereas women possessed the singularly identifiable "female malady," as Elaine Showalter (1985, 7) so poignantly identifies in *The Female Malady: Women, Madness and English Culture, 1830–1980*. Moreover, nineteenth-century psychiatry differentiated this distinction and classified the traditional English malady as aligned with civilized aspects of men, such as intellect and economical struggles, while women's malady was derived from their sexuality and affiliation with nature, both external and internal. Stereotyped as unable to contend with the rationale and cultural refinement of English men, women faced medical diagnoses affiliated with social-inferiority and inherent monstrosity.

This chapter builds upon these conventions of socially prescribed classifications and discusses the effects of restrictions on women's natural instincts as they manifest in contemporaneous gothic fiction. The impact of repression is illustrated in conjunction with psychosexual theories of the period, on figurations of the female mind-body in the Victorian Gothic. Among many of the impositions upon women in the nineteenth century, significant restrictions were placed on inherent inclinations favoring exhibitions of virtue. These socially mandated roles negatively impacted women's psychosomatic, biochemical, and neurological systems, thus resulting in such responses as hysterical conversion disorders. This relationship between neurology and psychosexuality demonstrates how psychology and physiology coalesce through varied displays of hysterical exhibitions. In nineteenth-century gothic texts, this manifests in the "monstrous" forms of madwomen, whose disordered mind-bodies are affected by, and in turn affect, their environments.

VICTORIAN FEMALE MADNESS: A PLAGUED DISCOURSE

Gender diagnosis disjunction is prevalent in the early-to-mid-Victorian identification of men with hypochondriasis and women with hysteria. While both disorders stem from a nervous disposition and inflict psychosomatic anomalies, psychic institutions created a dogmatic response for distinctive biology-based behaviors to avoid cross-categorizing gendered traits. Hypochondriasis, during this time was suggested as a predominantly male psychic reaction generated from ambition and desire for success, such civilized passions that Showalter (1993, 293) describes as "natural to men." Hysteria, on the other hand, was deduced as an affliction induced by the assumed natural feminine emotion: love. Stemming from the preconceived disposition of innate love and passion, hysteria was corroborated by the early-to-mid-Victorian medical sciences strictly as a female malady. This differential diagnosis segregates women's disorders from men's rationality and aligns them with irrationality and an inability for self-regulation. Thus, allowing a patriarchal structure to define and establish necessary processes for female behavioral regulations through literary classifications of hysteria.

Among many of the impositions women faced in the nineteenth century, significant restrictions were placed on inherent inclinations favoring exhibitions of virtue. These socially mandated roles negatively impacted women's neurological, psychological, and biological systems, inducing hysterical conversion disorder, or as Elizabeth A. Wilson (2004, 13) suggests in *Psychosomatic: Feminism and the Neurological Body*, transforming the "psyche into soma." In gothic texts of the Victorian period, this monistic amalgamation manifests in the forms of madwomen, whose disordered mind-bodies are affected by, and in turn affect, their environments. Thereby, the correlations between neurology and psychosexuality demonstrate how physiology and psychology coalesce through varied displays of hysterical conversion disorder. Conventions of socially prescribed classifications and their restrictions affect women's natural instincts and manifest in figurations of the female mind-body in contemporaneous Victorian Gothic fiction.

Early-to-mid-Victorian narratives used medical discourse to present social anxieties through mind-body exhibitions of female hysterics. Lives of the Victorian populace interceded and informed one another, and women struggled because their identities were intersected by the juxtaposition of the real and imaginary, the popular and obscure. Victorian medical science and literature were cyclical. Encapsulated within a feedback loop, medical and gothic narratives were responsible for informing one another. In this loop, the hysterical subject faces an identity conflict and struggles with the repressed intricacies of the construct of the female form. All of these circular social practices, as Michel Foucault (1976) claims, stem from the relationship of knowledge and power. The discursive construction of female ideologies, then, offer a framework for social methods and practices to inform what social relationships and behaviors women could have. As discussed in the previous chapter, discourses on sexuality created the ways in which society thinks about and deals with that specific topic. *Scientific sexualis*, or confessions of sexual discourse, informs the regulation of the body and the mind and how society thinks of them. For example, the image of the prudish Victorian construct is identified as conservative, silent, and hypercritical of sexuality expressed in society. Similar to the ideological framework of this prescriptive anti-sexuality, all social constructs are informed by discourses and are inclusive of popular psychological, biological, and neurological medical treatises and pseudo-sciences such as phrenology. Victorian medical discourse, then, functioned as a confessional tool for patriarchal institutions to define these traditional gender roles. Many of the scientific and medical texts generalized the female form so that women, their individuality, and agency are collapsed into, and identified by, their own reproductive organs and functionality. These popular beliefs proliferated through nineteenth-century literature, therefore assisting in the eradication of unique women's identities into basic essentialism. This speculation of oneness disseminated through Victorian rhetoric and deprived women of agency while implementing intransigent identities of volatility and instability. Similarly unstable, medical science, as a transitioning process in the Victorian period, depended on the modified story provided by the doctor's experiences, and was used to perpetuate this treatment of constructed gender roles. Therefore, hysterical figurations of madwomen, as diagnosed by male doctors, demonstrate the nature and sexuality of the varied interpretations of female insanity, according to the perception of institutional "experts." Stemming from this male miscomprehension of women's madness and forced repression of their natural instincts, hysteria, then, became the mind-body unifier in figurations of Victorian madwomen.

Primitive Instincts and Victorian Women

Women's role in Victorian society was juxtaposed by their innate connection to nature. Instincts exist in most living organisms and are inherent complex systems that control behavior. Based on habitual functions and characteristics, instincts connect all species back to nature and are derived from an ethological concept called fixed action pattern or FAP. Bernhard Ronacher's (2019) study on human behavior explains that FAP is a characteristic found in species that is hard-wired into the neural network initially created by a stimulus affectation. Rejecting the Cartesian separation of man and animal, modern neuro-science draws on other disciplines such as ethology (the study of animal behavior) to propose that human consciousness is behavioral and of the same type as consciousness in other species. Echoing Charles Darwin's (1871, 186) premise that "the mental faculties of man and the lower animals do not differ in kind" but in intensity, this theory undermines the distinction between man and animal, culture and nature, and other dualisms that posit wildness as other-than-human. This concept of neural networking and affect will be discussed in further detail in the following chapter as related to restructuring experiential events, but here it refers to experiences processed in the brain's neural network. The mind, inclusive of bodily connections and neural entanglement, is affected by environmental stimuli. Therefore, neural mapping, and parallel mind-body processing of these influences, alter consciousness. As inborn neuro-biological processes, fixed action patterns are responsible for reactive behavioral responses. Case in point, derivative

Darwinian studies on ethological evolutionary instincts explain that such behaviors as sexuality are psychologically developed processes formulated from engrained proclivities informed by environment factors during the developmental stage. While the desire for sexual gratification is inherently instinctual, with humans, social and cultural influences modify the reactive behavioral responses. The alteration of these intrinsic characteristics in early-to-mid-Victorian literature transposes recalcitrant female characters from nature to confined social spaces for control. Thereby, neural mapping and ethology of Victorian madwomen figurations demonstrate how repressed primal instincts inform re-mapping of neurons through reflex stimulation, resulting in the psychosomatic response of female hysteria.

Early-to-mid-Victorian scientific narratives medicalized women as negatively inhibited by their sexual proclivities. For example, Thomas Laycock (1840, 96), while constructing a theory of female hysteria and the nervous system, examines causal affections in *all* animals of higher and lower classification and identifies a "psychological phenomenon" produced by an intimate connection with the "reproduction of the species." These responses result in the instinctual attachment to offspring, uninhibited sexual desire, and outward aggressiveness, when repressed, that controls the behavior of the organism. Thereby, sexual impulse and the resulting gratification maintains similar importance to that of food, and either the fulfillment or refusal of this survival sensation affects innate human responses of either aggression or reservation. Reminiscent of Darwin's rhetoric, Laycock (1840, 95) draws a distinction of degrees between higher evolved human animals and "the human female," which intimates that both possess a skilled faculty of artfulness, or cunning deception. It is only after puberty, a phase when the entirety of the nervous system "is excited by the sexual stimulus," that these so-called gender-specific, and unusual qualities of women's constitution flourish (Laycock 1840, 72). Thus, according to Victorian evolutionary perspectives, these sexual desires are inherent in human women and were considered as parallel to the lowest animal species. Therefore, female instincts and reproductive systems were noted by several medical experts as the cause for psychological-physiological instability. In possession of influential nervous systems, and skilled dispositions for deceit, women were presumed by medical professionals as both corrupted and corruptible. These carnal passions were thereby assumed as the cause for many afflictions that resulted in either criminal or hysterical outbreaks.

Hysterical Conversions: Psyche into Soma

The direct connection between mental faculties to biological functions allowed social institutions to construct roles based on the assumed peculiarities of women's nature. As ascertained by Laycock, these so-called peculiarities consist of irrationality; overt aptitude and affection for children; preference for domestication; and innate purity and morality. Since hysteria was considered as an illness involving symptomatic passions, historically, medical studies warned against self-irritation of fragile nerves and promoted the belief that all women should conform to popular social and medical notions of biological womanhood. Due to this association between reproductive anatomy and brain function, women were designated as inherently unstable and susceptible to corruption. As early-to-mid-Victorian institutions encouraged the separation of women from their instincts, literature of the period illustrated how their corporeal (body) and incorporeal (mind) were monistic figurations informed by nature. The environment, or nature, is key to the creation of restrictive discourse about women and, as Stacy Alaimo (2010, 7–8) similarly suggests, is "crucial" to the analysis of "potent discursive formations." Ergo, the environs function as an influential factor that affects the physical and mental development of humanity. Establishing the strength of female biology in conjunction with the psyche, this informative juxtaposition reconfigures the balance of women and their inherent nature.

Women's psychological connection to their biological functions produce psychosomatic responses through hysterical conversion. A term coined by Sigmund Freud (1895), hysterical conversion, signifies how psychical passions manifest into physical responses, which is a significant characteristic of the disorder. Freud's exploration of this conversion is most famously referred to in his case studies on Dora, who was diagnosed with the affliction of hysteria.[1] In these psychoanalytic examinations of Dora, Freud interprets how the repressed psychological symptoms result in hysterical manifestations in the body. Subsequently, Freud's initial theory of hysterical conversion is a psychological principle connected to corporeality. While this monistic approach to the female mind-body, as Wilson (2004, 1) identifies, the immaterial-material is unified in one congruent structure and highlights that "the psyche is always already of the body." Whereas such early feminists as Sherry Ortner (1974) and Carolyn Merchant (1980) claim that such studies of the body are biologically reductionist, Wilson (2004, 3) arguably suggests it is in this evaluation that the "most acute formulations about the nature of the body and the character of the psyche" are presented. Owing to these psychosomatic effects, or somatic symptomatology, Freud constructed the foundation for his methods and theory of psychoanalysis. Therefore, drawing from Freud's conversion disorder, hysteria is explained as a neurological process resulting in bodily reactions and somatosensory dysfunctions.

The foundation of psychoanalytic studies predates research on the hysterical body but can be traced back through Freud's studies of biology. In this early research it was determined that cells in the spinal cord distribute fibers into the dorsal (sensory) and ventral (motor) roots. Tracing the intricate fiber mappings of these roots to the spinal cord, Freud established how nerve cells are foundational as they are the root at which the fibers connect. In this study, a pathway was provided for the future studies of the Neuronal Theory, which states that individual nerve cells communicate with other nerve cells through proximal connection. Although Freud later abandoned this neurological research for psychological studies, biology remained as the core for his research of hysteria and psychoanalysis. Thereby, Freud's determining factor for hysteria is not a division of the consciousness, but the potential for its "*capacity for conversion*"; a little-known disposition which he theorizes as a "psycho-physical aptitude" for transitioning elevated emotional responses "into the somatic innervation" (Wilson 2004, 11–12). This hysterical conversion disorder, then, argues that pain and stress can be repressed, however, emotions have the potential to convert into neurological manifestations. Furthermore, this evocation of biology explains how etiological psychopathology offers insights into instinctual sexual desires and conversion responses. It is this connection of the libido, passions, and neurological processes that influence the mind-body to produce psychosomatic events as hysteria.

Hysterical conversion in early-to-mid-Victorian figurations of fictional women originates in the libidinized nervous system. Under the influence of hysterical disorder, women in the Gothic visibly project their internal struggle through physiological events. Depending on the severity of the malady, hysteria's psychological responses (anxiety, depression, confusion) turn into physiological events. Known as hysterical conversion, common symptoms such as "paralyses, facial neuralgias, loss of vision or voice, tics, bodily pains, and chronic muscular contractions" occur during moments of mental provocation (Wilson 2004, 4). For example, these symptoms are identified through three specific figurations of fictional female hysterics. Emily Brontë's Catherine Earnshaw, experiences depression caused by separation from Heathcliff, and consequently suffers from "a tempest of passion with a kind of fit," resulting in a physical "paroxysm" (*Wuthering Heights* 1847, 425–427). Charlotte Brontë's infamous Bertha Mason, struggles with repressed instincts, thus transforming her mental anguish into fierce "yells and the most convulsive plunges" (*Jane Eyre* 1847, 213). Lastly, Septimus R. Urban's replicated Bertha, Agatha Jeffreys, impacted by tragedy, converts her psychical trauma into physical actions of "howling cries," maniacal laughter, and "rapid articulation and a vehemence of manner" (*Wronged Wife* 1870, 29). It is this very concept of hysterical conversion, turning psychic disturbances into somatic episodes, that has been neglected. Hence, hysterical conversion disorder, as illustrated in early-to-mid-Victorian Gothic fiction, is a repression of instincts that results in a mind-body rejection of social confinement.

As a psychosomatic affliction, conversion symptoms function as an all-inclusive structural process. A systematic ailment, hysteria impacts the neurological system resulting in spatial reactions with temporal emergence, which means that reactions occur in different parts of the body at indeterminate times or orders. It is this compulsion, or spontaneous manifestation, that segregates hysteria from behavioral responses or traditional psychological ailments. These uncontrollable symptoms, compulsions, and repetitions are monistic manifestations that signify how catastrophe moves into the death drive resulting in sensations of annihilation and instability. To survive within the confines of a restrictive social construct, Victorian hysterics or in this case, gothic madwomen, repress their passions which result in the involuntarily transition of these desires into psychosomatic responses through repetition and compulsory reactions. During this exhibition of hysteria, the effects are randomized in the individual's body therefore manifesting spontaneous behaviors and somatic actions. These physical symptomatic responses, as demonstrated by notable nineteenth-century obstetrician and gynecological surgeon Isaac Baker Brown (1866, 7), result in irritation on the female reproductive organs originated from "spinal irritation," which transition into such ailments as "amaurosis, hemiplegia, paraplegia; epileptoid fits or hysterical epilepsy, cataleptic fits, epileptic fits, idiotcy, mania, [and] death." While demonstrating such physical symptoms, there is no logic to determine which parts of the body are impacted, or the sequential order they appear, as potential neurasthenic responses.

"Neurasthenia," a term coined by George Beard (1869) as a structural weakening, or mechanistic fatigue, of the nerves, became a popular Victorian malady characterized by weakness, dizziness, and fainting. This mild neurosis, addressed by Silas Weir Mitchell's (1829–1914) "rest cure" later in the century, presents the stereotype of the pale, fainting Victorian woman seen today. Women faced with the "absence" or "inadequacy of sexual satisfaction" are notably afflicted with this psychosomatic illness (Wilson 2004, 17). Although some early-to-mid-Victorian medical "experts," such as Baker Brown, claim nervousness as a symptom of excessive masturbation, this nervous anxiety correlates to inadequate sexual relations. While a satisfactory event results in an adequate discharge that involves the synchronous release of "somatic and psychic tension," anything less than this complete evacuation will result in an accumulation of "somatic excitation" that impacts the subcortical resistance and influences the psyche (Wilson 2004, 17–18). Neurasthenia begins when sufficient, but not complete, discharge occurs; however, psychosomatic illness, or hysterical conversion, transpires when an expulsion of somatic excitation is not resolved. A weakening of the psyche is created by a weakening of the soma, not because one controls the other, "but because the soma and psyche are ontologically integrated" (Wilson 2002, 22).

Through this monistic process, the nervous system is libidinized, neuronal pathways are impacted, sexual energy circulates through the psyche, and thus, projects this behavior into the external world. This energetically charged nervous system transitions the mind-body into psychosomatic hysterical exhibitions, hence leading to illness and uncontrollable behavior.

Repressed Hysterical Exhibitions

For Victorian women to socially assimilate, the repression of their carnal instincts was required. Consequently, female desires were dictated, and forcibly inscribed into prescribed roles, by men. These passions, as Luce Irigaray (1985, 33) interprets in *Speculum of the Other Woman* (1985, 33), must originate with, and focus on, male necessities or women face classifications as "crazy, disoriented, lost" for failure to cooperate. Thus, female sexual expression is agentically impaired and forced to align with the discourse of men. Objectified as ontologically void constructs without passionate expression, women, then, remain isolated and repressed in their limitations or absences, therefore led "to follow the dictates issued univocally by the sexual desire, discourse, and law of man" (Irigaray 1985, 33). To achieve social stability, Victorian women were expected to suppress their instinctive drives and function as the prize (once again speaking to the language of Darwin) for pacification of male desires and tensions. In refocusing female libidinal energy into domesticity, women's passions, or motivations for desires, are confined by the marital, social, and parental obligations. While confined to these roles, sexuality is repressed through automation and repetitive lethargy. Furthermore, women's reclassification into what Irigaray (1985, 54) refers to as "narcissistic monuments," involves the personal negation, or desexualization of the libido, to prioritize focus on activities of agential and instinctual sublimation. Introversion of female sexuality, then, forcibly refocuses women's energies into male fulfillment and satisfaction. This sublimation of female passions causes the eventual rejection of confinement and creates mind-body hysterical responses. Moreover, the negation of primary instincts inhibits women's connection with nature, thus creating internal conflict.

Hysterical exhibition, a term I have coined based on Irigaray's ideas, is the result of repressed instincts. It refers to a display of psychosomatic responses induced by the separation of self from intrinsic proclivities. Induced by conversion disorder, hysterical exhibition is a visible expression of female disconnection from nature. Hysteria, as argued by Irigaray (1985, 60), is "stigmatized as a place where fantasies, ghosts, and shadows fester," and like all things relative to women, must be "unmasked, interpreted, brought back to the reality of a repetition." This unveiling returns the hysteric to reality "of repetition, [as] a reproduction, a representation that is congruent to, consistent with, the original," or the "master-signifier"—the prescribed female identity (Irigaray 1985, 60). Reducing women to their biological functions, patriarchal institutions struggled to rewrite female roles, by redirecting instincts to the confines of a productive bourgeois marriage. While psycho-sexual discourses attempt to affirm inherent female connections with nature, the prescribed models inadvertently reconnect women to their primal instincts. Although diagnosed as a psychological affective disorder, hysteria is a method of escapism and rejection of restrictive gender ideologies. This madness in Victorian society, according to Showalter (1985, 24–26), was treated as an ailment of "the highly cultivated and industrialized," and, in the higher classes unusual behavior was declared as "nervousness or eccentricity" until tendencies progressed into violence or suicide. Although the lower-classes experienced these exact pathologies, they were subjected to the chaos and squalor of public asylums. Women from the middle- and upper-classes were confined, and treated, within the home or at private medical houses to avoid familial shame. These middle- and upper-class women were reduced to functions that appeased male necessities or rebelled through psychosomatic events. Expected to perform within the confines of morality and domestication, antagonistic to natural dispositions, women avoided censorship of their instincts by repression and involuntary transformation to hysteria. Since women's bodies and minds suffer under the restriction of domestication while facing sexual dissatisfaction, they act as a reminder of latent instincts. For fear of "total repression and destruction" of their sexuality, women in the Victorian Gothic turned their desires into hysterical expression while reconnecting with their carnality (Irigaray 1985, 72).

This notion of hysterical exhibition also draws on the exploration of bodily excess, which argues that images of female grotesque bodies function as exhibitory figurations. Through this association, transformative grotesque bodies, as Mary Russo (1994, 7) suggests in *The Female Grotesque: Risk, Excess and Modernity*, are liminal figurations, as "doubled, monstrous, deformed, excessive, and abject," who disrupt materiality while strengthening their social position. As strongly associated with the psychic and somatic, grotesque bodies are essentially projections of the inner conflict. Similar to the popular dualist approach of the Gothic, this notion of bodily identity follows a divisive Cartesian approach that restructures the grotesque as immaterial and material fragments. However, while this stance highlights bodily reductionism, the exploration of social discourses further illustrates the impact on women's minds-bodies, resulting in grotesque exhibitions of madness. This rejection of stringent gender roles unifies the mind-body through hysterical exhibition and allows women to reclaim agency albeit in a gothic and grotesque register of aggressive monstrosity. The opportunities for agency and revolt are constrained within the early-to-mid-Victorian

Gothic texts and the mode of transgression, more broadly. Since figurations that border on monstrosity re-inscribe the typologies of madness identified by Showalter, they represent female madness as dangerous and deserving of punishment or incarceration and affirm the antithetical and negative stereotypes of women identified in the previous chapter.

Victorian medical sciences constructed a Cartesian division between body and nature, and a segregation of the mind from body. Medical institutions perpetuated this dualistic approach to illness by diagnosing mental disorders as derivative of either psyche or soma. However, despite the divide, these elements are unified through neurological communication and maintain the ability to influence, and create systematic functions in, women. Nineteenth-century medicine identifies this particular correlation between psychology and physiology by the influences of exterior phenomena such as the environment and internal sensations as emotions. For instance, the mind-body figuration, as a closed circuit of influence, is informed and affected by intrinsic affectations as well as the mercurial tendencies of the environs. Similarly, the Victorian hysterical form is in a perpetually unresolved informative loop with the environment, thus these affectual feedback processes produce a reactive systemic response. Therefore, affectations of the mind affect the body, and the body systematically affects the mind, while external forces concurrently influence both, hence substantiating how the mind-body-nature functions as a monistic system. Prior to the nineteenth-century research of biological and neuronal responses, mental illnesses were not explicitly categorized as physiologically relative. Medical diagnoses of hysterical or hypochondriacal disorders exemplify the psychosomatic correlation and unify the mind-body. The female body and its correlation to nature (whether human or nonhuman) is assumed as in constant fluctuation from environmental influences, therefore producing effects within the whole system. In some instances, women, according to Robert Brudenell Carter (1853, 139), were suspected to use hysteria as a "habitual deception" and "self-produce" the "novelty" illness as a method to gain control. Contrary to Carter's theory of hysterical women as impersonators, Andrew Scull (2009, 6) claims that there are those who concede that this "chameleon-like disease" molds itself to the "culture in which it appears" and imitates symptoms of other illnesses. As material-semiotic figurations, women affected by hysteria speak to the unification of a mind-body structure enveloped by social and cultural affectations. Signifying conflicts about female instincts and sexuality, the hysterical form mirrors the influential environment. Replicating the necessary surroundings, hysterical exhibition offers women a chance for expression from within their confinement.

Whereas Victorian medical experts emphasize inherent sexual dispositions of women as the causality, scientific theories restructure these traits into controllable moral behaviors. Furthering this argument on systematic female repression, the rejection of social subjugation results in hysterical exhibitions. Engaging in conversation with Freud, Irigaray argues that this mechanism for social constraint is induced by masculine discourse which perceives women as a negative reflection of itself. Furthermore, female subjectivity is then constructed through a singular gender model of men which inscribes women's regulation, thereby representing women as lesser copies devoid of pleasure, with only two options for action: silence or hysteria.

Female subversion in the form of hysterical madwomen in the Female Gothic challenges traditional Victorian values of domestic contentment. Women in these narratives, while facing supernatural forces and dark structures, do not pursue escape from these elements but, rather, from personal experiences. The following narrative selections, constructed in the gothic mode of transgression, expose internal conflicts between the traditional confines of oppressive marriage and desire for agency, thus resulting in figurations of madness, deemed monstrous by popular discourses. Poised between the binary roles of good and evil, gothic madwomen epitomize identity fragmentation while illustrating female victimization and subjugation in a restrictive society.

SOCIAL OBLIGATIONS AND SEXUAL REPRESSION IN *WUTHERING HEIGHTS* (1847)

Wuthering Heights is a story of women's psychological imprisonment. This gothic tale emphasizes unfulfilled passions and internal conflicts created by social expectations. Early readers of the novel, such as those expressed in *Douglas Jerrold's Weekly Newspaper* (1848) and *Atlas* (1848), were surprised, and disconcerted by the emotional response of Brontë's anti-hero, Heathcliff. The two anonymously written reviews discuss the readers' disgust and shock by the ferocity of Heathcliff's brutal expressions of passionate love.[2] His inclination for prioritizing instinctual desires over social obligations and morality counters traditional Victorian beliefs. Later readers found Heathcliff's passions as enigmatic, and he has since become a prototype and embodiment of the Byronic anti-hero of gothic romance (Alexander and Smith 2006). While these readings centralize romance and drama as the allure of the text, it is the constructs of female repression and their calamitous results that embolden the tale of *Wuthering Heights*. As ascertained earlier in the chapter, early-to-mid-Victorian women were restricted from exposing personal desires, therefore social convention necessitated the repression of natural instincts. Brontë's novel reflects the concept that Victorian social convention was in direct opposition to female desire. This conflictual binary of instinctual passions and conventional Victorian moral femininity are figured in Catherine's reactive sexual repression within the popular text and reconceptualized as a wild and passionate woman in communication with nature. *Wuthering Heights*, then, produces the female character as a sexual subject while concurrently demonstrating repression as is practiced by traditional, socially appropriate writing. Although this narrative emphasizes circumstantial events created by repression, Brontë's novel also reveals Victorian fears of female sexuality through Cathy's assumed monstrous transformation into a monstrous madwoman.

Early in the novel, Brontë introduces Catherine Earnshaw in the midst of Lockwood's investigation of her diary. Within the diary, Catherine's discourse offers explications of passionate desire and co-dependency with Heathcliff through tortured nights filled with denial and "headaches" (*Wuthering Heights*, 342). Albeit a young child, Catherine demonstrates awareness of social obligations and conflict through the inscriptions "*Catherine Heathcliff*" versus "*Catherine Linton*" (*Wuthering Heights*, 341). Brontë establishes Catherine as an educated, tragic heroine of Victorian society, under the obligation of social expectations, but haunted by innate desires for passionate expression. Whilst examining her secretive books, Catherine is introduced to Lockwood as a spectral child. Labeled as a "creature" in her "waif" form, Catherine terrorizes Lockwood as she attempts to gain entry into her former room (*Wuthering Heights*, 344–345). Brontë constructs this scene of Cathy's liminal position between the material and immaterial to symbolize the social and medical position of Victorian women. While such scholars as Martin Willis (2012) argue that Lockwood's weaponization of Cathy's books and his aggression against the specter is a metaphor for both oppression and women's restriction to education, these actions might be more obviously read here as a representation of the patriarchal fear of recalcitrant women. Depicted as a childlike spectral phenomenon, Catherine embodies Victorian anxieties of female passion and independence shrouded by an innocent façade. This figuration of innocence and rebellion speaks to what Lucie Armitt (2016) claims as the gothic girl child who is both alluring and dangerous, therein Catherine, as the embodiment of social anxiety, is Brontë's representation of female amorousness, intelligence, and rebellion. Symbolized as monstrous, Catherine's immaterial form reflects her fragmentation and liminality in life.

Wuthering Heights exemplifies gothic elements of repressed sexuality, fragmented identity, and liminality in the dark heroine. In Eugenia DeLamotte's (1990, 131) feminist reading of the nineteenth-century Gothic, *Perils of the Night: A Feminist Study of Nineteenth-Century Gothic*, she investigates how borders of the individual self are sources of anxiety because they are unreliable and "shifting" or "non-existent." Brontë's novel, then, identifies the anxieties of unstable personal boundaries through Catherine Earnshaw's indecisiveness, reactive psychosis, and dual identities. These identifiable borders and boundaries function as an "interface" for opposing sides: the dark negative, gothic mode on one hand, and the light positive, idealistically sublime mode on the other (DeLamotte 1990, 124). Emulating this gothic trope, Catherine personifies both the light and dark in her corporeal and incorporeal identities. Since immaterial figures as specters and other supernatural apparitions are formless and lack boundaries, Catherine, following DeLamotte's theory, transgresses the borders of life and death. In death, Catherine is in a constant state of liminality, transcends boundaries, and creates terror and anxiety in both characters and readers alike. In life, Catherine struggles to obtain the sublime through her connection to nature and Heathcliff, while meeting social expectations through an elite marriage. It is because of this connection that Catherine's repression of her primitive self is exposed in the emergence of nature as a mirrored destructive force.

Cathy's Fragmentation: Or Nature and the Self

Nature, in the sense of an untamed environmental space, mirrors the unrestrained passions of gothic women. As "undomesticated" or "untamed," nature, Stacy Alaimo (2010, 16) claims, is a model that serves "female insurgency." From childhood, Catherine is portrayed as an untamed and passionate girl dismissive of Victorian gender standards and emboldened by her connection to nature. Shortly after the arrival of Heathcliff, Mrs. Earnshaw dies, and Catherine finds herself in the unrefined rearing of an undomesticated household. Lack of maternal guidance allows Catherine to develop an identity in conjunction with her own natural instincts. Since Heathcliff is introduced during her ontogenetic development, Catherine affiliates her primal side with Brontë's wild villain. Unimpeded by social regulations, she is "mischievous and wayward" (*Wuthering Heights*, 352). Catherine's behavior in the company of Heathcliff, according to Nelly, promised that they would "grow up as rude as savages" (*Wuthering Heights*, 357). Whereas their amusements through the moors portray uncivilized barbarity, Brontë's dark heroine exhibits unadulterated satisfaction. Therein, Catherine's fondness of Heathcliff and ability to express intrinsic desires result in her spirits, "always at a high-water mark, her tongue always going—singing, laughing, and plaguing everybody who would not do the same. A wild, wicked slip she was—but, she had the bonniest eye, and sweetest smile, and lightest foot in the parish" (*Wuthering Heights*, 354–355). Although exhibiting a visage of femininity, Catherine is the antithesis to self-restraint and morality. While allowing herself to indulge in uncivilized activities, this "aggression," as noted by Irigaray (1985, 20), is exhibited as both harmful and masculine. Women who are perceived as inherently antagonistic and contravene traditions, infringe upon, and disregard the expectations of social customs. It is with this association of destructivity that

Catherine is identified as a woman who necessitates social reformation and restriction. Subject to the influences of the Linton family, Catherine's connection to her instinctual self is all but severed. This separation of the self, or the attempt at the incorporation of what Elizabeth Grosz (1995, 122) refers to as "men's materiality," results in her isolation as a negative image of a diminished male reflection. Similar to Irigaray's response to Freud, this regulation of women removes autonomy and equality, thus casting them into supportive roles. Compared to this containment within a structure of figuration, not built for, or by women, they find themselves isolated and alone within this construct. Finding herself voluntarily subjugated within the social sphere of the Lintons, Catherine undergoes this precise homelessness and erasure of self within her new role.

The acquisition of the conventional Victorian role of femininity requires the repression of natural instincts, which results in the manifestation of psychological disturbances. This redirection of aggression is a masochistic feminine transition to avoid violation of social expectations. For women to acquire a function or role, it is necessary for the introversion of their antagonist traits. This intersective pairing of opposing traits will ultimately result in self-destruction since she does not obtain an authorization for the outward projection of her individuality or aggression. Catherine's acquisition of her role as Mrs. Linton, then, establishes the renunciation of her savagery and represses passionate impulses. Marriage to Edgar Linton redefines, and revokes, Catherine's agency through restriction and self-denial. Her destructive tendencies and primal behavior, as displayed at Wuthering Heights, are then turned inward.

Catherine's instinctual repression results in the division of self. Catherine and Heathcliff's relationship is based on codependence and an insecure ontological assurance. The intensity of their bond nullifies each as independently autonomous beings. As a result, their unification of identities presents the concept of ontological insecurity, or doubt of one's own substantiality. Typically, ontologically secure persons recognize their experiences as unique and fundamentally real. These individuals rarely question or doubt their own identity or autonomy and possess an inconsistency in authenticity, substance, or worth of identity. Catherine, however, as ontologically insecure, does not have independent autonomy or an ontological sense of security, thereby is dependent on a coextensive relationship to Heathcliff. She identifies with Heathcliff as part of her natural self; he is an embodiment of her primal instincts, therefore, Catherine is unable to separate her being from his. The repression of her instinctual side, and separation from Heathcliff, as suggested by Nelly, is "the greatest punishment . . . invented for her" (*Wuthering Heights*, 355). As a significant part of her own identity, Catherine's deprivation of Heathcliff results in instability and removal of agency.

This insecurity of self allows Catherine to identify Heathcliff as an integral part of her monistic structure. In the most famous proclamations in Brontë's novel, Catherine professes "I am Heathcliff!" and "he's more myself than I am," which offers her recognition of their symbiotic affiliation (*Wuthering Heights*, 379). Catherine claims that she and Heathcliff's souls "are the same" while denouncing Edgar's as "different as a moonbeam from lightning, or frost from fire" (*Wuthering Heights*, 379). From her perspective, Catherine's and Heathcliff's souls unify and align with the elements of nature. She recognizes an inherent connection to her natural instincts and desires, thus incorporating Heathcliff, not as an affinitive companion, but as a segment of her own being. However, while exhibiting intense passion for one another, the irony occurs in the concept that while they identify the identical, yet individual, nature of one another, both characters recognize their unattainability (DeLamotte 1990). If Catherine and Heathcliff are in fact a unified structure, the rejection of self can lead to psychological destruction. This instability is a central characteristic to insanity and suggests that it is Catherine's lack of self-recognition itself which signifies a psychological upheaval. Her sociopathic and narcissistic approach to the external existence of humans, as separate from the monistic ontological figuration of Catherine-Heathcliff, is an early identifier of pending mania. Her latent instincts and passions for self-indulgence, as inclusive of Heathcliff, deviate from social acceptance. By this exclusion of others and identification of self with Heathcliff, Catherine's insanity is exposed. Unable to differentiate herself from Heathcliff and separate her social position from inherent passions, Catherine evokes nature in her hysterical exhibition.

Identified as a space that informs, and is informed by, female passions, nature operates as "the ideal site" for exhibiting their anxieties about social expectations (Alaimo 2000, 18). Catherine's rejection of self and separation from Heathcliff results in a tumultuous affectation of temperament reflected by the environment. Since they are two beings sharing a significant bond to nature, and one another, through instincts and habitat, the severance of Catherine and Heathcliff's relationship is reflected in a violent climatic response. In their exploration of the ecoGothic, Andrew Smith and William Hughes (2013, 8), examine how the bodily form is the "site of Gothic fear." The body, then, as the figuration of physical injury, sexual enclosure, and physiological affectations, as Smith and Hughes (2013, 8) suggest, can be affiliated and "remembered in a literary landscape." This conjunction of affectations is simultaneously prevalent in Cathy and the tumultuous atmospheric conditions at Wuthering Heights. On the night of Catherine's martial acceptance, Heathcliff overhearing his devaluation, discreetly vanishes. Brontë's imagery of the weather on the night of his departure, not only suggests the preliminary deconstruction of Catherine's psyche but also portrays nature's destruction of itself. In the event of the wild couple's separation, the evening is noted as being incredibly dark for summer and "the clouds appeared inclined to thunder" (*Wuthering Heights*, 381). While an approaching storm threatens Wuthering Heights, Catherine's agitation grows incrementally. Ignoring Nelly's persuasions for serenity, Catherine "kept wandering to and fro, from the gate to the door, in a state of agitation" (*Wuthering Heights*, 381). Increasingly unsettled by Heathcliff's failure to return, the moment the "growling thunder" and "great drops" of rain begin to fall, Catherine succumbs to a nervousness and responds by "crying outright" (*Wuthering Heights*, 381). Acknowledging Heathcliff's disappearance, she abdicates from rationality and surrenders to volatile passions. Operating as a gothic figure, full of instability and social anxiety, Catherine's torment projects onto the environmental landscape. Her internal struggle to find resolution results in a storm "rattling over the Heights in full fury," bringing with it, "a violent wind, as well as thunder, and either one or the other split a tree off at the corner of the building; a huge bough fell across the roof, and knocked down a portion of the east chimney-stack, sending a clatter of stones and soot into the kitchen fire" (*Wuthering Heights*, 381). The fragmentation of identity is reflected in both Catherine's tortured animosity and sequential stages of destructive nature. Heathcliff's exodus from Catherine leaves her to acquiesce and submit to the role as Mrs. Linton. Permanently divided from her true nature, as well as nature itself and her kindred companion, Catherine succumbs to lype-monomaniacal hysteria and dies. Symbolically represented as the catastrophic division of women from nature, Catherine's death is expressive of Brontë's wider critique of female repression by society.

Nature and Nurture: Instincts and Social Roles

Catherine's acceptance of a traditional female role restricts her access to nature. Since Victorian women were assigned roles based on their reproductive functions, and assumed as susceptible to uncontrolled sexual desires, social institutions created moral imperatives to restrict their biological nature. For instance, Catherine's five-week residence at Thrushcross Grange introduces Brontë's dark heroine to the luxuries of the Linton family's society and treatment. Frances Earnshaw, Catherine's sister by marriage, seeks to raise the young lady's "self-respect with fine clothes and flattery" and often visits the Grange to offer guidance (*Wuthering Heights*, 361). During this event, Catherine faces social refinement, improves her appearance, and appropriates respectable mannerisms. Upon her return home, Nelly claims that Catherine is no longer a "wild hatless, little savage" but a "very dignified person, with brown ringlets falling from the cover of a feathered beaver, and a long cloth habit which she [is] obliged to hold up with both hands that she might sail in" (*Wuthering Heights*, 361). Brontë's portrayal of Catherine's new aesthetic suggests a vision of Victorian femininity through her lighter appearance, which also reflects etiquette and grace in her movements. Catherine's newly acquired fashions, albeit presenting dignity and cultivation, result in restriction to the Heights. Prior to entry, Nelly is ordered to remove "her things" which symbolically reflect the eradication of culture to access nature (*Wuthering Heights*, 365). Although Catherine is cultivated while at the Linton residence, she struggles with her connection to nature and Heathcliff while at Wuthering Heights.

The depiction of Catherine's wildness restrained by feminine clothing suggests that Victorian women's acceptance of traditional female roles repress their natural instincts. Catherine's attempt to accept her role as a middle-class Victorian woman causes a breakdown of self because she ultimately denies her instincts, thereby repressing her nature which results in a catastrophic psychosomatic destruction. As highlighted in chapter 1, women who failed to perform within the boundaries of traditional female roles, encountered significant consequences. Thereby, assumedly unregulated female constitutions were prone to illness, and these women developed such maladies of melancholia or hysteria, which resulted in mind-body degeneration or death. Catherine's accedes to the role of Victorian "lady," a decision that restricts her natural instincts and vociferous behavior. Confined within this role, her violations of social rules cause mental degradation. Catherine's voluntary repression of her destructive disposition creates psychical conflict while inadvertently causing a disruption in her nervous system and resulting in physical anomalies.

Conventional Victorian gender roles of femininity create divisions in Catherine's identity, separating her from her natural self. Denounced by Nelly as an "unfeeling" and "selfish" child, Catherine struggles with her dual identity and relationship with society and nature (*Wuthering Heights*, 365). Brontë presents Catherine in a purgatory state, trapped between an instinctual bond to Heathcliff and an expectation to "conceal her emotion[s]" (*Wuthering Heights*, 365). At the age of fifteen, Nelly describes the wildness of Catherine's being as a "headstrong creature" filled with haughty arrogance and a "wicked spirit" (*Wuthering Heights*, 369, 372). While demonstrating "no temptation to show her rough side," she maintains the etiquette of a proper young lady in her acquaintanceship with Edgar and Isabella Linton (*Wuthering Heights*, 370). However, in their absence, Catherine displays intense affections towards Heathcliff while struggling with her emotions. Although attracted to the Linton's lifestyle, Catherine is ontologically connected to Heathcliff's wildness, a representation of individual freedom. Whereas the nurturing Linton household functions as a civilized structure to encourage the Victorian feminine behavior, the wild nature of Wuthering Heights promotes Catherine's unadulterated instincts. The Heights and surrounding moors, then, offers Catherine a return to nature and personal freedom as well as an escape from the restraints of social expectations. The moors, as a symbol of undomesticated freedom, outside of the cultural sphere, provides a space for Cathy to escape restrictive boundaries and intimately reconnect to nature. As a liminal figure between culture and nature, Catherine is confined between her desires for this reconnection to her natural self and the expectations of Victorian society. Despite the fact that Cathy covets a return to nature she consciously chooses a position which encourages social success and a defined role.

Acceptance of social assimilation and expectations of domesticity result in the repression of Catherine's instincts and removal of her natural agency. Prior to marriage, Catherine identifies social expectations and redirects her desires accordingly. While claiming to love Heathcliff, she admits to Nelly that "it would degrade" her to marry him, which signifies a rejection of an authentic self (*Wuthering Heights*, 379). After introduction into the Linton household, Catherine learns the importance of wealth, title, and society. In her emotional profession to Nelly, she parrots the diction found within Victorian conduct books and claims that her espoused "will be rich," and she will "be the greatest woman of the neighborhood" (*Wuthering Heights*, 377). Catherine announces that such accomplishments will make her "proud of having such a husband" (*Wuthering Heights*, 377). Echoing the standards of middle-class femininity promoted by Sarah Stickney Ellis and John Ruskin, Catherine's announcement aligns with the social conventions of womanhood, not her own personal desires. While justifying the motive for her marital plans, she decries her unhappiness with the situation. Simultaneously, Catherine claims passionate love for Heathcliff while declaring a desire for social ascension. In this moment she must decide to either accept the role of Victorian wife and sever the bond with her natural self or re-assume the role as uncultivated "savage" (*Wuthering Heights*, 361). Again, drawing from the discourse of the period correlating women to what Darwin declares as lower races, Brontë utilizes this language in reference to Catherine's independent nature and relationship with Heathcliff. As a young woman intimately associated with a "dark-skinned gypsy," who repeats "over and over again some gibberish that nobody could understand," Cathy's nature is analogous to Heathcliff's "otherness" (*Wuthering Heights*, 322, 352). Linking both Catherine and Heathcliff to what Anne McClintock (1995, 40) refers to as "the colonized," their unrestricted identities are presented within a stereotype, thereby projecting them into an "anachronistic space" that denotes "prehistoric, atavistic and irrational" behaviors. Echoing critical language reflective of colonial perspectives of Indigenous peoples, Emily Brontë's writing and the implicit racism of the depiction of Heathcliff will be addressed more fully in the discussion of Charlotte Brontë's Bertha Mason. While attached to Heathcliff, Cathy maintains a connection to nature and independence, however, in an attempt to obtain a position of acceptance, her identity transforms into a dark negative self. This transgression, and repression, of self leads to lype-monomaniacal illness resulting in psychosomatic exhibitions.

Hysteria and Hallucinations: Catherine's Descent into Madness

Emily Brontë's *Wuthering Heights* is a gothic response to Victorian society's repression of women and subsequent psychosomatic consequences. During a period when women faced indictments of mental instability, Brontë's Catherine is an intertextual response to Victorian psychopathological institutions. I say intertextual because prior to the publication of *Wuthering Heights*, Jean-Étienne Dominique Esquirol (1838) provided structural differentiation between stages of psychological maladies. Esquirol's classifications recognize five levels of maniacal psychosis from non-obtrusive symptoms to catatonic dysfunction. In the lesser stages, Esquirol identifies that lypemania-monomania, or a deep, abnormal melancholy with delirium, results in excitable passions and occasionally, death. Classified as "a disease of the sensibility," lypemania-monomania, compounded with the degeneration of hysteria, often progresses into exhibitions of insanity (Esquirol 1838, 200). Embedded in the text as a tragic gothic heroine, Brontë constructs Catherine's lifelong behavior and conclusive demise as a psychosomatic case study reflective of Esquirol's Victorian ideologies of mental illness.

Hysterical exhibition in *Wuthering Heights* accentuates how Victorian women were perceived as emotionally unstable and susceptible to illness. In this sense, Emily Brontë's use of maladies dramatically differs from the depictions of illness used by her sister. While Charlotte uses an excessive depiction of illness in the character of Bertha Mason, Emily's use of illness is constructed as a representation of social affectation against women in Cathy. Therefore, *Wuthering Heights*, utilizing Emily's perspective of female mental illness as symbolic, views the patriarchy as a powerful institution that perpetuates power, and preys upon the psyche and soma of women within the construct. It is through Brontë's rejection of culture and structured society that illness, or perpetual flaw, is metaphorically constructed into what Beth Torgerson (2005, 16) posits as "two supernatural creatures—the vampire and the ghost." Catherine's spectralization, then, is Brontë's exploration of women's self-alienation, while Heathcliff's vampirism emphasizes the "blood-draining qualities" inherent in Victorian culture (Torgerson 2005, 16). Although Brontë approaches culturally induced illness through metaphorical representations, it is Catherine's psychosomatic response that suggests realistic acknowledgments of social issues. Drawing on these psychic disturbances, Catherine's figuration of embodied wildness trapped in society, suggests ontological instability.

Anxieties of female instability from innate connections to the natural self are embodied within Brontë's heroine. The human form became a focal point for cultural and social contestation during the early-to-mid-Victorian period. The necessity for turning abstract social anxieties into concrete objects results in transitioning female forms into blueprints of traceable anomalies. As corporeal maps that exhibit internal conflict, subjected women's bodies, Grosz (1994, vii) asserts, are "reconfigurations" that expose attempted inversions to "displace the centrality of the mind, the psyche, interior, or consciousness (and even the unconscious)." All the immaterial effects, in this case hysteria, are explained through the visual exhibition of the material form. Locating mind-bodies as sources of conflict for social and sexual divisions allows for alterations in discourses about women. Consequently, nineteenth-century medical assumptions about female nature linked women's psyches to their psychical and biological forms resulting in nervous disorders, thereby creating an obstacle to fully access the public forum. Prescribed assumptions allowed institutions to construct hysteria as a disorder whose characteristics and identifiers were easily transposed and ascribed to individuals dependent on the situation. With this pendulum diagnostic moving between the socially accepted feminine construct and the monstrous pathologically corrupt derivative, as the "experts" determine, incorporation of external ideas from relevant and irrelevant sources result in symptomatic contradictions. These conflicts, which result in hysterical exhibitions, are correlated to the interrelationship of the uterine system, genetics, the psyche, and the ability to assimilate into cultured society, as surmised by medical institutions. It is through these contradictions of biopsychological functions that transgressions of prescriptive womanhood are constructed as wild and monstrous madwomen traditionally illustrated in the Gothic. Brontë's realistic representation of Catherine as the Victorian madwoman encapsulates both the social anxieties about female instability and the repression of suffering women.

Early-to-mid-Victorian social fears of behavioral instability and corruptible reproductive functions subjected women to male ratiocination. Informed by cultural narratives from middle-class popular literature, the medical identity of female insanity was, as Showalter (1985, 10) states, "perpetuated by three major Romantic images," one of which is reflective in Brontë's Cathy. A notable image of hysteria is William Shakespeare's (1609) morosely suicidal Ophelia, depicted as a melancholic woman, whose marginalization between love and duty drives her to fatal hysterics. Embodying the Ophelian stereotype of the despairing madwoman, Catherine is presented in a "loose, white dress, with a light shawl over her shoulders, in the recess of an open window" (*Wuthering Heights*, 425). Aligned with the medical discourse of Esquirol, the Ophelian stereotype is represented as Catherine's lype-monomania, or what later Freud refers to as melancholia.³ Subdued, with a "wild vindictiveness," a "bloodless lip," and "scintillating eye," Catherine is portrayed as an "unearthly beauty" on the verge of hysteria (*Wuthering Heights*, 426). Brontë's reference to Catherine's visage, not only recalls her introduction as the spectral child but also reaffirms her connection to nature through her "unearthly" depiction of wildness (*Wuthering Heights*, 426). Acknowledging this status of wild and monstrous madwoman as the result of liminality between culture and nature, Catherine's declaration of "I shall not be at peace" ends with a violent paroxysm and physical weakening (*Wuthering Heights*, 427). Identifying her primal instincts and connection to Heathcliff (nature), coupled with the repression of society and marriage to Edgar (culture) as the source of her anguish, Catherine's behavior results in a cataclysmic hysterical exhibition.

Catherine's pathologies are driven by inherent passion and instinctual repression resulting in maniacal responses. Lypemania-monomania is classified as two stages of a disease: the first presenting a partial delirium of depression and despair later progressing into insanity of periods of excitement and undeterred expressions of overt passion. Men, as Esquirol (1838, 37) argues, are more susceptible to the presentation of insanity than women; while women conceal their disorder, men are "more maniacal, more furious." Taking into consideration that Irigaray (1985, 55) stresses women as "mirrors" or "mimics" for men, it is appropriate that destructive masculine energies are presented in female hysterical exhibition. Catherine's display of initial lypemaniacal melancholic response occurs when her "wondrous constancy to old attachments" is interrupted (*Wuthering Heights*, 365). Classified as a miserable and melancholic disposition, lypemania causes the individual to be unassuming, afraid, and dejected. Brontë presents these traits in Catherine during her introductory stages of sophisticated social appropriation and separation from Heathcliff. Forcefully rejected from any interaction with her natural self, Catherine responds with "flushed" cheeks and tears that "gushed over" (*Wuthering Heights*, 365). Furthering her descent into mania, Catherine's loss of appetite is symbolically foreshadowed as she "slipped her fork to the floor, and hastily dived under the cloth to conceal her emotion" (*Wuthering Heights*, 365). In an attempt to repress what Nelly refers to as her "genuine disposition," Catherine struggles to maintain cordiality but lapses into "uncontrollable grief" and lypemania (*Wuthering Heights*, 373, 383). Pronounced as "dangerously ill" by the doctor, Catherine faces a treatment of "bloodletting," a restrictive "diet," and "full observation" to "ensure that she does 'not throw herself down the stairs, or out of the window'"

(*Wuthering Heights*, 383). The significance of the gothic madwoman as a material-semiotic figure reflects specific characteristics and effects of lypemaniacal responses which Brontë employs to exhibit the progressive degeneration from Victorian repression in women. Using Heathcliff's desertion as a pivotal provocation, Brontë transforms Catherine into this transgressive figuration of gothic madwoman.

Catherine operates within the gothic narrative as a liminal figure. Madwomen, as pivotal characters of Victorian Gothic novels, transgress lines and boundaries within the narrative. As individuals who contravene conventional Victorian femininity, figurations of madwomen reject social expectations of controlled passivity. The madwoman, as Laurence Taliarach-Vielmas (2016, 34) argues, is characterized as ambiguous and "blurs conventional representations of femininity through its contradictions, and evokes mystery and fear." In *Wuthering Heights*, Catherine blurs these lines between society/nature, good/bad, and sane/insane. Tormented by repression and contradictions, she assumes the position as madwoman, and navigates her liminality. Women and madness, from this perspective, are comprised of both feminine ideals and their antithetic characteristics. In this sense, madwomen, as embodied contradictions of sensitivity and confined immorality, are reflections of the heroine's experience. Initially exhibited as lypemaniacal, or melancholic, Catherine experiences "seasons of gloom and silence" after the loss of Heathcliff and uninhibited desire (*Wuthering Heights*, 385). However, upon his reappearance Cathy is subjected to the return of repressed passions forcing her into the contradictory role of liminal figure. Heathcliff's homecoming, after Catherine assumes the role of domestic housewife, provokes further destruction of her identity, causing reversion back to a maniacal state. Cathy's confinement in the restrictive male-constructed society causes her to uphold the depiction of madwoman as she "flirt[s] with madness" (Talairach-Vielmas 2016, 33). While not altogether flirting with a mental disorder, "*hysteria is all that she has left*," therefore Catherine embraces her escape into madness (Irigaray 1985, 71). Divided between a lawful marriage aligned with societal compliance and a devotion attuned to passions, Catherine's liminal position between society and nature, creates psychological disjunctions.

Catherine, then, is marginalized between the desire for her natural self and the social position of femininity. As a figure confined within two spaces, Catherine is forced to deny inherent traits and passions. Disturbed by internal conflict and external social demands, Catherine becomes the madwoman who projects her repressed emotions through hysterical exhibitions. Incarcerated within the Linton's private sphere, Catherine, is trapped in the traditional roles as wife and soon-to-be mother which denies all aspects of her wild nature, thus disallowing Heathcliff any relevancy in her new life.

Married and pregnant, she finds the conventions of femininity suffocating and uncontrollable. Performing as expected, or doing "as she is asked," Cathy's suppression, of what Irigaray (1985, 72) refers to as the "economy of her primal instincts" is suspended. While Catherine's passivity epitomizes the Victorian female construct, her desires are repressed by marital confines and her true self is fragmented. Owing to the separation from Heathcliff, thus from her natural identity, Catherine begins to demonstrate nervous agitation and psychosomatic illnesses. Sandra Gilbert and Susan Gubar (1979, 280) suggest that Heathcliff's reappearance "represents the return of her true self's desires"; however, Catherine's status removes her prior autonomy and denies access to her former agency. As she is an upper-middle-class wife and mother, Cathy is unable to revert back to her former independent self. Trapped within marital and impregnated confines, Catherine's autonomy as a moral Victorian lady requires her to deny all passions towards Heathcliff, thereby rejecting a connection to her natural self. It is through this repression of instincts that the mind-body processes emotions in the limbic state, causing women to disregard the desire for her "first object" and the ownership "of her own sexuality" (Irigaray 1985, 71–72). Initially functioning as a mirror for Edgar's insecure masculinity Catherine represses her passions for domestic assimilation, therefore her instincts are in stasis, or limbo, and unrepresented as authentic. Catherine's desires are suppressed, or redirected, to assume those of her husband, thereby ensnaring her within a social construct "that denies her autonomy" (Gilbert and Gubar 1979, 280). Restricted of personal freedoms, Catherine repression of instincts later results in psychological fragmentation.

Catherine's reintroduction to her natural self produces a hysterical response generated from social pressures and repressed passions. Heathcliff's return juxtaposes Catherine's position between culture and nature, and forces acknowledgment of her repressed passions. Faced with powerlessness, Catherine has no option and must succumb to a lype-monomaniac state. Set up in a position of Victorian middle-class expectations, Catherine's status, forces her to fragment her own identity into a dichotomy of either cultural refinement and marriage to Edgar or wildness and nature with Heathcliff. The reappearance of Heathcliff, instead of functioning as a cure for Catherine's lypemania, provokes her mental degeneration. The absence of power results in an abeyance of instincts, "converting them into hysteria," thereby, Heathcliff's return initiates a re-emergence of Catherine's instincts (Irigaray 1985, 72). This excitability, then, energizes the transition of nervous pathologies and their exchanges, consequently libidinizing the neurons. Stimulation of an inhibited sexuality causes Catherine's neuroses to "short-circuit" her "systems of representation" and circulate "through the ego and the external world" (Wilson 2004, 22). The reawakening of instincts, simultaneously stemming from psychical and neural repression, directly locates Catherine's psychopathology with somatic imprinting. Her limbic, or intrinsic emotional, response causes Catherine to deviate from social norms and threaten self-punishment. Struggling to regain power, Catherine claims helplessness and uses starvation to "break their hearts by breaking [her] own" which results in a self-destructive event (*Wuthering Heights*, 401–402). Unable to reobtain her former life, Catherine's unstable neuroses degenerates into the hysterical madwoman.

Fully submerged in a state of psychosomatic exhibition, Catherine transitions from recovering lypemaniac to functional hysteric. Once presenting episodes of melancholy and fear, Catherine now assumes the degenerative role of manic petulance and audacity. Characterized by fits of delirium and excitement, lype-monomaniacal behavior, Esquirol (1838, 56) argues, consists of a "cephalalgia" (pain in the head), "insomnia" (trouble sleeping), or "somnolence" (strong desire for sleep). Presenting these episodic events, the individual also manifests "presentiments, dreams, and strange ideas" and an inclination for movement and irritability (Esquirol 1838, 56). Catherine's limbic response and voluntary starvation result in nervous weakness, culminating in a forced lypemaniacal hysterical exhibition. Rejected from interaction with Heathcliff and perplexed by Edgar's ignorance of her self-punishment, Catherine's mind-body weaken and exhibit psychosomatic responses. Suffering from cephalalgia and claiming, "a thousand smiths' hammers" are beating in her head, Catherine announces her "passionate temper, verging, when kindled, on frenzy" while "dashing her head" against the sofa (*Wuthering Heights*, 401). Voluntarily adopting the self-punishing behaviors as "a struggle for control," Catherine's masochistic approach results in "three awful nights" of insomnia (*Wuthering Heights*, 404). Characteristic of Esquirol's lype-monomaniac, Catherine's "feverish bewilderment" transitions into madness and delirium, thereby manifesting dreams of "lying in [her] chamber at Wuthering Heights," which illustrates her desire to return to nature (*Wuthering Heights*, 404). In her inability to escape the confines of domesticity and restrictive Victorian womanhood, Catherine's exodus into madness allows her to refute authoritative control and reconnect with nature by demanding that Nelly "open the window," albeit in "the middle of winter" (*Wuthering Heights*, 404). Embracing her hysteria as a way to avoid "total repression and destruction" of her agency, Catherine performs as a madwoman to escape social conventions while simultaneously indulging in her natural desires (Irigaray 1985, 72). In her final moments, Catherine explicitly blames both Edgar and Heathcliff for her "broken" heart and proclaims, "you have killed me" (*Wuthering Heights*, 426). Catherine's accusatory statement demonstrates how the forced division of women's identities between social ideologies and the natural self is destructive. Brontë's figuration of Catherine as a gothic madwoman responds to the discursive context of Victorian womanhood that reifies women as agents of morality incapable of passionate desire.

Catherine is a material-semiotic response to institutional discourse, whose repression of natural instincts and confinement within conventional Victorian boundaries result in her acquiescence of hysteria. Unable to indulge in desires and obliged to pursue a socially prescribed role, Catherine embraces madness as a means for escape and expression. Catherine's monistic structure of mind-body-nature-woman is forcefully separated to abide by Victorian feminine ideals, thus transgressing into a monstrous figuration seeking agency and singularity of self. This division of self, or woman from nature, is a common occurrence in gothic fiction as identified through Catherine Earnshaw's transgression to hysteria.

JANE EYRE'S (1847) MONSTROUS WOMAN IN THE ATTIC

Jane Eyre, a narrative about a young girl's achievement of independence, contains a darker side about female confinement and neglect. Struggling on a journey of self-exploration, Charlotte Brontë's protagonist, Jane, finds herself employed at Thornfield Hall, home of Edward Rochester. During her residence, she develops a romantic relationship with Rochester, only to discover that his current wife resides in a cell on the third floor. Presumed insane, Rochester's wife, Bertha, is forcibly imprisoned, neglected, and theriomorphized. Operating within the gothic mode, Brontë's monstrous madwoman embodies early-to-mid-Victorian anxieties about transgressive female sexuality and their inherent connection to nature through biological functions. Brontë's novel, as Sally Shuttleworth (1994, 11) suggests in *Charlotte Brontë and Victorian Psychology*, shares a dynamic preoccupation with Victorian psychology that addresses excess in the "workings of insanity, and nervous disease, and the unstable constitution of female insanity." This conjunction of sciences and literary subjectivity construct the psychological science of the authentic self where manifestations of behavior are perceived as distortions of the unconscious thought. Informed by Victorian psychiatry, then, *Jane Eyre* identifies the dangers of women's sexual passion using cultural and medical discourse on the hysterical anti-heroine, Bertha Mason.

Victorian women epitomized domestic refinement and purity, as demonstrated through presentations of moral disposition and proper etiquette. As discussed in the prior chapter, Victorian ideologies centered the middle-class lifestyle as the function of morals, hospitality, and guidance. For the mistress of the house, private domiciles were moral sanctuaries free from social corruption and public debauchery. Fulfilment and accomplishment were achieved through motherhood, marriage, and proper domestication. While men spent much of their time on professions, therefore limiting time at home, women, on the other hand, were responsible for familial guidance, the moral development of children, and the supervision of the household affairs. In failing at, or rejecting, these expectations, women were labeled as immoral, corrupt, or psychologically impeded. It is, then, these antagonistic roles of Victorian womanhood and psychological instability that, Shuttleworth (1994, 4) claims "are played out in Brontë's fiction" to intensify struggles and expose secrets. Charlotte Brontë demonstrates the severe repercussions of these female expectations through Bertha Mason, whose embodiment of instinctual repression should also be read as a vociferous attempt for reclamation of agency. Here, spousal neglect and instinctual restriction in Brontë's *Jane Eyre* are responsible for Bertha Mason Rochester's monstrous manifestations of sexual repression transformed into psychosomatic episodes.

The Repression of Bertha Mason

Jane Eyre is a tale of female struggle and success within a patriarchal system. While Brontë's novel accentuates the growth of the protagonist, Jane, it removes agency from Bertha. Whereas some scholars critically analyze Jane, Rochester, or their relationship, Bertha faces obscurity as a shade of the main heroine; a reminder of patriarchal failure; or an obstacle for the couple to overcome to achieve happiness. As the protagonist, Jane is the focus of Brontë's novel; readers witness her journey to overcome classism, genderism, and the ability to gain independence. Most importantly, as noted in Gilbert and Gubar's influential feminist work, *The Madwoman in the Attic* (1979), Jane must learn to overcome her sexuality, rage, and immaturity to develop her own agency in a gender-suppressive society. Restricted by her gender and role in society, Jane represses her sentiments behind a docile façade. Her inability to express personal passions results in what Gilbert and Gubar (1979, 359) define as a threatening "avatar" or Jane's "dark double": Bertha Mason, the forgotten monster in the attic.

Bertha is theorized as exhibiting the ferocity of an abandoned child, struggling to find the balance between personal success and social assimilation. The psychological repression of the novel's anti-heroine allows a projection of a metaphorically spectral figure who acts in ways Jane cannot. Bertha's functions and manifestations at Thornfield have been argued as relevant, or directly connected to Jane's repression and rage. The dual personalities, as reflected by Bertha and Jane, offer an example of behavioral dos and don'ts, not only to the reader, but to the protagonist as well. The violent actions of the unstable madwoman teaches Jane lessons on feminine appropriation and "how not to act" in order to succeed in Brontë's (re)construction of the period's social structure (Gilbert and Gubar 1979, 361). While seeing the plausibility of Bertha as Jane's instinctual self, the identity and authenticity of Brontë's anti-heroine is erased. Donna Heiland (2004, 121), similar to Gilbert and Gubar, suggests that Jane resides in fantasy while tenanting Thornfield, while Bertha "descends like a malignant spirit" to terrorize the governess and the master of the house as a reminder of the "real." Depicted as a Burkean figure of the sublime, not a figuration of the uncanny, she emerges, "large, dark, terrifying—with the potential to overwhelm" (Heiland 2004, 127). While still not in possession of her own identity, Bertha operates according to Jane's necessities. Lastly, the aggressive madwoman functions as a mirror of Rochester's masculinity that denotes overt lust and desire. A literal and symbolic "residue" of Rochester's crime, Bertha acts as a haunting reminder of his "sexual fall" (Hoeveler 1998, 213). However, in allotting her the role of a figuration that illuminates other characters' motivations, psyches, and histories, critics erase Bertha's agency as an individual woman with her own passions and desires. While these theorists perceive Bertha as a vehicle for Jane and Rochester's mobility, others argue that her identity is shaped by imperialist marginalization.

An antithesis to the moral injunctions and domestication illustrated in chapter 1, Bertha Mason rejects the Victorian ideal of virtuous femininity. Identified by a Creole identity and sexual disposition, Bertha is marginalized within the Victorian English social standard. Refusing to develop the popular theory that Bertha is Jane's dark double, Gayatri Chakravorty Spivak (1985) argues that her native status is depicted as not entirely animal-like, but a terroristic subject to imperialism. Evaluating Victorian perceptions of Indigenous sexuality as in possession of savage and beastlike propensities, this notion suggests that enforced subjectivity and categorical British identity aligns this otherness to humanity. This construct, then, allows the so-called heathen to be humanized so that society can implement a level of control. Suggesting that Bertha is a figuration created by the politics of an imperialist society, she functions then as an amalgamation of human-animal, while also acting as the gatekeeper to regulate the influence of both. Correlating this indeterminate line of human and animal with Brontë's anti-heroine the boundaries act to "weaken" Bertha's "entitlement" in accordance with the law (Spivak 1985, 249). Similar to Spivak's argument, Sandra M. Gilbert (1998) identifies Bertha's otherness as associated with her instinctual drive. Defined as both "beautiful but dissolute," Bertha's Creole heritage, Gilbert (1998, 360) argues, is "most likely of European descent"; however, her life in the West Indies offers the speculation of biracialism. Although not clarified in Brontë's text, Bertha is undeniably Other to Jane in both appearance and behavior. Described as an eminently "fine woman, in the style of Blanche Ingram: tall, dark, and majestic," Bertha's implication of exotic "otherness" creates tension for traditional white Victorian womanhood (*Jane Eyre*, 221). This pathologization of colonized women allows society to fixate on their bodies as figurations of anachronism. Similarly, Victorian society's simplification of these figures result in a perception of subhumanity and a necessity for imperial domination. Indeed, Indigenous women are aligned with the imperial perspective that they, like the Earth, need "to be discovered, entered, named, inseminated and, above all, owned" (McClintock 1995, 31). Bertha's exotic otherness, then, presents an ominous intersection between high-class society, womanhood, and the sexual instincts of lower classes and the Darwinian-applied savage. As a white Creole woman, she is marked as indeterminate and sexually primitive, thus negating her as fit for traditional Victorian womanhood. Deficient in the characteristics of conventional British femininity, as promoted by Coventry Patmore and John Ruskin, Bertha is unable to assimilate into the role of middle- and upper-class wife. Therefore, restricted from accessing this domain, she is neglected and becomes the model of the monstrous gothic madwoman.

Madness is a manifestation of rejection against the confines of social repression. Ignorant of Bertha's instinctual passions, Rochester provokes psychological disturbances through neglect. Allured by her beauty and desirability, Rochester indulges in carnal pleasures with Bertha as he claims: "she flattered me, and lavishly displayed for my pleasure her charms and accomplishments. All the men in her circle seemed to admire her and envy me. I was dazzled, stimulated; my senses were excited, being ignorant, raw, and inexperienced, I thought I loved her" (*Jane Eyre*, 221). What he professes as love is, in reality, Rochester's attraction for Bertha and need for sexual conquest. Reflective of the colonized women, Rochester's imperial adventure results in his enthusiasm to claim, re-identify, possess, and dominate the Jamaican native. Claiming that he was "cheated into espousing," Rochester's need for carnal domination enticed his necessity for a marital union (*Jane Eyre*, 212). While entering into the bonds of matrimony, Bertha not only assumes the role of Victorian wife but acquires Rochester as the restrictive master over her natural disposition. What begins as a mutual affection between two passionate individuals, leads into a degradation of freedom and a marriage of "one of ruler and subject" (Summerscale 2012, 49). No longer a relationship of equality, Rochester assumes the role of possessor while Bertha is forcibly sublimated and objectified. As their marriage is founded on sexual desires, Rochester demonstrates a loss of interest and claims that the "honeymoon [is] over" (*Jane Eyre*, 222). Locked within the legal confines of matrimony, Rochester imprisons his wife, thus transforming their relationship into that of owner and discarded possession. Declaring that Bertha is "intemperate and unchaste," Rochester labels her as the feared hysterically immoral woman

84   Chapter Two

to alleviate personal guilt (*Jane Eyre*, 222). As a result of Rochester's rejection and his forced confinement, Bertha is unable to access her agency as a sexually expressive woman and submits to the hysterical exhibition of a madwoman. Therefore, Bertha's madness is a result of neurological dysfunction created by nympho-erotomania.

Bertha's Singularity: How Mind Becomes Matter in Female Hysteria

Brontë constructs an instinctually motivated gothic madwoman from early-to-mid-Victorian psychiatric discourse. Revealed in a letter to William Smith William, Brontë confesses familiarity with James Cowles Prichard's *Treatise on Insanity* (1835). In this correspondence, Brontë claims that she used this diagnosis of moral insanity to construct her anti-heroine. Informed by Prichard's research, Brontë created her madwoman to disrupt the stereotype of the discursive madwoman trope and to bring awareness to the division of the female mind-body. While claiming that the "character is shocking," Brontë also notes that Bertha's realistic madness is "natural" (Shuttleworth 1994, 14). Afflicted by moral insanity, the individual suffers from degradation of morality and, as Brontë notes, that all morality and humanity is erased and replaced by a monster. Prichard suggests that in the state of moral derangement, the mind expresses incessant excitement and strong expressions. This conduct, as Prichard (1835, 19) asserts, results in "[a] female modest and circumspect becomes violent and abrupt in her manners, loquacious, impetuous, talks loudly and abusively against her relations and guardians, before perfect strangers." While not definitively "modest," Bertha displays characteristics of the Victorian ideal during Rochester's courtship when "she flattered [him], and lavishly displayed . . . her charms and accomplishments" (*Jane Eyre*, 221). Accompanied by chaperones, Bertha also exhibited the guise of chastity through her "very little private conversations" with Rochester prior to marriage (*Jane Eyre*, 221). After four years of "liv[ing] with that woman upstairs," Rochester identifies that "her character ripened and developed with frightful rapidity" demonstrating "vices" that were "so strong, only cruelty could check them" (*Jane Eyre*, 222). Examining this approach that Bertha's madness is a natural event, Esquirol's theories of mania establish how it is in fact, the *repression of nature* that creates this hysterical exhibition. Although informed by Prichard's medical research, Bertha also reflects the characteristics of a hypersexualized nymphomaniac with erotomaniacal tendencies. A conjoined disorder "characterized by an excessive sexual passion," it stems from both "the organs of reproduction" and a psychical "sentiment" (Esquirol 1838, 335). The nympho-erotomaniac is frequently violent and "utters nothing but abuse, obscenity and blasphemy" (Esquirol 1838, 378). Bertha demonstrates this lack of "virtue in her nature" through passionate indulgences and animalistic ferocity (*Jane Eyre*, 221). Reminiscent of Showalter's three romantic images of female insanity, Bertha's exhibition as sexually motivated madwoman correlates to the violent Lucia, or Lucy. Linked to the fear of female sexuality, the dangerous Lucy is from Sir Walter Scott's (1819) *The Bride of Lammermoor*. Denied her own passions and forced into a socially acceptable marriage, Lucy descends into insanity, stabs her intended, and succumbs to her illness.[4] Perceived as a woman controlled by carnal instincts, Lucy's mental instability correlates to her reproductive functions. Informing the medical diagnosis of eroto-nymphomania, this stereotype is in conversation with Bertha Mason.

Brontë's madwoman presents hysterical exhibitions as a result of her neurological dysfunction. Shuttleworth (1994, 148) suggests that Brontë foregrounds three popular concerns within Bertha: "the mechanics of self-control, the female body and sexuality, and the insurgence of insanity." Aligning Bertha's character with the popular medical discourse of the period allows Brontë to construct her outside of Cartesian dualism. The rise of monomania, partial insanity, and hysteria, then, removed the division of mind from body and placed it solely in the brain. Consequently, such ailments as unhappiness and illness, no longer perceived as part of the soul, became recognized as a condition of the nervous system. Since these disorders are not restricted to the immateriality of the spirit, the parameters of psychiatry advanced its research to incorporate physiology into studies of madness. No longer defined by the stipulation that the mind is separate from the body, Bertha demonstrates the unification through the neurological dysfunction induced by nympho-erotomania. Failing to transfer the "origin of her desire," to her husband/master, Bertha is punished (Irigaray 1985, 33). Therefore, as the representative of his wife's sanity and satisfaction, Rochester enforces a secretive imprisonment.

This imprisonment demonstrates Rochester's disregard for Bertha's desires and also functions as a symbol for the societal restriction of female sexuality. Rochester's remorse and "longing for renewal of [his] soul" leads him to "repudiate the containment of her crimes" and disassociate himself from Bertha's "mental defects" (*Jane Eyre*, 223). Confinement in both marriage and on the third floor, deprives Bertha of intimate expression and personal satisfaction. Initially placated in her sexual desires by an attentive husband, Bertha is forced to repress her carnality upon her abandonment. Quarantined to a cell-like room, restricted from all passionate intimacy, Bertha develops a psychosomatic neurosis. Originating from an instinctual desire, Bertha's rejection of sexual release influences a nerve-sensory response causing chemical instability and aggression in her motor functions. This disruption in Bertha's neurons is interlinked and disseminated throughout the psychosomatic system. As a psychic trauma of neglect and rejection, it results in psychosomatic vulnerability that results in transitioning Bertha's illness into an exhibition of conversion hysteria. Rochester's absence and Bertha's fifteen-year instinctual internment leads to violent expulsions of intense behavior. Deprivation and rejection of intimacy causes manifestations of hysterical conversion influenced by such erotomaniacal delusions.

As a vicious hysteric, Bertha Mason's madness is precipitated by an erotomaniacal response. Erotomania, as a subset disorder, is usually coupled with a primary psychological disorder, resulting in irritable or dysphoric moods and violently erratic psychosomatic behavioral events. Prolonged neglect in amorous women and the unexpected decline in sexual intimacy and intercourse creates this psychological imbalance. The core condition of this illness creates delusions of being loved, or infatuated by, an unattainable person. Typically, this disorder occurs in an event of major loss or severe loneliness. Rochester's initial promiscuity, and then forced neglect, creates a psychosomatic conflict within Bertha. While indulging in expressions of carnality with her new husband, Bertha continues to assert a connection to her primal instincts. During these events of initial matrimony, she is free to satiate her passions; however, when prompted by Rochester, Bertha does not repress her excessive temperament. Women, to ensure their roles as Victorian constructs, are to return back to chastity and assume the "sublimation required" through "asceticism, decency, [and] shame" (Irigaray 1985, 125). This sublimation functions as a defense mechanism used to transform socially unacceptable impulses, or the sexual libido, into acceptable behaviors which, after repetition, naturally convert into initial reactions. Bertha's rejection of domestic purity causes Rochester to forcefully repress her sexual expression. Intensified passions coupled with the deprivation of carnality, results in the reticulation of a libidinized nervous system causing psychosomatic illness. Bertha's mind-body repression culminates in hysterical exhibitions of vociferous animality and violence.

Bertha's repressed sexuality transforms into female vilification and animality. Struggling with a prurient disposition, she faces a psychosomatic weakening. This weakness of the physical form derives from her psychical trauma of erotomaniacal repudiation. Unable to discharge her destructive sexuality, Bertha's hysterical conversion results in reverting back to a primal state. Similarly, this transition portrays Bertha as a figure of limitless desire. This absence of an object to focus her passions on, the only outcome for Bertha is a "murderous" one (Milbank 1992, 144). This repression of sexual instincts is too powerful for containment, therefore it threatens to disrupt the conscious. This re-emergence of hidden elements into the consciousness, influences the psyche-soma through the intricacies of the nervous system and allows for such symptomatic events as "paralyses, amnesias, strangulated affects, nervous tics, and infantile fantasies," or in this case, dangerous assaults (Wilson 2004, 1). While Bertha demonstrates maniacal expulsions of rage through arson and mutilation, all of her attacks reflect a return to her natural self. Bertha's first offense, resulting in the attempted murder of her captor, uses a destructive organic element: fire. Creating a "blaze" in Rochester's room reflects the re-emergence of Bertha's repressed instincts (*Jane Eyre*, 109). Later transgressions display a significant resurgence of primal instincts through animalistic behavior. On the night when the moon "was full and bright," unbeknownst to the protagonist, Bertha echoes "savage," "sharp," and "shrilly sound[s]" from the confines of Thornfield Hall (*Jane Eyre*, 149). Assuming that Bertha's devastating cries are that of an animal, Brontë's heroine claims the source as "the thing" (*Jane Eyre*, 149). On a similar night, the protagonist draws "so near a wolf's den" and experiences "a snarling, snatching sound, almost like a dog quarrelling" (*Jane Eyre*, 151, 157). Referred to as a "goblin," "wild beast," and "tigress," Bertha's humanity is revoked (*Jane Eyre*, 151, 157). Reminiscent of Catherine's wild savagery in *Wuthering Heights*, Bertha's figuration reflects her connection to nature. While assuming a feral disposition, Bertha is thrust into the role of voracious monster and "suck[s] the blood" from Richard Mason (*Jane Eyre*, 154). Targeting her brother as responsible for allowing Rochester's subjugation, she attempts revenge but is re-confined. Bertha's reconnection to a natural, more primitive, self allows her to exhibit an uninhibited tenacity to seek freedom. Illustrated as a Victorian wife controlled by carnal instincts, Brontë uses Bertha as a gothic representation of a sexual contaminant in the domestic sphere.

Gothic expressions of violence and animality represent early-to-mid-Victorian fears of female sexuality. Similar to the gothic madwoman, the figure of the vampire is a liminal figure of civility and animality. In this sense, the female vampire exhibits the paradox of the construct created from social anxieties and the rigid social boundaries that refuse change or individuality (Wisker 2016). Similarly, DeLamotte (1990, 21) argues that vampirism symbolizes corporeal danger, or "transgression against the body, the last barrier protecting the self from the other." Epitomized as sexually transgressive figures, female vampires symbolize malignancy and threaten social boundaries of stability and control. Therefore, the female vampire, much like the madwoman, exposes the tensions of a society that created the figurations. Noted by Jane as the "foul German spectre," Bertha navigates through Brontë's novel as both the madwoman and the vampire (*Jane Eyre*, 154). Constructed as dual gothic monsters, Bertha illustrates the excess of social concern with female sexuality and mental instability, while destabilizing the connection between women and nature. Identified as a "mystery" established in "fire" and "blood," Bertha's vampiric behavior, "masked in an ordinary woman's face and shape," operates in "the deadliest hours of night" (*Jane Eyre*, 153). Brontë's representation of Bertha with "red eyes" and a "blackened inflation of the lineaments" suggests vampiric hunger and necessity for nourishment (*Jane Eyre*, 153). Women in *Jane Eyre* possess a desire, but it is either repressed (Jane) or perversely exploited (Blanche and Celine) to obtain rewards through self-spirituality or financial gain. Bertha's inherent desires for carnal satisfaction, in turn, is the dramatized sexual desires that these women repress (Gilbert 1998). Rochester's proclamation of Bertha's explicit nymphomania and destructive behavior has inexplicably tarnished his family name and honor through affiliation while repressing her desires, resulting in her madness. Brontë constructs Bertha's animalistic carnality and violent behavior as an expression of rage and rebellion against a repressive social system. Furthermore, Bertha's vampiric behavior and attack on her brother, as John Maynard (1984, 107–108) claims, is a peculiar "sexual form of violence" which emphasizes her illness as a "dangerous sexual extreme." Arguing that female sexuality disregards boundaries, Bertha's attack incorporates fear of sexuality and familial relations. Embodying social anxieties of excessive female carnality, Bertha's madness might be read, then, as an act of rebellion against social repression. Her marginalization as the nymphomaniacal madwoman, coupled with rejection, creates a psychosomatic response in the neglected Bertha. It is through Rochester's actions that Bertha is overcome by her instincts and submits to animalistic behavior.

Double Standards: Rochester's Sexuality and Bertha's Rejection

Brontë's figuration of Bertha's mirrored promiscuity results in marital disjunction. Recent narrative studies of nineteenth-century biological reproduction show the stark boundaries of male and female characteristics and how they are informed by nature and culture. This separation of sexual expectations assists in appointing women as "guardians of moral control" while allowing the "inevitability of male wanderlust" (Wilson 2014, 221). Women, while responsible for repressing their own instincts, are also expected to imitate men through their journey to "compensate for voids in the ego" (Irigaray 1985, 55). However, Bertha's mirroring of Rochester does not result in a revering wife, but in a contradiction that echoes his own corruption. While Rochester desires a supportive wife to fit the role of domestic caregiver, he is alternatively rewarded with a replication of his own sexual voracity through Bertha.

Bertha rejects the traditional moral role of virtue and, instead, rivals Rochester's sexual tendencies. Her outward expression of primal instincts reflects Rochester's desires therefore he tires with the demands of a sexually competitive marriage. Rochester's proclamation of his "vile discoveries" of Bertha's character, that "developed with frightful rapidity," demonstrates his intolerance of a sexually empowered wife (*Jane Eyre*, 222). Rochester expects to dominate the role of sexual master while possessing a virtuous and morally apt wife. However, Bertha's "vices sprang up fast and rank" and he could only "devour [his] repentance and disgust in secret" (*Jane Eyre*, 222). While in the West Indies, Rochester remains bound to a wife with a "gross, impure, and depraved" nature and indulges in sexual excesses (*Jane Eyre*, 222). Disgusted by her "pigmy intellect" and "giant propensities," he claims that "no professed harlot" possesses similar language and behavior (*Jane Eyre*, 223). Brontë's language about Bertha's intellect and bodily form once again alludes to imperial references about colonized women. Aligning with the fetishization of "primitivism" and "overexposure" of sexual organs, Brontë exposes Rochester's imperialistic attitude (McClintock 1995, 42). Though not admitting outright that Bertha emulates his own sexual capacity, Rochester blames her hereditary traits for madness. Upon arrival to England, he confines her to the third floor, abandons his duties as husband and master of the estate, and escapes to the continent as an enigmatic bachelor. Exasperated by a woman whose primal instincts suggest an adversarial relationship, Rochester rejects Bertha, seeks "the Continent," and goes "devious through all its lands" (*Jane Eyre*, 225). Declared by Rochester as antagonistic to his desires, Bertha is designated as immoral and confined to a life of instinctual repression.

Unable to attain freedom of sexual expression, Bertha communicates, and escapes, through nature. Similar to Catherine's environmental response in *Wuthering Heights*, Bertha's anguish and jealously is reflected in the weather at Thornfield. In their exposition of Mary Shelley's *Frankenstein* (1818), Smith and Hughes (2013, 3) propose that the "dystopianism" of the Gothic environment elucidates how nature represents "a space of crisis," that functions as "a point of contact with the ecological." They assert that this "key issue" coincides with the creature's discovery of a language that "'owns' the ecological and so anchor it as a site of coherent meaning" (Smith and Hughes 2013, 3). Similar to Shelley's creature, Bertha finds her language through the ecological environment. Whereas Smith and Hughes (2013, 4) suggest that "representations of the landscape" offer an ecocritical acknowledgment that encapsulates identity, gender, or class, the landscape in *Jane Eyre* represents the transgressions of Bertha's identity, gender, and class. Brontë presents Bertha with a limited vocabulary and an inability to communicate her desires to Rochester. Throughout the novel, Bertha's verbal correspondence is restricted to laughter and howls with one incident of a spoken threat against her brother. Unable to articulate a response, Bertha's repressed emotions are mirrored by the tumultuous weather. Most notably, during Rochester and Jane's engagement, "the weather changes" and interrupts the new couple's intimate moment (*Jane Eyre,* 186). The tabooed romance is disrupted by a "livid, vivid, spark" leaping from a cloud, followed by "a crack, a crash, and a close rattling peal" that represents the unspoken fury of the current Mrs. Rochester (*Jane Eyre*, 186). Powerless to warn Jane against the engagement or to claim Rochester as her lawful husband, Bertha's rage is symbolically portrayed by nature. The destructive storm, on the night of Bertha's agonized revenge, results in the infamous splitting of the "horse-chestnut" tree in the orchard (*Jane Eyre,* 186). While such theorists as Maynard (1984) argue for the split as a symbolic delay in Rochester and Jane's unity, it ecofeministically signifies the destruction of female repression. Tormenting the protagonist with a continuous wind accompanied by a "wild melancholic wail," Bertha's emotional turbulence results in calamitous weather until the wedding (*Jane Eyre,* 201). She discovers the ability to communicate using her connection to nature that is mirrored by the landscape and climacteric conditions. Finding her voice within the natural realm, Bertha is still unable to escape her confines as a Victorian woman and seeks her freedom in death. In the final retaliation against her captors, Bertha sets Thornfield ablaze and "spring[s]" off the roof (*Jane Eyre,* 310). Resulting in a violent death, she frees herself from the repressive torment while alleviating the anxiety of female sexuality in the patriarchal setting. Free of the burden of a sexually voracious madwoman, Rochester is now allowed to pursue his desires. Brontë utilizes Bertha's death and Rochester's freedom to demonstrate the imbalance of gender expectations in society. Whereas Victorian men have the ability to indulge in their desires, the only option for female independence, is death.

ECHOES IN THE ATTIC: *THE WRONGED WIFE: OR THE HEART OF HATE* (1870),

Originally published as a serial tale in 1863 by Septimus R. Urban, James Malcolm Rymer's pseudonym, *The Wronged Wife: Or the Heart of Hate* made its appearance in the *New York Mercury* as *The Vendetta: Or a Lesson in Life*. Later republished in *Frank Starr's Fifteen Cent Illustrated Novels* in 1870, with the new title. Well-known as a British author and editor, Rymer visited America for several years to write under his pseudonym. While many other publications by Rymer achieved popularity—*Varney, the Vampire* (1845–1847), *The String of Pearls* (1846–1847), and *Ada, the Betrayed* (1845), this tale falls short of such success. Similar to these other stories, this tale maintains the characteristics and tropes of a penny dreadful. Lacking the sanguinity and luridness of traditional pennys, it tells the adventurous story of righteous revenge, insanity, and governmental villainy.[5] Although Rymer emphasizes the adventurous masculine relationship between a naïve governor's son and a vengeful assassin, this penny clearly focuses on the gothic madwoman, Agatha herself, and her grandmother, called in the text, simply Mother.

The novel, while centralized around a plot of revenge, expounds female illness and its consequences. Sir Hannibal Murkington, originally known as John Jeffreys, seeks to avenge the attempted rape of his future wife through the assassination of the Wentworth family. While in the military, Jeffreys prevents two officers from assaulting the young Corsican woman, Agatha. Shortly after the assault is deterred, Jeffreys and Agatha are married; however, jealousy and humiliation intervene, and revenge is sought against the couple. One of the offenders, Colonel Wentworth, frames and accuses Jeffreys of theft, thus sentencing him to an execution. Jeffreys, shot in the presence of Agatha and her grandmother, survives his execution. Though the wound does not end his life, the shot brings grief and madness onto the Corsican family. Agatha, forced to witness the attempted execution of her husband, succumbs to manic hysteria. Reflective of Showalter's third image of stereotypical hysterics, Agatha echoes the characteristics of Crazy Jane, or the neurasthenic madwoman. Crazy Jane is based on a servant girl who is rejected by a lover (either through his death or abandonment) and she, in turn, faces madness. Paralleling Agatha Jeffreys, the novel uses the medical stereotype of Crazy Jane to join the discourse of female-induced anxiety. Entrapped within a permanent state of hysterical exhibition, Agatha projects her identity into a surrounding family and environment which demonstrates her return to nature and influence and manipulation of others. Unable to regain her senses, Agatha vicariously enacts revenge on the Wentworth family through Mother and Jeffreys, using the environment as a method for communication.[6]

Agatha's Discourse: Female Madness and the EcoGothic

Much like *Wuthering Heights* and *Jane Eyre*, *The Wronged Wife* situates expressions of female psychosomatic disorders with tumultuous environmental activity. As illustrated in hysterical women, the feminized gothic landscape, Jane Mitchell (2018, 61) suggests, mirrors the abject, "wild, untamed, and uncontrollable" repression of instincts. Both the home and the environment embody the terrors of female restriction and transform the domestic ideal into a fearful and unstable domain. Confinement, both literal and metaphorical, and destructive imagery in Urban's narrative is used to construct women's affiliation to their natural surroundings. Agatha, whose representation echoes that of Catherine Earnshaw and Bertha Mason, entertains an innate connection to her natural surroundings. Prior to her psychological incarceration, she spent her time "wandering in the valleys of Corsica" with her betrothed (*Wronged Wife*, 85). After her manic event, she demonstrates a connection to, and a longing for nature. In most gothic novels, Smith and Hughes (2013, 5) point out, that "the desecration of the natural world is met with psychological trauma." This affect, then, traces back to an oppressive source or powerful institution. Thereby, the structure functions as a mirror of "feminised nature" subjugated by the patriarchal system (Smith and Hughes 2013, 5). In this case, Agatha is attacked by representations of the patriarchal system and retaliates through her ecological surroundings. While Urban's novel involves both the natural environment and traumatic event, the *Wronged Wife* depicts a cause-and-effect relationship.

The wild element of nature reflects in Agatha's madness. In Dawn Keetley and Matthew Sivils's study on the ecoGothic, *Ecogothic in Nineteenth-Century American Literature* (2017), they suggest that the pervasive worry of environmental degradation is a result of loss of control. Centralization of the wild environment in the Gothic, Keetley and Sivils (2017, 3) argue "is born out of the failure of humans to control their lives and their world." This instability of threatening nature reflects in associations between female madness and the tumultuous environment. In Urban's narrative, nature is represented as a vengeful entity akin to Agatha's madness. Similar to Bertha, Agatha displays a connection to nature through wild and violent nightly psychosomatic aggressions. Presenting her hysteria as theriomorphic behavior, Agatha's aggressions become "worse when the moon is at the full" (*Wronged Wife*, 26). Simultaneously reflecting the natural lunar cycle and the female "moon-change," commonly referred to as menstruation, Urban's exhibition of Agatha as a monstrous creature with "unearthly screams," suggests female instability and monstrosity (*Wronged Wife*, 49). Agatha's figuration as madwoman mirrors Victorian anxieties about reproductivity and women's direct affiliation to nature. Intertwining Agatha's biological functions with the natural environment results in, what Keetley and Sivils (2017, 7) suggest is "an agentic force that challenges human's own vaulted ability to shape their world." While void of her own independence and identity, Urban's madwoman projects her wildness through Nature's agency, provoking trepidation about female unpredictability.

The environmental climate operates as a manifestation of repressed emotions for madwomen in the Gothic. The illustration of nature as dangerous, Simon Estok (2019, 47) argues "is central to ecoGothic texts." Ergo, Urban's tale designates Agatha as a representative of ecophobia that Estok identifies in gothic and horror texts depicting climate crisis. Whereas ecophobia is a fear, or sensation of powerlessness against environmental change, it also stems from loss of control. Agatha, as an agent of Urban's natural environment, operates as both the human and nonhuman threat to society. This ecophobia is presented in Agatha's most emphatic and hysterical moments, as the weather reflects her internal turmoil through atmospheric conditions and threatening storms. Echoing society's inability to control or repress nature, Urban mirrors this loss of control through images of wildness in Agatha and the natural environment. When she nears death at the end of the tale, the "darkness deepens in London" and a storm sweeps over the city (*Wronged Wife*, 94). It is in this moment that Agatha suffers from confusion and separation from Jeffreys. Escaping from her confinement, she searches for her husband while the "rage of elements" occurs around her (*Wronged Wife*, 94). When Agatha succumbs to a watery death, there are "vivid flashes of the forked lightning" and a "reverberating roll of the thunder," announcing her departure from life (*Wronged Wife*, 94). Following the desire to return to nature as demonstrated by Catherine and Bertha, Agatha sinks in the river and obtains her freedom, albeit in death. Similar to Emily and Charlotte Brontë's presentations of madwomen, Urban uses Agatha's death as the final resolution for peace in his novel. His depiction of the mad Agatha ensconced by a tempest and falling within the depths of the Thames suggests the culture-nature divide constructed for women. Following the similar conversation of his predecessors, Urban's discourse about the Victorian madwoman demonstrates the volatility of repression and inescapability of social confines.

Transgression and Vengeance in the Female Gothic Novel

A novel with a façade of masculine heroics and retribution, *The Wronged Wife* operates within the Gothic to identify female repression and villainy. As typical of penny and dime novels, Urban's narrative, while not a traditional gothic text, retains characteristics reflective of the genre. These novels typically occur within the domesticated confines of the home or similar location and expose questions of transgressive identities. Through this transgression, women assume the roles of villain and heroine, and demonstrate the instabilities of prescribed femininity and female nature. Urban creates Agatha within the paradigms of the Female Gothic tradition positioning her between the binary roles of victim and monster. Driven to hysteria by spousal separation, Agatha mirrors Charlotte Brontë's madwoman. However, while Bertha's erotomaniacal illness is based on the forceful suppression of her sexuality, Agatha's insanity is caused by the attempted execution of, and unwilling severance from, her husband.

Agatha, a figuration of Victorian medical sciences depicted as a threatening and monstrous madwoman, refuses confinement and suffers from fragmentation. Urban's construction of the evolved madwoman demonstrates a resistance for confinement. This Ophelian-turned-Crazy Jane trope, reconstructed by "medical research's" incorporation of the "heart and brain," led to a display of madness/badness (Talairach-Vielmas 2016, 442). No longer illustrated as silent and morose, the gothic madwoman embodies the dual functions that demand resolution. Reflecting this dichotomy of mad/bad, Agatha's behavioral transgressions appear in her manipulative and influential techniques. Projecting her repressed animosity into psychosomatic responses, Agatha controls Mother through disjointed hysterical exhibitions. Thereby, Mother embodies Agatha's hysteria, impotent rage, and repressed destruction. While incapable of enacting revenge on the profligatory source of her psychosomatic interment, Agatha functions through her grandmother. Communicating through hysterical exhibitions of "a wild, mournful voice" and "strange, unearthly sounds," Agatha controls the emotions and conversations within the house (*Wronged Wife*, 25). In Wilson's (2014, 18) research, she notes that neurasthenia acts in an affective manner, where one "inadequate body generates another." While this is demonstrated through influence of weakened sexual dysfunction, similar affectations occur in sympathetic responses. A psychological trauma results in the affected synapses, cortical pathways, and neurotransmitters of the witness. This maps onto the story and explains the susceptibility of Mother to Agatha's incoherent demands. While explicating wild mournful cries "like a lightning flash of misery," Mother interprets Agatha's pain as a motivator for action (*Wronged Wife*, 25–26). Upon hearing her raging and "loud maniacal laughter," Mother declares a "supreme vendetta," or blood feud, against Agatha's tormentors (*Wronged Wife*, 49).[7] Although portrayed by Urban as a victim of loss and mental subjugation, he demonstrates retaliatory vengeance through Agatha's manipulation and projected communication.

Forcibly repressing her passions and instincts, Agatha's identity fragments and influences the surrounding characters. Mirroring Brontë's Bertha, Agatha is confined by hysteria and unable to verbally communicate. Whereas Catherine and Bertha's depictions as madwomen confront social anxieties of female sexuality and loss of agency through self-inflicted aggression, Agatha presents a fiendish behavior. A madwoman, no longer defined as "an empty sentimental trope," Agatha embodies madness as both the "angel and demon" (Talairach-Vielmas 2016, 42). Maintaining a façade with "long fair hair hung in wild disorder about a free form of matchless beauty," Agatha's visage claims innocence (*Wronged Wife*, 29). In her silence, Agatha presents the trope of angelic serenity; however, when disturbed, she displays a demonic "articulation and a vehemence of manner that were fearful to listen to" (*Wronged Wife*, 29). When in her vociferous exhibitions of hysteria, Agatha projects her rage into a grotesque demonstration of vengeance.

Confined by the physical and mental boundaries of hysteria, Agatha indicates a necessity for communication. The Female Gothic in this sense, provides strength and rationality for women to navigate a mysterious, patriarchally driven world. Agatha, then, with a psychosomatic ailment that suggests isolation and loneliness is perceived as dependent and weak. As Anne Williams (1995, 139) asserts, these women are only viewed as vulnerable to a society that assumes "independence" and "conquest" as "supreme signs of accomplishment." The severity of Agatha's madness encapsulates her within the nonfunctional psychosomatic position of hysterical permanency. While Agatha is trapped within the role of a hysterical woman, she negates fragility through her vicarious influences on both Mother and Jeffreys. Rejecting the aspirations of Victorian womanhood, Agatha seeks vengeance to reclaim sanity and satisfaction. Unable to convey this initiative herself, Agatha and her grandmother operate as a unified transgressive structure. According to DeLamotte (1990, 21), transgression applies when the figuration "poses the similar threat of spiritual or psychological violation and the fusion of two separate identities into one." While captivated by the bonds of madness, Agatha does not transgress boundaries by fusing into a singular identity, she projects her desires onto her relations. In the confines of hysteria, Agatha's only form of communication is through screaming and songs therefore, affected by these cacophonous sounds, Mother functions as the performative corporeal form.

As head of the household Mother, a functional symbol for Agatha's represented rage, is portrayed as a grotesque, ninety-eight-year-old woman whose size "at each year of a protracted life becomes less and less" (*Wronged Wife*, 26). Urban's figuration of this grotesque figure is, what Russo (1994, 9) refers to as, a "cultural projection of an inner state." Whereas the grotesque figure is associated to a strong response to the psyche, Mother does not reflect her own psyche, but that of Agatha. Tormented by her granddaughter's cries, Mother's form reflects the corruption of Agatha. Illustrating an image of grotesquery, as a figure of excess and monstrosity, Mother exhibits the disconnection between Victorian discourses "of the biological body and the law" (Russo 1994, 9). In Avril Horner and Sue Zlosnik's (2016) study on older women in the Gothic, they argue that the older, or elder, woman has a neutral agentic identity. However, Mother, as Urban's gothic figuration of the older woman, is in possession of her own agency and acts as a pivotal character for Urban's plot. Functioning as her granddaughter's vengeful guardian, the "hag," admonishes unfavorable behavior through her "glaring eyes" and ferocity (*Wronged Wife*, 26). Aligning with Carol Margaret Davison's (2009) sentiment that fear of mothers is deeply embedded, Mother embraces a ferocity and vitality that illuminates a "brilliance about her eyes that betoken[s] the lamp of life to be far from extinct" (*Wronged Wife*, 26). Urban's depiction of grotesquery and malevolence in the grandmother mirrors Agatha's passions and rage. Represented as a grotesque crone figure, Mother, and her mad granddaughter, Agatha, create an unsettling response of female capability and monstrosity for the reader. Structuring Agatha and Mother in the gothic mode of transgression, Urban creates a unique representation of doubling. This "doubleness," creates a level of discomfort, as it demonstrates a divide in which the spaces, as a spectacle, are both frightening, yet "attractive" (Russo 1994, 18). While this grotesque doubling applies to the concept of twins, it also pertains to the conjoined relationship between Agatha and Mother. Both women are duplicitous figurations of grotesquery: Agatha as a gothic madwoman, and Mother as the aged hag. These models are indicative of the assumed link between female transgressive behaviors and bodies are both "dangerous, and in danger" (Russo 1994, 60). Urban's figuration of both women as monstrous suggests that all female forms and dispositions, outside of prescribed roles, are sites of excess and social destruction.

The figurations of hysterical woman and grotesque hag are embodiments of Victorian anxieties of expressive and demonstrative women. While Urban constructs both Agatha and Mother as destructive characterizations of social fears, he concludes the novel with their demises. Agatha, in her confused hysterical state, drowns in the river. Mother's death results from her advanced age, of which she is found "paralyzed" and "unresponsive" outside of her granddaughter's room (*Wronged Wife*, 91). Following Horner and Zlosnik's proposal that older women in the Gothic are typically expendable, Mother is utilized to achieve a goal and then disregarded. Urban's eradication of these monstrous women, similar to the destruction of Bertha and Catherine, suggests fears of female expressivity and their potency. With Agatha and Mother's annihilation, Urban creates resolution in his narrative while simultaneously alleviating tension in the reader following the moralistic schema of the popular mode in which he is writing, which, as I've noted, ensures virtue is rewarded and vice is punished.

Throughout the early-to-mid-Victorian period women's functions were correlated to their reproductive functions. Without the interference of social regulation, as so-called scientists and pseudo-scientific commentators claimed, the instability of women could resound in psychological illnesses. Female maladies such as monomania, erotomania, and hysteria were perceived as results of oversexualization in women. Women who refused to conform to social conduct and indulged in their primal instincts were diagnosed as madwomen and inherently problematic—a potential danger to society. Although Victorians typified these women as inhabited by irrationality caused by malfunctioning systems, it is the social repression of natural instincts that produce these manifestations of psychosomatic events resulting in the monistic, monstrous figuration of the gothic madwoman.

NOTES

1. Dora, whose actual name was Ida Breuer, was a case study whose interpretations were formulated and interjected by Freud. As many of his sessions were unrecorded, Freud shaped Dora's narrative based on his own recollection and experiences of their sessions. This case study was a definitive example of the history of failure for analysis. Dora's case study allowed Freud to later refine his analytical techniques and understand transference, or the projection of feelings onto the analyst, as a necessity for psychoanalytic theory.

2. See Christine Alexander and Margaret Smith, *The Oxford Companion to the Brontës* (Oxford/New York: Oxford University Press, 2006). Both reviews, anonymously written, were found with three others in Brontë's desk.

3. Freud later develops the concept of mourning versus melancholia. Similar to Esquirol's interpretation of the lype-monomaniac, Freud asserts that the features of the melancholic are noted as diminished interest in activities, an inability to love, and denouncement of self-worth and abilities, with an expectation that negative events and punishments are deserved. While Catherine exhibits all of these symptoms presented by Freud in the late nineteenth, early twentieth century, her figuration as a madwoman, echoes the concurrent medical discourses promoted by experts of the mid-Victorian period.

4. See Sir Walter Scott's *The Bride of Lammermoor* (1819). The story is about Lucy Ashton and her love for Edgar. Disallowed marriage to Edgar by her stepmother, the villainous Lady Ashton, Lucy is forced to wed another. Witnessing her betrothal to Francis, Edgar rejects Lucy who, in turn, descends into madness, stabbing her husband-to-be.

5. Urban's novel, although published in America, maintains a British setting. The author does not openly disclose the year, however, he portrays a London scene in which the Princess Royal, accompanied by the Queen, are in a carriage preparing for her marriage to the King of Prussia. Whereas the engagement of Princess Victoria and Prince Frederick William occurred in 1855, the wedding followed in January 1858. Therefore, it can be surmised that Urban places his setting towards the end of 1857 and the beginning of 1858.

6. See Jane Austen, *Persuasion* (New York: Millennium Publications, 1818/2014), 26. Following the practice of the penny genre, Urban's novel incorporates characteristics from high literature. For example, Urban's incorporation of the Wentworth family directly correlates to Frederick Wentworth in Jane Austen's *Persuasion*. Depicted as "remarkably fine young man, with a great deal of intelligence, spirit, and brilliancy," Austen's Wentworth is idealized as self-made through hard work and persistence. Urban antithesizes this depiction of the Wentworth family and portrays them as greedy, indulgent, and lazy.

7. Vendetta is an Italian word which refers to a long-standing fight between clans or families. The supreme vendetta, on the other hand, calls for a "blood revenge," which means vengeance, or murder, against all direct family members.

Chapter Three

Neglect, Rage, and Reaction

Female Criminality and the Victorian Gothic

> Once a woman has descended from the pedestal of innocence, she is prepared to perpetuate every crime.
>
> —J. B. Talbot 1844, 142

During the early-to-mid-Victorian period, criminal women were considered emotional, irrational, and susceptible to corruption. Such actions that involve promiscuity, rebellion, or manipulation were designated as monstrous reactive exhibitions involuntarily caused by psychological and biological reactions. These women who yielded to their inherent instincts were classified as unfeminine, mad, and responsible for the corruption of patriarchal ideologies. While Victorian institutions claimed that such unstable female characterizations were affected by mental and physical disorders, these charismatic and felonious women rationally manipulated a society that rejected, abused, and neglected them.

Building on the previous discussions of natural instincts and social repression mentioned in prior chapters, monstrous women in the Victorian Gothic exhibit the conjunction of the immaterial mind with the material body through the exploration of criminal malfeasance and their reactions to environmental influences. This ongoing research focuses on the effects of conscious rejection of the ideological Victorian standards placed on women. Illustrating how the mind-body work synonymously, this section demonstrates how female identities transition into exhibitions of aberrant behavior caused by cognitive social manipulation and monstrous criminal ontologies. By examining the causes of female deviance, it allows an identification of how affective environmental conditions and neurological consciousness drives early-to-mid-Victorian women to break social traditions and elicit physical responses through acts of nonfeasance, thereby illustrating how psychology and physiology unify and display monstrous reactions through material figurations.

This chapter, then, focuses on the characters' deliberate rejection of social restrictions and scrutinizes female mind-body reactions to repression and deprivation of human instincts in the early-to-mid-Victorian Gothic. The main overarching theme emphasizes the migrating shift of female gothic identities as connected to their environmental surroundings through affective experiences. These Gothic novels and ephemeral penny publications bring into focus the women who break from the binds of social restriction, displaying what has been labeled as criminal tendencies. In the Gothic, women often find themselves victims of oppressive male protagonists, however, in the following literature, they emerge as devious antithetical monsters to traditional Victorian womanhood. These women affirm their biological affiliation with nature to avoid the suppressing construction of social artificiality. Typical for the Victorian period, as also reflected in the Female Gothic, these novels focus on the conflict of female identity and transgressive behaviors. Despite the quantity of criminal characteristics available in gothic fiction, there has been little research about the individual analysis of conscious criminality, character function, and material reaction. The female figurations represented in this chapter are exhibited as Victorian angels in the house but perform as devious Others to, what Stacy Alaimo and Susan Hekman (2008, 2) state, "deconstruct the dichotomy itself." Each of these characters operate within the Female Gothic under the guise of the feminine ideal while dismantling Victorian ideologies.

BECOMING THE FELONIOUS OTHER

Victorian culture displayed an anxious belief that women were something other; individuals who were ready to fall victim to their natural instincts. Unless subjugated by social regulations, women were feared as having the potential to infiltrate the domestic realm and destroy the heart of society. However, while women's morals and ontologies were informed and re-created according to the standards of conduct books, medical journals, and theological tracts, concern over female deviance remained. In Andrew Mangham's comprehensive work *Violent Women and Sensation Fiction: Crime, Medicine and Victorian Popular Culture* (2007), he inspects how this popular literature influenced the social suspicion of women. For example, the infamous angel in the house imagery, a popular nineteenth-century perspective of Victorian femininity, was in fact sullied by the influx of murder cases involving women; most notoriously, those criminal events that involved attacks on children or spouses. While such manuals from Sarah Stickney Ellis and Isabella Beeton encouraged women to epitomize Victorian feminine ideals as wives and mothers, this well-received literature illustrated how there was a "ghastly, destructive energy living beneath female spaces and feminine graces" (Mangham 2007, 48). Each progressive phase of women's life—from puberty, to pregnancy, to menopause—was argued as being more reactive or violent than the previous stage. Ultimately, each biological milestone was suspected as a reactive becoming, another reason to construct boundaries of subjugation. In this sense, there remained an underlying suspicion of women, and early-to-mid Victorian society proliferated the belief that they were suspected as instable and on the constant verge of madness. Criminal women, as figurations of chaotic nature and overt sexuality, then, violated feminine expectations and threatened the fragile social order. Thereby, the notion of these volatile women allowed society to dichotomize feminine identities into the domestic angel and wicked Other, thus informing the popular discourses of the period. This division of female ontologies caused a cultural shift that reformed the hegemonic attitude of early-to-mid-Victorian society toward women that reflected in the discourses of the period.

Women of the Victorian Gothic, subject to these prolific discourses, are trapped within the biological confines of their own bodies as fixed subjects. In roles as vulnerable victims and dangerous *femme fatales*, these women are constructed as static figurations of "being," centralized around their reproductive functions and natural traits.[1] Limited in dynamic transitions, these women are fixed characterizations that rarely transgress their assigned boundaries. In her exploration of the Deleuzian concept of "being" versus "becoming," Rosi Braidotti (2003, 44) argues that the body is the focus of "embodiment" in the "feminist struggle for redefinition of subjectivity." Thereby, the female mind-body figuration as the concept of being is a phallogocentric restriction of subjectivity formulated for gender division, while its becoming is a movement away from the essentialist constructs of female identity. Antithetical to being, becoming allows the "feminine Other" to remove itself from the shadow of the "phallogocentric identity" (Braidotti 2003, 50). Subjugated by static categorizations of confinement and/or fragmentation of self, women in the Victorian Gothic are challenged by an inability for ontological transformations. Whereas the material-semiotic female figurations in Victorian Gothic novels face the restrictive mode of constructed being, their felonious identities are a result of becoming and the rejection of social confines.

Women with Many Faces: Degeneration and Female Criminality

Occurring in the nineteenth century, Jean-Baptiste Lamarck's and Charles Darwin's influential theories of genetic variations and evolution began to inform investigative research on criminality. This research, later known as Biopsychology, biological psychology, or psychobiology in modern studies, examines how human and animal biology affect thoughts, emotions, and behaviors. It identifies how influences on the nervous system and changes in brain chemistry situationally dictate human behavior. Proponents of these new nineteenth-century sciences hypothesized that the inherent characteristics and genetic lineage were responsible for criminal behavior. Thus women, already assumed as innately corrupt, were designated as vulnerable to these felonious dispositions. As Judith Knelman (1998, 110) submits in her examination of notable female offenders in the Victorian era, criminality was regarded as a behavior "outside a person's control," as a series of reactive actions informed by the individual's genetics, surroundings, or neurological impulses. Drawn from the prolific essentialist discourses of biological functionality, driven by experts such as Lamarck, Darwin, Thomas Laycock, and Robert Brudenell Carter, Victorian criminology located female malfeasance as an effect of inherent instability. Popular scientific beliefs of the time claim that women's passions, no matter their moral code, were based on "involuntary motor responses" and would emerge violently and unexpectedly (Knelman 1998, 110). Already viewed by society as dominated by their primal instincts, women were presumed as susceptible to any influential, hence corruptible, internal, and external sources. In both scientific and medical discourses, women were classified according to the standards of Western Cartesian thought that segregates the mind from body. This dichotomization delegated women's minds, their identities, and behaviors, as subordinate to their reproductive functionality, thus they were expected to align with the biological functions of the body. Their bodies, defined as sexual and reproductive objects, were then held as standards for the expectations and consequences of the functions of social roles. While society blamed women's biological pathologies for transgressive incursions, many violent female criminals fought the temptation for felonious activity; however, they were driven by the repressed status, thus unable to resist. Medical witnesses to such offending outbursts, however, argue that these women, albeit motivated by impulsivity, were aware of their desires for deviance and moral identification of right and wrong, but proceeded to indulge in this criminal activity. Such criminals, uninhibited by physical or psychological restraints, led to the later scientific hypotheses that identifies the dual aesthetic applied to the dichotomous behaviors of female offenders.

Early criminologist Cesare Lombroso, inspired by Darwin's evolutionary theories, suggests that the criminal persona is inherited and identifiable through physical traits and characteristics. While Lombroso's positivist criminology, as appropriated through Social Darwinism, flourished in the *fin-de-siècle*, the grounds of biological corruption and instability emerged in discourses of the early-to-mid period. It was up until the mid-Victorian period, as Lucia Zedner (1991) points out, that the primary incursions of female criminality were solely "moralistic." As Lombroso's *Richerche sul cretinismo in Lombardia* (1859) and later work, *L'uomo delinquente* (1876) began to shape mid-to-late nineteenth-century rhetoric of "occasional" versus "born" criminal behavior, the corruption of morals and expectations proliferated in discourse of the mid-1800s. Villainous women, regarded as immoral, thereby considered more dangerous than criminal men, were held against the standards of Victorian womanhood and judged as both lawbreakers and deviants from the standards of middle-class femininity. For example, Henry Mayhew (1862, 444), sociologist and founder of the infamous *Punch* magazine, offers an exposition of prison life and argues that in female transgressors, "one sees the most hideous picture of all human weakness and depravity." Arguably, this popular perspective resounded through Victorian society because women, exhibiting behavior classified as rude and crude, were antagonistic to the ideals of them "as the most graceful and gentle form[s] of humanity" (Mayhew 1862, 464). Holding similar views to those of Mayhew, Mary Carpenter (1864, 32) a philanthropist and social reformer who specialized in prison rehabilitation, likens the female criminal to an evil perversion who has "diseased" her nature. This assumption was also echoed by Marianne E. Owen (1866, 153) in *Cornhill Magazine*, who claims that women who "are generally so bold and unblushing in crime," are remiss of the ideals of womanhood, and are "more justly compared to wild beasts than women." As supposedly vulnerable beings, women impacted by such corruption makes them a more significant danger to Victorian society than men. This rhetoric of influential perversions and bestial comparisons pervaded narratives of the mid-Victorian period and offered a foundation for later phrenological studies of female criminality.

Lombroso's later work with William Ferrero, *The Female Offender* (1895) establishes that the criminal distortion in feminine appearance and behavior stems from genetic degeneration because "the primitive type of a species is more clearly represented in the female" (Lombroso and Ferrero 1895, 109). This phrenological-based hypothesis on criminology maintains a social-class dimension that suggests the lower-class appearances of physical degeneration speaks to their supposedly inherited "lower" traits, thereby justifying the social order rather than investigating poverty as the source of criminality. Emulating popular rhetoric of the contemporaneous sciences and medicine,

Lombroso and Ferrero's discourse, then, echoes Darwinian language about the inferiority of women while building on the mid-Victorian perspective of female criminality. According to Darwin's *The Descent of Man, and Selection in Relation to Sex* (1871), women are viewed as biologically stunted compared to men of the species, a theory that Lombroso and Ferrero both appropriate and promote. Women, as surmised by Darwin (1871, 324), are naturally designed as both lesser objects and "prizes" for the "strongest party [to] carry off." This notion of female passivity suggests that most women are inherently subdued and incapable of performing violent and murderous acts. Adopting this presumption, Lombroso and Ferrero (1895, 110) argue that the reason for the rarity of malfeasance is the congenital notion that "they are less inclined to crime than men." The lesser distinction of ferocity in women is attributed to their innate connections to ancestral behaviors, or those naturally born that way. As classic constructivists who resort to reductive essentialism, Lombroso and Ferrero stipulate that it is women's inherent propensities, not social factors, that dictate their malfeasant behaviors and activities.

Atavism, as pertaining to this criminal construct, and the accusation that "savage females, and still more, civilized females" are naturally more timid than men, which is responsible for the essentialist limitation of violent behavior in women (Lombroso and Ferrero 1895, 110). Once again, invoking the language of the period that references the "savagery" of the supposed "lower races" implied by Darwin (1871, 326–327), Lombroso and Ferrero apply this to all criminal women. Furthermore, this assumption influenced nineteenth-century criminology to conclude that the only women capable of enacting criminal offenses are occasional offenders. In these occasional female offenders, anomalous physiognomies are absent, thus these women possess the ability to assimilate within the Victorian domestic sphere. Such identities of these assimilative criminal malefactors include swindlers, adulteresses, bigamists, or calumniators, all offenses and roles "which require an attractive appearance" (Lombroso and Ferrero 1895, 110). Thereby, occasional offenders, then, are exclusively discerned on account of their malicious behavioral traits. On the other hand, the born criminal, lacks this ability for social deception and is physically atypical.

Inherently affected, criminal-born women were classified by society as unfeminine, monstrous, and animalistic. Perceived by science and society as connected to nature, therefore intrinsically corrupt, these women who disregarded social regulations were presumed to exhibit bestial characteristics of mental agility, and physical strength similar to wild and feral animals. This characterization evolves from Darwin's (1871, 326–327) assumption that women who possess the male characteristics of "powers of intuition, of rapid perception, and perhaps of imitation" are aligned with the so-called lower races and inappropriate for "civilized" society. Once again referring to Darwin's rhetoric of women as inferior "savages," Lombroso and Ferrero argue that pathological immorality or deviation from societal traditions are attributed to hereditary anomalies. Victorian women, by the standards of Sarah Stickney Ellis, were cultivated to enjoy low-energy activities such as tea parties and dinner events, especially when it reflected on the quality of their domesticity. Employing Darwin's derogatory diction referencing women, theoretical criminology claims that this disregard of social traditions is caused by the biologically flawed "savage" who is born into the modern world (Lombroso and Ferrero 1895, 97). Women's minds and bodies were assumed as inherently less powerful than that of men, therefore the hereditary abnormality was also considered to be conducive to the frailty of female genes. The habitual criminal, then, is subject to aberrant atavistic and pathological tendencies, marginalized between savagery and lunacy. This degenerate position is suggested to affect the psychological and physical peculiarities, which are notably discovered as simultaneous reactive functions in a criminal figuration. Reinforcing this psychosomatic perspective of Victorian criminology, Lombroso and Ferrero (1895, xvi) argue that where "deep-seated physical anomalies" are abundant in an individual, they are found with "nervous and mental anomalies" all conducive of a "morbid character." These inherent physical abnormalities coincide with psychological dysfunction, thus producing adverse criminal responses. Therefore, anomalies are more commonly witnessed when the criminal presents an absence of morality, rejection of social conventions, or temperamental instability.

Arguing that women's excess of instability, vanity, aggression, or vengeance is responsible for criminality, Lombroso and Ferrero (1895, xvi) stipulate that these behaviors become habitual as they are "akin in their nature to the orgies of uncivilized tribes." The language of this argument for abnormalities, and their direct reference to tribal orgies speaks to the Victorian fear of excessive sexuality. This association of biology, Indigenous women, and deviance echoes the imperialist perspective that Anne McClintock (1995, 42) refers to as the medical "overexposure" of sexuality and the pathologization of "female sexual pleasure." As scientific experts, Lombroso, Ferrero, and Darwin fetishize women's bodies, reverting all behaviors and characteristics to the perspective of primitivity or propagation of instinctual drives separate from cultural norms. Promoting the popular rhetoric of the period that reduces women to their biological functions, these scientific theorists expand upon this standard by incorporating the imperial perspective of other-than-English sexual excess into their arguments for degenerative female dispositions. This Victorian distinction of the born criminal demonstrates how psychological, and conscious purpose have the potential to resolve in the physical form of women's deviance. Although Lombroso and Ferrero's discourse essentialized Victorian criminality to female functions and attributes, environmental affectations informed the habituation of their deviant behaviors. Women's connection to nature, then, functioned as a technique to reject social confinement. Therefore, material-semiotic figurations of criminal women in gothic fiction are affected by, and utilize, the environmental (natural, cultural, and social) to manipulate social situations.

Affective Ecocriticism: Environmental Influences and Victorian Women

Affective experiences, similar to transgressive gothic identities, perpetually fluctuate between the borders of becoming and substantive being. Affectivity, according to Braidotti (2010, 210), is an event that "activates an embodied subject, empowering him or her to interact with others." An affective experience occurs when an individual is influenced by external emotions, feelings, or motivations. Stemming from Spinoza's monism, as all beings both human and nonhuman, material and immaterial, are derived as modes from the substance of Nature's *conatus*, they inherently affect each other through behaviors and actions. These affects have the ability to originate from other individuals, animals, or environmental conditions. In experiencing this affective state, the influenced individual is then moved into a transformative state of becoming. This metamorphic process keeps the subject in a spatiotemporal transitioning phase of influence. While in a constant state of affectation due to ongoing influences, the individual never resolves to be in a fixed state. In his investigative research of affect and social aesthetics, Ben Highmore (2010) claims that the affective experience is both situated in the metaphysical and physical. For instance, he uses such examples as "our feelings are hurt" or "I am touched by your presence" to demonstrate this interconnectivity of the somatic and sensory responses (Highmore 2010, 119). With affectation, there is a juxtaposition of the physical and metaphysical when the sensory system perceives and submits sensations that transition into neurological impulses as a result of outside influences becoming internalized in the human form. Illustrating this meaning using the example of bruising, these varied forms of bruising, then, occur as an experience when there is both physical conflict as well as the involvement of mental humiliation. The ashamed individual is not just literally bruised, with the skin displaying discoloration, but metaphorically as well, with a behavioral presentation of a wary disposition, hence, the ego is bruised. The influential affective interaction described is demonstrated as an indeterminate experience posited as both material and immaterial. While this example creates a definitive correlation of the physical forcefully manipulating the metaphysical, not all affective experiences are quite so obvious. Other exposures to affective interactions are more subtle and used as motivation to encourage human reaction.

Affect correlates environmental influences on the internal emotions of an individual and the non-linguistic responses to external stimuli. For example, Kyle Bladow and Jennifer Ladino's informative collection *Affective Ecocriticism: Emotion, Embodiment, Environment* (2018) identifies how the mind and body become the sites of environmental affectation through sensory and emotional responses. Bodies, in this sense as both nonhuman and human, are the salient figures that unite the concepts of ecocriticism, affection, and morphic ontologies. Drawing from this theory, ecocriticism is demonstrated through affective experiences and how the environment (whether social, natural, or cultural) influences the behavior and identity of the character. Similarly, Stacy Alaimo (2010, 4) argues that the understanding of the "human self" is consequently determined by "recognition" that the environs is the "very substance" of self, thereby reinforcing the substantiality of the monistic figuration of woman-nature. Furthermore, this ecocritical perspective suggests the embeddedness of humans in nature rather than their separation from it. This has obvious ecological implications, but also reminds us that the denigration of women and nature as Other to man and culture is an artificial process that can be reversed, even if this operates ambiguously in Victorian Gothic literature. Whereas, notable affect theorists, such as Silvan Tomkins (2008), tend to address affect as an occurrence only within bodies and by internal influences, Bladow and Ladino redirect the emotion-impacting theory to an external occurrence.[2] In their research, they identify how the surrounding environment, whether natural or social, is profound for shaping emotional responses (fear, anxiety, anger, etc.) through cognitive processing. Affect, while precipitating these basic emotional responses, also effectuates more complex reactions such as ecophobia, environmental disgust, or desirable inclinations toward nature. In this sense, affective ecocriticism examines familiar affects in relation to the environment and identifies how spatiality influences and creates new affects for human cognitive processing.

Affect is a guide that informs the mind and body into a complex state of perpetual becoming. This particular metaphysical perspective of "becoming," according to Giles Deleuze and Felix Guattari (1986, 5), is to create something new. In this state, individuals open themselves to new influences and relations. Affectivity, as noted earlier in the chapter, motivates the individual into the state of dynamic becoming. It is through this important guide that characters consciously shift identities to replicate necessary behavior for assimilation. While typically analyzed in parallel with human emotion, affect is ultimately distinct. The conceptualization of the human emotion is a social expression, whereas affect occurs as an unprocessed preconscious event. While being prelinguistic contributors to the individual's ontology, affect experiences are neither in the purview of human awareness, nor controlled by the consciousness. The issue with perceiving affect as a precognitive process is that it is mistaken for an ephemeral or autonomous reaction, not selected, or acknowledged by the mind. While theorists, such as Donovan Shaefer (2015), suggest that affect is predominantly precognitive, others, like Megan Watkins (2010), argue that affect is actually a motivator for the consciousness. She distinguishes this consequent affect recognition of a preconscious occurrence as an influence that leaves no lasting impact within the individual. The issue of correlating affect with a precognitive process allows temporary arousal in the individual, but these affective sensations are assumed to quickly disappear without impacting the host entirely. This affective experience, or *affectio*, in its pre-cognitive state is fleeting; however, the interaction allows a trace, or residue, to remain within the being. The "greater the power" of the affect, such as "pain or pleasure," as Benedict de Spinoza (1663, 7) suggests, the longer the residual impact on the individual. It is through this retained impression that the mind-body can begin to change and reconfigure the consciousness to adapt accordingly.

Affects arising from environmental influences allow the individual to transition and acquire new roles. While the mind-body is impacted and able to reconfigure, the affective experience presents an opportunity for identity performances. The identity, as a result of social influence, occurs by the being's interactions with other elements, actions, and beings. Although an individual's identity is learned through socialization, what stops that person from creating multiple identities to use at will? Therein lies the subject's adaptation to performativity. This performativity happens when a phenomenon materializes into existence as a consequence of significant meaning placed on the subject. While typically correlated to Judith Butler (1990) and gender, performativity was later reidentified by Karen Barad (2003) as a material process. Linked to the "materialization" of human bodies and the "socio-political interpellation," performativity is about bodies and "the material-discursive practices" involved (Barad 2003, 810). In the process of developing an identity, the subject is heavily influenced by, and susceptible to, their surroundings, thus absorbing many possible traits responsible for affecting ontological development. As a result of this process, the affected individual consciously establishes a desired identity, dependent on the social situation, of which to perform. Therein, this performativity has an ontic status that involves the consciousness, identity, and informs the subject's state of becoming.

Neural Darwinism: Mind and Body Merge

Consciousness is the unification of the material and immaterial responsible for the monistic mind-body. Gerald Edelman's (1987) *Neural Darwinism: The Theory of Neuronal Group Selection* (1987), as its namesake suggests, draws its argument from Darwin's theory of natural selection. The brain, as recognized by Darwin, is the key to development and evolution of the human species based on its adaptability to environmental stimuli. Neural Darwinism, then, builds on this evolutionary hypothesis and claims that the human brain's adaptability is on account of a vast system of neurons that is capable of uniting into complex structures (Edelman 1987). This nexus of neural networks makes adaptation to environmental and sensory stimulations possible. While evolution and elasticity of the brain are genetic products of natural selection, these neural connections are established through bodily actions. Influenced by repetitive external stimuli, the neurological system (nerves and reflexes) informs the synapses and neurons in the brain, resulting in mental causation, or a conscious state. As a reductionist, however, Edelman rejects dualism and asserts that mind-consciousness is a material phenomenon originating from the intricate neuronal processes within the brain. While this method is a reductive monism, narrowing mind-body to the sole matter of the brain, it also determines how figurations of the mind-body are instantiations of the same substance. It is with this scientific hypothesis of mind-matter that Edelman created a theory of neurology based on the dynamics and structure of the material brain. Thereby, this acceptance of both genetically inherited anatomy and somatic selection allows an establishment of a structured group referred to as the Dynamic Core.

The Dynamic Core is the necessary neural structure that allows for humans to experience consciousness. The initial stage of the core theory is defined as the developmental selection stage that connects the neurons and synapses through somatic selection. During this phase, the initial structure of the "brain circuits" are impacted by genetic restrictions, however, this "epigenetic process leads to extensive individual variance" (Edelman, Gally, Baars 2011, 2). This concept of epigenetics, the heritability of changes to gene expression caused by environmental factors, allows the evaluation of personal environmental affects on heritable genes. While offering some credence to Lamarck's (1801) debunked theory of evolution, epigenetics emphasizes the causation on an individual within their lifetime.[3] Through epigenetics the connection between nurture and nature can be identified, as this science demonstrates how the environment influences and modifies both behavior and the evolutionary form. This occurs when an environmental event affects cellular processes, causing lasting consequences even after the event diminishes. Genetic material, then, reforms into affected structures, thereby creating new cellular structures and processes. Furthermore, this convergence of synaptic connections is not only the primary source for continued selection but is also responsible for individual human development. The following stage, known as experiential selection, occurs after the initial formation of the neuroanatomical structure and persists throughout the individual's lifetime. During this process, the connected synapses between the neural nexus groups strengthen and weaken as a result of influential experiences. While these changes are contingent upon existential interactions, the amplitude and influence of these experiences are restricted by the "inborn value systems" (Edelman, Gally, Baars 2011, 2). Therein, these experiential changes are limited by human's material capacities. Since the boundaries of the neural nexus are ever in flux, the secondary repertoire's strengths and weaknesses are indeterminate. The final stage of the Dynamic Core, indicated as the re-entry tenet, or neural structuring of the brain, is responsible for subjective conscious human behavior. This re-entry process allows the neural map to transmit and reciprocate differentiated signals from various points throughout the brain structure. Defined as the "dynamic spatiotemporal coordination in circuits" necessary for cognitive integration, this phase is responsible for "adaptive conscious behavior" (Edelman, Gally, Baars 2011, 2). This integration, then, allows the neuronal map to synchronize with receptors and transmitters, thus allowing a fully established subjective experience.

While it offers a preliminary conjunction of immaterial and material through psychological reactions and disorders, this neuronal group selection creates a monistic unification. It is through this process that the mind-body aligns and does not rely on dual interactions of the singular mind and singular body. The physical operations of the cerebral and cortical mechanisms allow autonomous, reactive, and attentive control over the consciousness through sensory input. Additionally, causing the nexus of cortical neurons and synaptic structures to create a tangible network where the incorporeal consciousness operates, and is influenced by environmental stressors. Therefore, as exhibited in Victorian Gothic texts, through their rejection of gender stereotypes, Victorian women gain agency in their adaptability by developing new neuronal mapping circuits. Female consciousness, as influenced by environmental affects, rejects the restriction of societal structures, dismisses conventional social roles, and becomes the embodiment of instinctual desires. With these newfound capabilities, criminal figurations, as demonstrated in the following narratives, infiltrate social spaces, and retaliate against strict patriarchal standards.

IGNIS FATUUS, OR THE WILL-O-WISP, IN *THE STRING OF PEARLS* (1846–1847)

The String of Pearls, also known as *The String of Pearls: A Romance*, and later known as *Sweeney Todd and the String of Pearls*, is a penny blood published in serialization between 1846 and 1847 in *The People's Periodical*.[4] Although this story was published in the early Victorian period, it is set in

1785 and, according to Rohan McWilliam (2015, v.), is noted as a "contribution" to the Newgate Novel genre because of its tales of adventure and criminal activity. *The String of Pearls*, a macabre Victorian penny blood with gothic characteristics, was responsible for the creation of a new urban legend. The story introduces the reader to Sweeney Todd, a barber who operates a successful parlor on Fleet Street in a busy London center. While Todd offers an *ignis fatuus*, or deception, in the guise of a prosperous establishment, true animality occurs behind closed doors. With the use of an ingenious, mechanical barber's chair, Sweeney Todd murders his unsuspecting customers and plunges their bodies to the depths beneath his shop. Once in the bowels of the establishment, Todd uses subterranean passages to drag the corpses of his desecrated victims to the cellar of Mrs. Lovett, where she converts the bodies into succulent meat pies.

The String of Pearls, as Robert L. Mack (2007, 731) argues, gave birth to "one of the most recognisable figures" during the Victorian period and, in turn, Sweeney Todd became the most enduring. While the novel introduces one of the most notorious serial killer teams known to gothic fiction, there remains very little discussion about the material-semiotic criminal characterization: the felonious Mrs. Lovett. Whereas Todd himself has received notoriety in theatrical productions, made an appearance in *The Man from Ironbark*, and is rumored as an urban legend, Mrs. Lovett's role is limited as his minor domestic accomplice, or not considered at all.[5] This minimal emphasis on her criminal figuration in critical works and adaptations threatens to consign Lovett to obscurity.

Criminal Relations and Lovett's Affectations

Mrs. Lovett possesses a secret that she disguises through a reputable social identity. While not part of the upper-middle-class, Lovett still functions in the respectable position of lower-middle-class shop owner. Since penny literature was created for increasingly literate working classes of Victorian England, Rymer constructs his characters as a way to highlight the corruptness of the city in the Gothic mode while simultaneously providing a form of escapism from city living. Therein, Lovett, as a villain in a penny blood, reflects a position that addresses both the traditional middle-class gothic readership as well as the incoming working-class audience.[6] When introduced to Lovett, as Mack (2007, 125) highlights, Rymer emphasizes the infatuation of her male patrons by suggesting that "Lovett's shop exerts a magnetic centripetal pull on anyone who happens to be close to it." The fragrance of the succulent meat pies permeates the Bell Yard and encourages the young men to fill the counters at lunchtime. However, while the scent of the pies entices the patrons into the shop, the other "portion of the secret" for their attraction is Mistress

Lovett, the proprietor (*String of Pearls*, 28). The shop owner is described as a Victorian angel that radiates as a "buxom," "young," and "good-looking" woman who enamors the "young scions of the law" (*String of Pearls*, 28). When claiming a seat at Lovett's counter, the young men devour their pies and daydream "that the charming Mrs. Lovett had made that pie especially" for each of them (*String of Pearls*, 28). Albeit visually appealing, according to Victorian aesthetics examined by popular voices as John Ruskin and Coventry Patmore, Lovett embodies a deceptively clever criminal persona illustrative of Lombroso and Ferrero's occasional offender.

The figuration of Mrs. Lovett is an untraditional rendition of the gothic figuration who mimics middle-class characteristics. As a novel written for the working classes, Rymer's penny blood reflects similar, yet distinctive, characteristics from the traditional gothic and melodrama texts, which, according to Vicki Anderson (2005, 76), typically feature "sensationalistic . . . detective stories, westerns, outlaws, bandits, villains, lost loves, damsels in distress, *femme fatales* and melodramatic plots." As both a sensational *femme fatale* and a transgressive gothic monster, Lovett characteristically embodies sexuality, ambiguity, and instability, and performs according to both instincts and social expectations that promote desirable femininity. Figured as a monstrous *femme*, Lovett idealizes the monistic immaterial-material embodiment of Victorian fears of women, a representation of the *femme* that conceals her true identity, purpose, and essence. Therefore, Lovett also figures as a *femme* because her motivation and origin is shrouded in mystery, as there is little-to-no character development. Although depicted as a devious murderess shrouded by the charismatic domestication of femininity, she is not the traditional gothic woman. Whereas figurations of women in, and readers of, the Gothic are generally middle-class, Lovett is created in a literary source published for the working class. Therefore, as an amalgamation of both classes, she is represented as a lower-middle class character. Mimicking the middle-class private sphere, Lovett's commercial space is constructed as a domestic environment. Whereas Lovett's private domain coincides with that of commercialization, it is shrouded in the conventional domestic affairs of cooking, cleaning, and serving. Albeit not the conventional middle-class woman, Lovett operates according to those expectations of femininity to purposefully infiltrate and navigate through acceptable society.

Although Lovett is noted as being "fair" and generous with her recognitions as she "bestows smiles upon her admirers," other patrons do not care for Lovett and frequent her establishment exclusively for the pies (*String of Pearls*, 29). Select patrons sense a shrouded malignancy within Lovett. As one of the sole interpreters of her characterization, Mack (2007, 125–26) claims that Lovett, is "one of the main attractions of the shop"; however, she "inspires a divided response." The customers who resist her charms suggest that she leaves an unsettling affect in the environment, that her "smile was cold and uncomfortable—that it was upon her lips but had no place in heart—that it was the set smile of a ballet-dancer, which is about one of the most unmirthful things in existence" (*String of Pearls*, 29). In disagreement with her admirers, these patrons recognize that Lovett approaches her clientele with tact and impartiality; therefore, they are not altogether seduced by her much-desired Victorian guise. These particular customers, although enamored by the savory meat pies, could sense "what a merely superficial affair her blandishments were, and that there was 'a lurking devil in her eye' that, if once roused, would be capable of achieving some serious things, and might not so easily be quelled again" (*String of Pearls*, 29). While Lovett is blessed with quintessential feminine Victorian attributes, the more observant patrons retain an abject suspicion toward her authenticity. Lovett's inauthenticity as a Victorian lady is represented in her "set and inflexible smile of the manikin or effigy"; it is this "demonic grin" creates suspicion and hesitancy in some of the younger clientele (Mack 2007, 126). This recognition of a hinted devilish visage presents the reader with the suspicion that there may be an underlying wickedness to the shopkeeper. Lovett's subtly sinister behavior hints at the viciousness of her environment, relationships, and habitual practices.

Impacted by environmental and relational affective experiences, Lovett refines her criminal identity for further adaptation into an expectant society. Her restriction to the private sphere is informed by the Victorian ideals of female domesticity; however, lacking the desire to participate in the familial life, she rejects the social structure and adopts a criminal lifestyle. As biocultural beings are informed by their environment, humans demonstrate how traces of their surroundings are reflected in their identities and actions. In this sense, both the individual and the environment impact one another and leave traces of the interaction behind. It is through this interaction the individual reshapes his or her ontology in accordance with the environment's residual trace. Lovett, then, attempts to inhabit the domestic space while emulating the expectations of lower-middle-class society. As an ambiguously deceptive figure, Lovett imitates middle-class respectability to shroud her monstrous behavior. Although she boasts the physical aesthetic necessary for assimilation, her behavior is negatively altered by her environmental surroundings and abhorrent relationship with Sweeney Todd. The barbaric actions introduced into Lovett's house/shop confines her to the role of criminal while leaving traces of social acceptability on her visage. Rather than adapt to the role of the Victorian "angel," her consciousness corrupts the role through a secret criminal identity and perversion of the domestic sphere.

Conscious Adaptability: Affective Faces and Spaces

Lovett's adaptation to her surroundings is formed in the primary consciousness. This process of assimilative consciousness is responsible for regulating the importance of the cortical stimulus to adjust to the complexity of its own requirements for adaptability. While affected by her surroundings, Lovett's consciousness guides her behaviors and actions to obtain a goal. In the re-entrant loop process, habituation and connection to situations are key to establishing primary conscious responses. For example, this is observed in Lovett's repetition of human butchery and commodified cannibalism. Operating simultaneously in dichotomous roles of deviant felon and respectable shopkeeper, Lovett's consciousness functions according to "the relative salience of external events" and "internal value schemas" (Edelman 1989, 99). Necessary for survival, and the successful outcome of "goals," environmental affectations inform the consciousness, "therefore affect[ing] behavior" and "action patterns" (Edelman 1989, 99). Transgressing from the role of socially compliant shopkeeper to that of a vicious criminal for eight years, Lovett's neural mapping adapts to affective experiences for personal survival.

Lovett's association with Todd is an undisclosed, yet affecting, connection. While there are several indications of their secretive meetings, Rymer only introduces the duo's direct interactions at the end of the novel when they meet "with all the familiarity of old acquaintances" (*String of Pearls*, 266). This "mysterious bond of union" is presented as a dependency-based relationship highlighting monetary gain and social destruction (*String of Pearls*, 266). However, when scrutinized, it is implied that this particular method of criminality is forced upon, rather than accepted by Lovett (*String of Pearls*, 265). When access to their conversation is granted, the reader discovers that the pie maker and barber have been in the human butchering business for eight years. Rymer, unfortunately, never provides the origins of their relationship or how they established their felonious network. However, in this meeting it is disclosed that Lovett, while fully immersed in these criminal proceedings, grows impatient and demands "ample independence" from these malevolent acts (*String of Pearls*, 266). Negating any signs of her womanly Victorian façade, Lovett assumes an agitated and angry stance, assailing Todd with the desire to end these atrocities as she "run(s) the frightful risk" while he reaps the reward (*String of Pearls*, 266). For a woman who has been in the human baking business for nearly a decade, she appears unnerved by the presence of Todd. It is only through this experience that that Lovett's identity is discerned as an affectation caused by this relationship.

Lovett struggles to maintain both identities as the lower-middle-class woman and the nefarious butcher. Any "sensory input" interferences in the "normal functioning" to the cortical response of the neural mapping, as Edelman, Gally, and Baars (2011, 2) argue, "disrupt[s] the contents of consciousness." Therein, any environmental affects inform the mapped consciousness of the individual, resulting in reactive responses. In the case of Lovett, the instability of her environment and interactions influences her performative abilities. During the exigent conversation with Todd, her identity as the wicked criminal slips and her vulnerability appears. This moment of weakness, as Lovett "sank into a chair, and trembled so violently," informs the reader that the conflict of the experience overwhelms Lovett's conscious mind, thus her body reacts (*String of Pearls*, 267). She declares in a faint voice to Todd "I am forced to drink, or I should kill myself, or go mad, or denounce you"; it is through her alcohol intake that Lovett maintains the deviant façade she adopted eight years prior (*String of Pearls*, 267). Drawing from Lombroso's argument that a "minor degree of alcoholism" is "ascribable" to lunacy in female criminals, Lovett's consumption is used to deter from her thoughts of madness (Lombroso and Ferrero 1895, 289). While she demonstrates psychological and physiological frailty, she perpetuates a strong rationale by claiming her sanity and using it as a threat. Marginalized between these dichotomous identities, she illustrates a refusal of traditional gender ideologies through her explicit admonitions of sanity. Lovett struggles to rebel against conventional feminine stereotypes by participating in severe criminal activities with Todd. Lovett, although she is one half of a serial killer couple, maintains domestic traits, albeit in a corrupted form. While Todd participates in the slaughter and procurement of contents for Lovett's pies, she is solely confined within the artificial social exhibition of charismatic shopkeeper and domestic purveyor of food.

Lovett's magical pie shop, while smacking of enticing delicacies and feminine enchantment, operates as an establishment to conceal criminal activity and monstrous deceit. Additionally, anxieties of Victorian society were formed from the notion that "every home and every woman could harbor the potential for extreme violence" (Mangham 2007, 9). Drawing from this belief, the pie shop, as both her professional and domestic environment, functions to conceal Lovett's nature. In an establishment that echoes the eco-Gothic hybrid construction of the human and nonhuman, both human nature and the environment interact to create an affectation to signify the deviance of Lovett's criminal monstrosity. This gothic environment that disguises the transgressions of Lovett is responsible for creating a relative sense of "unease engendered" by threatening and "uncanny" characteristics (Parker and Poland 2019, 11). This unsettling sensation occurs when customers, not captivated by her appearance, "swore that Lovett had quite a sinister aspect" (*String of Pearls*, 29). Reflecting her deviant nature, the façade of Lovett's establishment compels young men to indulge in their appetites while the conditions within suggest malicious villainy. Lovett's shop, with its "prodigious 'din of tongues'" demonstrates an ambience of scandal and secrecy that Mack suggests (2007, 125) "transforms" it into an environment resembling "a sort of Babel of vicious and even vaguely criminal activity." The shop is used as an expressive social convention filled with conversations of daily exploits and ploys of grandeur. While presenting the illusion of social assimilation through the prosperity of her popular establishment, the power of Lovett's affective environment is created in the corrupted realm of the shop's subterranean vaults.

Exploring configurations of gothic spaces and the law, Sue Chaplin (2016), argues that hidden spaces are used to examine women's marginalized positions under the overburdening power of a patriarchal structure. These enigmatic, and typically subterranean, areas represent danger, confinement, and "marginalised positions" therefore positing women as *"buried within"* the borders and laws of its boundaries (Chaplin 2016, 140). Constructed in a Gothic environment, hidden under the realm of patriarchal control, these spaces are not only used by women to articulate the terrors of womanhood, as Chaplin suggests, but utilized as a means of freedom, as demonstrated in *The String of Pearls*. Therefore, Lovett's establishment, secreted away, and mysteriously concealed as a cornerstone of social success within the heart of London, is her way to transgress social dichotomies. Rymer creates Lovett's cellar as the key to her malicious nature, similar to that of murderous Todd's barber/butcher chair. All items, or locations, are concealed to preserve the authentic identity of the possessor. In the vaults of the notorious pie shop, the reader is introduced to themes of captivity, terror, and murder long before the exposure of Lovett's involvement and atrocious constructions. It is through the perspective of her imprisoned cook, that the reader gains access to the fiendish identity of Lovett. Jarvis, upon his acceptance to Lovett's service, recognizes his situation as "mysterious" and acknowledges that his new employer has a "strange manner of talking" (*String of Pearls*, 97). Lovett interacts daily with her patrons and maintains her feminine façade; however, when in a position of power, her relation to the subterranean prison unveils the "hidden meaning" of her behavior (*String of Pearls*, 98). This shrouded identity offers the impression that Lovett "had the assistance of the devil himself in conducting human affairs," when she rebukes Jarvis's refusal to work and threatens to "cut" his throat (*String of Pearls*, 178). The disclosure of her "true" nature seals Lovett's fate and revokes her place in society as a proper Victorian woman. The declaration of Lovett's dual ontologies as the malicious criminal concealed by a pretense of Victorian domesticity, resolves in her personal destruction. Upon Jarvis's explication that "Mrs. Lovett's pies are made of *human flesh*!" she is then identified by society as both the respectable, and adored, shop owner as well as a murderous fiend (*String of Pearls*, 284). This recognition of Lovett as both the charismatic woman and corrupter of Victorian morals aligns her with Lombroso and Ferrero's occasional offender. While she offers a pleasing aesthetic and resists the so-called aberrations of degeneracy, she infiltrates and mimics feminine stereotypes, thus collapsing the construct's boundaries and dooming herself for eradication.

Whereas Todd is brought to justice and hanged outside of Newgate Prison, Lovett meets her end by the hand of her accomplice. Reminiscent of Charles Dickens's Newgate serialization, *Oliver Twist* (1837–1839), Lovett's fate echoes the sympathetic figure, Nancy. As a fallen woman, Nancy is also involved in a criminal network, however, unlike Lovett she demonstrates characteristics of kindness and maternity, which lead to her inevitable demise. As echoed by Mrs. Lovett, Nancy is also "struck down" by her male accomplice (*Oliver Twist*, 298). Following the traditional construction of penny publications, Rymer draws from Nancy's situation and offers his rendition in the figuration of Lovett. Like Nancy, Lovett's fate is not lawfully resolved as an executed criminal for her eight years of butchery, nor rehabilitated into a Victorian woman. Instead, Lovett is poisoned by Todd, who compares their ongoing relationship to hunter and prey, claiming he "must dispose of one whose implacable disposition I know well, and who would hunt me to the farthest corner of the earth, if she were not at peace in the grave" (*String of Pearls*, 261). In order for Todd to leave England with the stolen money and goods, he must extinguish Lovett's vengeful animosity. Although Rymer synchronizes Lovett's timely poisoning with her arrest, it is ultimately the exposure of her transgressions and ambivalence that causes her to sink "insensible to the floor" and succumb to death (*String of Pearls*, 285). While she utilizes the environment and relational affections to refine her dual identities, the forced unification of the wicked woman and Victorian lady results in Lovett's demise. Rymer's destruction of Lovett's criminal figuration responds to anxieties of transgressive female behavior. The death of Lovett by the hand of a serial killer absolves civic responsibility for the punishment of a Victorian lady, while simultaneously assuring readers that devious women will fail in their attempts at social assimilation.

CHIMERICAL ONTOLOGIES IN *THE DARK WOMAN:* *OR DAYS OF THE PRINCE REGENT* (1861)

The Dark Woman: Or Days of the Prince Regent is a penny dreadful by Malcolm J. Errym, published in 1861.[7] The story occurs in the early nineteenth century during the reign of George IV as His Royal Highness the Prince Regent.[8] This penny dreadful, ostensibly realist in mode, shares similar characteristics with its blood predecessors of occultist gothic and criminal elements. Blending these literary facets, the penny dreadful exhibits criminality as heroic and glamorous by illustrating how sensational crimes, such as murder and cannibalism were highlighted by the tropes and themes of gothic fiction. Utilizing the contextual figurations of heroic criminality and adventurous male exploits of the genre, Errym demonstrates these tropes in his anti-heroine, Linda, to construct a tale of maliciousness precipitated by rejection and deceit.

The Dark Woman centers around Linda Mowbray, also referred to as the titular Dark Woman. Linda is introduced as the enigmatic first wife of the Prince Regent, George IV, and mother to their lost child. Upon her announcement of pregnancy, Linda is ultimately rejected and declared as a madwoman by the Prince. This proclamation of insanity allows George to forcibly confine Linda to an asylum and strip away her traditional role as wife, mother, and princess. While Errym does not provide explicit details about her requisite sanctum, he does disclose that Linda faced "sixteen long years of a hapless agony in her prison house" (*The Dark Woman*, 323). The residual effects of emotional shaking and glances of paranoid terror Linda's presents are the only implications of her suffering while imprisoned. Due to the "carelessness of one of her keepers," she escapes from confinement and ferociously retaliates against society and the Prince Regent (*The Dark Woman*, 323). The reader discovers that Linda, with another surname de Chevenaux, is also the shrouded leader of an underground criminal network, Paul's Chickens. Unbeknownst to the Regent, Linda uses both identities as aristocrat and criminal mastermind to manipulate situations and other individuals to obtain information. Therefore, Errym's obscure penny dreadful, *The Dark Woman* is a tale of a Victorian woman's passion and revenge against the rejection and abuse of society by the utilization of gothic tropes, affectation, and the environment.

In *The Dark Woman*, Linda uses environmentally influenced mimicry to affectively challenge and infiltrate high society. This mimesis, as Luce Irigaray defines in *This Sex Which Is Not One* (1985), is a process of conscious resistance where women imitate stereotypes about their own sexual expectations sanctioned by men. To undermine such stereotypes, Irigaray proposes that women should purposefully assume the role of the stereotypical feminine construct and perform according to the socially prescribed behavior as a means to infiltrate and command the domain from within. Using mimetic responses, women have the ability to recover their identities through exploitation without being reduced to a stereotype. For women to act within mimetic roles it allows the resubmission of self to align with the notion of self-perception according to that of masculine logic. It is this adaptation and repetition of actions that allows the mimetic woman to remain hidden. These imitations are performances of the feminine role used to infiltrate and restructure perspectives about the expectations of women. Thus, the strategy of mimesis is used as a method for women to reject social boundaries and reclaim agency. In Errym's dreadful, Linda's connection with the natural environment and affective experiences is exhibited through such mimetic responses.

The Dark Woman engages with her environmental surroundings and uses mimesis to juxtapose the two identities: wicked criminal and Victorian lady in response to a repressive societal structure. Equally evaluating the idea of mimesis as a form of foundational representation for culture and nature, Alaimo (2000, 6) proposes that it is women's alignment with nature that is essential to the "culture," or society "that erects itself upon them." Linda, then, uses this innate connection to reinvent and restructure her identity as a liminal figure that represents her as either unified with nature or idealized in culture. Operating as, what David Del Principe (2014, 1) refers to, "a site of articulation for environmental and species identity," Linda embodies society's fears of nature and woman. Juxtaposing characteristics of both human and nonhuman identities, Linda uses mimetic strategies of performativity to transcend the restrictive figuration of being. This performative mimetic manipulation operates as a role for female imitation to avoid male subjectivity and dominance. Wherein Linda ontologically represents the expectations for cultural assimilation, she instinctually operates according to her natural connection and free will. While purposefully adopting the visage of the innate villain, she assumes various ontologies through environmental affectation and mimetic adaptation.

Linda's mimetic shift occurs through a conscious reaction informed by affectations of her surroundings. The Dark Woman is a transgressive character immersed in a full criminal ontology who accepts her bond with nature. She uses this position to fluidly transform from a lady of the aristocracy to the chimerical "fiend" of London's seedy underbelly (*The Dark Woman*, 12). In Lombroso and Ferrero's recognition of criminal deceptions in women, they specifically note that women's crimes were usually intentional with a definitive purpose and their intellect varies depending on the individual. While some (mostly born criminals) may demonstrate a lack of intelligence, others (such as occasional offenders) possess a significantly alert acumen that allows them to observe and achieve objectives. Thereby, popular Victorian criminal discourse claims this as the reason for women's limited impulsivity in criminal actions. In Errym's dreadful, Linda is meticulous with her strategies and opposes compulsions; she embodies the observant intellect discussed by Lombroso and Ferrero. The Dark Woman is a collector of identities and utilizes them for adaptation and coordination with her environment, whether natural or cultural. This mimetic strategy employed by Linda is based on a conscious awareness of surrounding milieu and other imitative individuals.

"Corporeally based forms of imitation," as Anna Gibbs (2010, 186) notes, can be used involuntarily and voluntarily. These reactions, and desires for imitative behavior, are founded upon primitive instincts that transition into emotional responses and visceral actions through affect contagion. This model of corporeal imitation, in conjunction with Irigaray's mimetic response to stereotypical behavior, is relevant here. The Dark Woman infiltrates and corrupts expectations. Unbeknownst to the reader, it is undisclosed whether Linda's label as The Dark Woman was personally acquired or delegated by society. While the popular definition of the term "dark" recalls images of coloration and lighting, it also refers to the exhibition of evil characteristics and desires. As an embodiment of these traits, Linda juxtaposes the Victorian ideologies of criminality and conventional femininity in a singular figuration. In varied situations, Linda consciously chooses a specific mimetic form of imitation to assimilate into the proper environment and to provide a necessary performance. While affect and mimesis are considered two entirely different concepts, the informative affect contagion is at the center of mimetic replication. The synchronous method of affect and mimesis between physical bodies and the natural world creates a monistic figuration, which allows the levels of behavior to coordinate accordingly. This affect occurs between individual entities and acts as a bioneurological method of transmission from form to form. Linda, in her daily interactions, voluntarily observes the actions and behaviors of others and assumes the necessary role for social mobility. In the process of her mimetic transformations, Linda synchronizes her "facial expression, vocalization, postures, and movements" with others, which allows her to fully assimilate (Gibbs 2010, 186). Thereby, Linda's response to the environment and ability for mimetic replication allows her to embody the persona of the wicked criminal behind an upper-class Victorian aesthetic.

The Dark Woman's appropriation of criminality demonstrates monstrous abilities and supernatural-like affiliations with the environment. As a character situated in a position that interconnects "human bodies and nonhuman natures," Linda is a dynamic figuration that is informed by surrounding situations, while also projecting her own passions into the environment. Echoing the natural representation illustrated by Catherine Earnshaw's impact on the weather in chapter two, Linda also extends her emotions into the natural environs. In several of her criminal incursions, the environment reflects Linda's repressed rage and inherent mastery of nature. Similar to Cathy's emotional outpouring at the loss of Heathcliff, whenever Linda experiences moments of vulnerability, the environment becomes tumultuous and dangerous to others while appearing "to have no effect" upon her (*The Dark Woman*, 111). During the moments of absolute anguish or vindictive actions, such as Linda's strategic murder of the entire "Paul's Chickens" network, the weather transitions into "furious gales of wind" casting a "pitchy darkness" in the sky (*The Dark Woman*, 80). Since Linda is one and the same with nature, it is in these moments of repressed torment that she demonstrates a supernatural control on the environment. While using environmental elements intertwined with gothic themes, Errym's figuration of female criminality is a manifestation of nature embodied within a villainous role. Utilizing women's assumed connection to nature, Errym's criminal figuration presents Linda as a dynamic character with a transformative identity. Aligning her natural disposition to that of the environment, *The Dark Woman* offers a new approach to female criminality in the Gothic.

Female Criminality and Mimetic Transformations

Errym's *The Dark Woman* demonstrates the popular fear of the female criminal's potential. In the Female Gothic, identities of female malfeasance are amalgamations of social and cultural issues that challenge such facets as "national identity, sexuality, language, race, and history" (Wallace and Smith 2009, 10). *The Dark Woman*, then, reflects such anxieties through a *femme* exhibition of mimicry and deceptive social manipulation. While women in the Gothic suffer from fragmentations of agency, as demonstrated through both Catherine Earnshaw and Bertha Mason, Errym's figuration of female criminality acts independently and has freedom of choice. Employing her talents for environmental manipulation and mimicry, Linda assumes situationally dependent identities: Linda Mowbray, Linda de Chevenaux, Countess de Launy, Countess d'Umbra, Thomas Waller, Astorath are all distinctive identities of the Dark Woman, created from the rejection and neglect of a Victorian woman. The most notable aspect of the Dark Woman's sub-identities is that a special necessity is demonstrated dependent on the gender of the role. While assuming a male identity, Linda passes undetected in society and demands obedience from others. Performing in the role of Thomas Waller, she is permitted to escape a crime scene when authorities search for a female perpetrator. In her imitation of Astorath the Astrologer, she assumes the role of a self-proclaimed omniscient advisor to the gentry. Although Astorath, before his demise at the Dark Woman's hands, was considered a gimmick by society, the superstitious Prince Regent still sought his guidance. Therefore, when Linda obtains this identity, she directly manipulates and controls situations while working to corrupt the royal figure. Whereas the Dark Woman uses male identities to demand authority, she uses female identities to manipulate victims' desires through sexuality or assumed vulnerability. Linda's ability to mimetically transition into these various ontologies works to transgress feminine expectations, exact revenge, and allocate authoritative positions for herself.

The Dark Woman assumes various roles to secretively destroy the social structure. When introduced to the anti-heroine, she is disguised as a figure in a black mask and cloak, it is only through the removal of the "singular-shaped hat" that she is identified as a woman by the "contour of her head" (*The Dark Woman*, 8). Referring back to the popular phrenological pseudo-science, or study of the cranium in reference to character, Errym makes Linda identifiable by the "circumference" and "shape" of her head (Lombroso and Ferrero 1895, xvi). Although she reveals her femininity, she remains shrouded behind a mask. It is due to the familiar recognition of George IV that the mysterious woman's true identity is revealed. The shrouded woman is only recognized when her "figure is thrown into strong relief," backlit by crimson light and the authorities call out "It is the Dark Woman!" (*The Dark Woman*, 13). Throughout the novel, when Linda assumes this role of criminal deviant, she utilizes her ability for mimetic replication to assimilate into the necessary environment to create an impeccable affect. She perfectly imitates the criminal ontology with this masked visage and projection of a voice that is "deep and impressive," which suggests a "wildness of tone" (*The Dark Woman*, 15). Similar to Mrs. Lovett, the Dark Woman consciously adjusts and metamorphoses her social identity while affected by environmental necessity.

When Linda transitions into the role of the felonious Dark Woman, she leads and instructs a gang of criminals in a subterranean structure beneath a church. In these deserted vaults, Linda cannot assume her role as the aristocratic lady but undertakes the "extraordinary character" known as the Dark Woman (*The Dark Woman*, 13). Reminiscent of Mary Russo's (1994, 1) description of the "grotto-esque," or "grotesque cave," the subterranean dwelling used by both the Dark Woman and Mrs. Lovett are symbolic of women's telluric, or earthly, materiality. Traditionally presented as a biological metaphor of female sexuality and materiality, these bases of operations invert the hospitable womb of traditional motherhood. Whereas, classical women's bodies are designated for reproduction, grotesque bodies, metaphorically depicted as the Dark Woman's cave, are spaces for destruction. As reflective of a grotesque womb, the sanctum is "[l]ow, hidden, earthly, dark, material, immanent, visceral," an antithetical space of social corruption for the Dark Woman (Russo 1994, 1). In her underground retreat, she mimetically transitions identities and controls the hidden network of thieves and deviants. Maintaining a reputation as a "human basilisk," the Dark Woman, reflective of the monstrosity of her grotesque cave, possesses the power to destroy lives (*The Dark Woman*, 128). Linda's comparison to the mythical beast implies that she has the power of enacting death while also presenting the imagery of temptation. As a serpentine mythological creature, the basilisk, a feared beast with the power to kill by a single glance, also refers to the serpent's temptation of Eve in Christian theology that ultimately led to the Fall. The assumption that she is a beast of nature with abilities of intrigue and destruction suggests that Linda retains attributes for survivability, integration, and corruption.

The Dark Woman maintains the conscious ability to regulate the continuous environmental changes and developed experiences allow her neuronal structure to reacclimate and learn new patterns, thus allowing her adaptation to selective events. Linda's attentiveness and immersion in her habitat occurs through the Dynamic Core. Based on her continuous adaptivity to varied situations, the use of Linda's neural connections strengthens and reacts more consistently. With the demands of the ever-changing environment, neurons construct the necessary neural circuits for survival. Following Darwin's theory of natural selection, Edelman (1987, 22) decries that "synapses in the brain," similar to "animals in their environments," contend for survival, therefore those synapses that thrive are successful, "while those that are not used perish." Linda's repeated subjection to these environments result in a remapping of her neural circuit structure. Portrayed as possessing the "most remarkable change that ever pantomimic presentation knew," Linda's systematic remapping is prevalent in her ability for immediate environmental adaptations (*The Dark Woman*, 18). Conveyed by Sixteen-String Jack, a former member of Paul's Chickens, that Linda "has the power of personation of many different characters, and that in unexpected places she will be found assuming the characteristics of people widely dissimilar," her ability for environmental acclimation is refined (*The Dark Woman*, 18).[9] This exposure permits her neuronal grouping system to release specified transmissions and hormones necessary for adaptation creating a dichotomous embodiment of identity contradictions.

The Dark Woman embodies the binaristic gothic structure of good and evil in a singular individual. These dichotomies, embodied within the monistic gothic female figure, create contradictions and tensions because the identity is simultaneously being and becoming while the tragic woman seeks to establish agency. The *Dark Woman* exhibits the anxieties of transgressive female identities exhibited in the Gothic, however, while she dynamically shifts identities, Linda situationally introduces new ontologies. Following a gothic trope, the Dark Woman performs her wicked actions when the sun sets. While she transitions into a malefactoress in the hours of the night, Linda assumes an aristocratic role in the light of day. Upon emerging from her refuge, Linda is introduced to the readers in her socially acceptable role as Countess de Launy, a widow of an old French noble. Although, the Countess never received a formal invitation, her reputation is known throughout the Court as powerful and immensely rich. Errym's reveal of the Countess is demonstrated through a descriptive unsheathing "with nimble fingers" that "loosened from round her neck the outer robe, or dress, that she wore" (*The Dark Woman*,

18). With this dramatic unveiling, Linda transforms to fit the environment and acceptable identity of conventional femininity.

The Countess, as she emerges from her grotesque environment, transitions into an antithesis of the criminally maligned Dark Woman. Similar to Mrs. Lovett, Linda's criminal figuration also aligns with the sensational *femme fatale*. According to Mary Anne Doane (1991, 1), the *femme* is a "figure of a certain discursive unease" because, for her, "the most striking characteristic perhaps, is the fact that she never really is what she seems." Linda, then, in her transgressive performances embodies both the monstrous and *femme* characteristics. Beneath the dark deviant exterior, Linda exhibits the illusion of Victorian femininity as "she appeared in a splendid dress of pearly satin, richly embroidered with roses" and a "a mass of beautiful ringlets of light brown hair, with just sufficient warmth of colour in it to redeem it from the commonplace, fell about her neck and shoulders" (*The Dark Woman*, 18). Her metamorphosis from the monstrous subterranean villain into the appealing aristocrat allows Linda to manipulate and destroy society from within the appropriate sphere. Her transformation from the Dark Woman to the Countess de Launy encapsulates the upper-class aesthetic of the picturesque Victorian woman. Whereas the Dark Woman is veiled in "dark-coloured gloves," "peculiar hat and mask," and exhibits a rigid depiction of malicious animosity, the Countess is discussed in terms of her delicateness when the lightest "touch" removes the disguise from her face (*The Dark Woman*, 18). The diction used to unveil de Launy's angel-like appearance notes a light feminine touch in removing her outer garments while also focusing on the cascade of colorfully warm full hair, which Errym distinguishes from the lower classes. Errym's attention to the Countess's jeweled splendor of "costly jewels" that "sparkled on her fingers," a "neck encircled by a row of costly pearls," and "diamonds [that] glittered in her hair," not only refers to her place within the upper-class but also to the overindulgence of the period (*The Dark Woman*, 18). Portrayed as the refinement of class and beauty in this assumed role, de Launy cunningly influences and manipulates.

While influential to other aristocrats in this position, Linda adopts Lombroso and Ferrero's criminal aesthetic with her transition to the Dark Woman. As previously stated, born criminals present an abnormal physiology that distinguishes them from normal society. Among these distinctions, Lombroso and Ferrero (1895, 97) stipulate that "the hair of criminals and prostitutes is darker than among normal" and they contain masculine characteristics, all of which Linda uses to her mimetic advantage. While disguised in her role as the Victorian "angel," the Countess meets with an admirer, the Secretary of State, Lord Ilchester and enquires about local criminal activity. Ilchester, in his attempts for flattery and attention, discloses that Paul's

Chickens are led by an "old, plain, masculine, cruel, and vindictive" mastermind who is quite dreadful, "commits murder without hesitation," and stops at nothing "to carry out her purposes" and "goes by the name of the Dark Woman" (*The Dark Woman*, 19). Ilchester's declaration about the criminal leader fits the Victorian popular imagination as Lombroso later contributed to criminology. During Ilchester's explication of information to the Countess/ Dark Woman, he passionately declares "Oh, Countess! When I look at you, in all your feminine beauty and contrast you with such a persona as that Dark Woman, I wonder how nature can produce two such opposites, and that they should both be called woman!" (*The Dark Woman*, 19). Ilchester's identification of the dichotomous identities created from nature refers to the patriarchal implications of what Alaimo (2000, 2) refers to as, the "historically tenacious entanglements" of women with the "long imagined nature." However, analyzing Ilchester's statement through Alaimo's (2000, 10) redefinition of nature as "untamed and unruly," and Braidotti's (2003, 44) "redefinition of subjectivity," the dual figurations of Linda emerge as nature's insurgents against social confines and fixed roles of being. Transforming between antithetical identities that represent femininity/light and deviant/darkness, Linda's ontology juxtaposes the distinction between society and nature, that also reflects the figurations of she-wolves discussed in the following chapter. Utilizing her ability for transgressing boundaries, Linda as an occasional offender, not a born criminal, does not display notable signs of degeneration. Illustrated as a "brilliant and beautiful being," the Countess is a picturesque ideal of angelic beauty and delicate grace while harboring a cunning intellect (*The Dark Woman*, 18). Through this illusion of perfection, as exclaimed by Ilchester, she infiltrates and corrupts the Victorian stereotype of conventional womanhood.

The Dark Woman's nefarious manipulation of personal identity is attributed to deception by the Prince Regent. Though Lombroso and Ferrero argue that criminal women are monstrous, they also acknowledge that their misconducts and felonious actions are derivative of situational, and complicated, origins. Early in the novel Errym reveals that Linda claims to be the mysterious first wife of George IV from nineteen years prior. When confronted with this accusation, the Prince Regent admits his devious sexual manipulations by stating that he "would have done anything in the world to get possession of her" therefore he devised a "real marriage" to claim her (*The Dark Woman*, 140). While the Regent confesses to Linda that the registrar's certificate is fraudulent and their marriage is illegitimate according to the Royal Marriage Act, she refuses his rejection and declares her intention of revenge against him.[10] The Prince's dismissal of their legal marriage and the involvement of procreation results in a deceptive conversion of Linda into a fallen woman. Linda's proclamation against the Prince accuses him of stealing "the sunshine from this poor heart" and replacing it with "strange fires" (*The Dark Woman*, 9). This explicit statement of removing life-sustaining light and replacing it with infernal flames demonstrates the fierce animosity emboldened by the Dark Woman. It is the Prince's negative impact on Linda's emotions that encourages her transition into the criminal monster. The involuntary repudiation of Victorian ideals and instant conversion into the immoral, as demonstrated previously in the figuration of Bertha Mason, aligns Linda with her enraged, and bestial nature. Sharing similarities to Rochester's manipulation of Bertha, the Prince's rejection of Linda results in her retribution. Therefore, Linda's proverbial fall from grace causes her to assume the role of the monstrous Dark Woman. In his exploration of female offenders, Ian Ward (2014) orients fallen women with criminality and discusses how there are two distinct categorizations of fallen women: the fall within marriage and the fall outside of marriage. The sexual transgression that occurs within the bond of matrimony is defined as a criminal deception with limited, or no violence. This criminal action typically occurs through bigamous or adulterous relations. The other categorization of fallen women affects the unmarried and their crimes were significantly more sensational. The Dark Woman, while deceptively cast in the space between married and unmarried, assumes the role of this particular violent and vengeful criminal, which results in a state of limbo and irresolution.

This narrative charting the Dark Woman's mimetic identities and fluid assimilation into the aristocracy offers no resolution. In Errym's last chapter of *The Dark Woman*, the reader is witness to the confrontation between Linda and George. Linda seeks resolution in her quest for equality and recognition, however, there is no justification for the criminal woman. In the final moments, Linda sneaks into St. James's Palace to accost George and announces her true identity as "the Dark Woman, and dark as Erebus are the feelings now of my heart" (*The Dark Woman*, 414). Linda's embodiment of emotions that rival the Grecian primordial deity of Chaos, allude to the purpose of her intrusion. In his shocking realization that the Dark Woman is Linda, George claims, "so you have at least, Linda, made up your mind to murder me" (*The Dark Woman*, 414). It is in this moment of recognition, the Dark Woman's resolve dissolves from threatening destruction to tearful tremors. George opportunistically takes advantage of Linda's vulnerability and declares:

> My intrigue with you of so many years ago has turned your brain. You are no more Princess of Wales than I am Emperor of the Moon. No other madbrain but yours would have for a moment hatched such rank absurdities. You will have again to find a home in some asylum, where you may rave to the walls, or to the ears of those who will be as indifferent to you. (*The Dark Woman*, 416)

Linda, forcibly cast out of the murderous role, is once again declared as insane by George, the same individual who incarcerated her decades ago. In this statement he inflicts derogatory connotations of disinterest in Linda and once again suggests an asylum. With the Regent's accusation of her "madbrain," Linda transitions back into the identity of the Dark Woman and claims that George is a "traitorous villain" (*The Dark Woman*, 416). Both characters advance on one another, seeking to claim ownership of a deadly poniard—a light knife similar to a parrying dagger, most commonly carried by upper-class noblemen or knights—however, the novel ends with the Dark Woman and George standing "face to face with each other, each holding down to the floor a weapon that might have been most dangerous" (*The Dark Woman*, 416). Errym offers no resolution to the Dark Woman's character and strategically leaves a cliffhanger with the Prince Regent declaring that he is trapped in a room with a madwoman. With this simple explication of insanity, Errym disqualifies all of the Dark Woman's cunning social manipulations and transgressions of gender stereotypes and casts her back into the role of fragile Victorian woman.

Errym's lack of resolution frustrates the pending closure to the Dark Woman's story. As she is left in stasis with George, her storyline is left open, and many questions unanswered. While undeniably a monstrous figure, the Dark Woman should face destruction to avoid social contamination. In his inability to complete the tale, Errym leaves Linda to continue her corruptive navigation through the pages of Victorian society. Errym's figuration of female criminality rejects social constructs of femininity through use of performative and exhibitive mimicry and manipulation. His narrative follows the common trope of unfinished penny novels therefore *The Dark Woman* is unresolved, leaving the reader to question the outcome of Linda.

DECEPTIVE CRIMINALITY IN *LADY AUDLEY'S SECRET* (1862)

Lady Audley's Secret, a highly controversial sensation novel published by Mary Elizabeth Braddon in 1862, responds to a fear of female instability within society. In constant fear of social upheaval, economic changes, and domestic destruction, Victorian society maintained a belief that their moral values were under siege. Family and the domestic realm, with women as indoctrinated hearth angels, became idealized as the sanctuary for Victorian ideals. Early-to mid-Victorian society mandated identities to restrict immoral behaviors and women's natural instincts, and in their attempts to adhere to these restrictions, many middle-and upper-class women inadvertently deviated from these boundaries through popular fiction. Lynn M. Voskuil (2001), one of the many Victorian scholars who recognize the social concerns created by Braddon's sensation novel, decreed how these texts, *Lady Audley* in particular, was largely popular due to society's fascination with the female protagonist who disregarded gender expectations. This social intrigue is founded on the threat caused by Braddon's novel, or the contradiction that is Lady Audley herself. It is this controversy of Lady Audley's authenticity that is pushed to expose the severity of ideologies, highlighting the paradoxes of middle-class gender constructions. This overt interest in the bigamist anti-heroine and her abnormal criminal behavior alarmed Victorian traditionalists over the possibility for women to corrupt the domestic sphere. While several theorists investigate how "Lucy's" ascension from governess to baroness is a desirable drive for economical wealth and social respect, others claim that Braddon uses her heroine to subvert Victorian boundaries.[11] "Lucy," however, is a product of abuse and neglect. Her criminal behavior is not hereditary madness but a logical and decisive reaction as a direct result and rejection of restrictive social pressures. Whereas *The Dark Woman*'s Linda transformed both her appearance and behavior to manipulate society, "Lucy" uses her visage and trained demeanor as the conventional Victorian woman to assimilate into social situations. Being *compos mentis*, or fully sane, "Lucy" consciously processes her environmental surroundings and uses these affective experiences to cultivate her physical and psychological exhibition as a figuration of criminality.

Sensation fiction, a genre of non-realist literature reflective of Victorian concerns, operates as a point of fragmented ontologies that responded directly to the society that produced it. These texts, as Lyn Pykett (1994, 67) points out, were generally believed to be "written by wicked women, about wayward girls and wicked women," which were then consumed by contumacious women signifying the potential for this behavior through such reading material. The actions taken by women in the sensation genre revolve around socially prohibited behaviors that involve immorality or criminality. The most notable female protagonists embody a duplicitous nature stemming from deception, jealousy, or greed typically disguised in innocence.[12] The plot, or conflict, of the sensation novel, usually resolves in the exposure of the fair Victorian woman as the source of deception or crime. The unveiling of the deceptive sensational heroine exposes her doubled identity and converts it into a singular individual, thus threatening Victorian assumptions and expectations of women, domestication, and physical appearances. Similar to the Gothic, sensation fiction offers transgressive identities made visible through actions such as adultery, madness, bigamy, murder, or female monstrosity. Indeed, these modes are linked and mid-Victorian sensation novels and penny bloods and dreadfuls maintained their evolutionary roots in the gothic genre. Sensation fiction revises the Gothic through what Andrew

Smith and Williams Hughes (2012, 8) define as "excessive codification of the body" that presents characters as liminal or spectral figures who transgress between the dead and the living. While Braddon's heroine is not a spectral form or factually classified as dead (as surmised by her tombstone), she is in fact a liminal figure trapped between the margins of a transgressive identity. "Lucy" presents the ambiguous inauthenticity of human identity that needs to be investigated and exposed. It is through these gothic spaces of secrecy and fragmentation that Laurence Talairach-Vielmas (2012, 31) believes as the singular site where "fragments and truth can be recollected and reunited." Braddon's sensational text, blended with Victorian social conventions and gothic elements, navigates through "Lucy's" identities and crimes to delve into the corrupted core of her duplicitousness. It is through "Lucy's" unveiling that the reader is exposed to her manipulative criminal strategies.

Braddon's novel begins with a tale of a sweet and ethereally beautiful governess who becomes the object of desire for a man of the gentry. During her employment, she is introduced to, receives a proposal from, and eventually marries the older aristocratic, Sir Michael Audley. Although "Lucy" is initially reluctant to return Sir Michael's advances, she accepts his proposal and joins the household as Lady Audley, the angel of the house. According to Martha Vicinus (1981, 134), "Lucy" "never pretends to love Lord Audley" but uses the marriage as a means to secure her own role within the upper-class domain, thereby achieving a status in Victorian society as well. After her incorporation into the domestic realm at Audley Court, "Lucy" hints at an underlying corruption to her feminine ruse. This deception is almost immediately recognized by several family members, most notably Robert Audley. Throughout the novel, Robert investigates the identity of Lady Audley while also exploring the disappearance of his friend, George Talboys. Although there are several subplots occurring concurrently between characters, they all eventually conclude at the moment when Robert discovers Lady Audley's guilt. "Lucy" Audley, then, confesses to her crimes of bigamy, manipulation of various identities, and the attempted murder of her first husband, George, thus disclosing her infiltration of the upper-class Victorian home.

"Lucy" Audley's ontological shifts and desire for assimilation are caused by the suppression of her instincts. Several theorists, however, argue that Lady Audley's struggle for ascension is related to her obsession with class and wealth. For example, Anna Royal (2013, 1) claims that "Lucy" "redefines herself" from her once "humble origins," and while she does not explicitly reject the role of dutiful "angel," she masquerades in this position while concurrently attempting to further increase her social equity. Therefore, Lady Audley's purpose for secrecy and manipulation is because of her desire for social power, ambition, and economic value. "Lucy" capitalizes on her position and uses her grandiose surroundings to shroud herself, not only in secrecy but in wealth to secure her new identity as lady of the house. The wealth and material possessions of Audley Court create an affective environment that allows her to retrain her persona from that of governess to that of baroness.

As a figuration of criminality, "Lucy's" monstrous nature poses a challenge and collapses the human-nature boundary. Presenting a character with what Jack Halberstam (1995, 17) refers to as, an "inversion of identity," Braddon's "Lucy," in this case, instead of rejecting the conventional Victorian womanhood, seeks to achieve this social role. Abandoned by her destitute husband and exploited by a greedy father, Braddon's protagonist adopts a newly created identity of "Lucy" Graham to navigate through society. Adopting strategies, after Ruskin's standards, taught by her working-class father, "Lucy" procures the station of governess and adheres to the affects of a middle- and upper-class lifestyle. Initially condemned by society and spouse, "Lucy" becomes a social climber and develops a new ontology to ensure her success and assimilation in Victorian society. Braddon's figuration of "Lucy" who originated in the lower-class and strategically appropriates skills of conventional femininity and criminality for social ascension, speaks to Lombroso and Ferrero's speculation of the occasional offender. Arguing that occasional delinquents present little, or no, "characteristics of degeneration," it is contended that their offenses multiply in their "opportunities of evil doing" (Lombroso and Ferrero 1895, 111). Since occasional criminals are remiss of the attributes of born criminals, they participate in such crimes as adultery, or other acts that necessitate and enchanting appearance. "Lucy," then, with her training and child-like innocence, adapts to the role of Victorian lady who embodies beauty and goodness. Exhibiting gracefulness, youth, and a resistance to this degeneracy, she assumes the position as governess and conventional role of femininity. For example, "Lucy" instructs her charges "to play sonatas by Beethoven, and to paint from nature after Creswick," and afterward "walk to the humble little church three times on Sunday" (*Lady Audley*, 6–7). Not only is "Lucy" aesthetically suited for Victorian perfection, but she also assumes the role of Coventry Patmore's "Angel" perfectly. It is this artificial persona, or what Tabitha Sparks (2012, 29) calls a "misrepresentation as an angel," that allows "Lucy" to "infiltrate the highest echelon" of society. It is "Lucy's" desire and drive to achieve the Victorian ideal that illustrates her deviant and dangerous nature. Declaring "no more dependence, no more drudgery, no more humiliations . . . every trace of the old life melted away—every clue, to identify buried and forgotten," "Lucy" assumes the role as Lady Audley (*Lady Audley*, 12). This transgression of Victorian borders occurs through the artificial identity assumed by Braddon's protagonist.

While shrouding her criminality in respectability, she uses her feminine mask to master the environment and manipulates her way through experiences. Presented as an angelic and innocent beauty, "Lucy" utilizes her childish characteristics and appearance to obtain access to a house of nobility. As Herbert Klein (2008, 165–66) suggests, "Lucy" epitomizes the ideal role of "the child-bride" who maintains an element of spousal subordination, thereby suggesting the trope that Lord Audley is not only a husband, but a father figure. Exploiting her angel-like façade and mastery of conventional feminine techniques, "Lucy" influences and enchants those around her in order to present a false sense of belonging. Her depiction of innocence and vulnerability "exerts an almost magical sexual attraction over men," most notably Sir Michael, granting her access to high society (Klein 2008, 166). Furthermore, her childish behavior and angelic allure are used to conceal her deviance and monstrously criminal ontology. Her skills of concealment and social manipulation allow her to successfully transcend from a life as an impoverished and rejected wife and mother to the adored child-bride of the gentility. While "Lucy's" overall aesthetic is representative of the early-to-mid ideals of Victorian womanhood, her beauty, while appealing and angelic is wrongly interpreted as moral innocence. This misconception of beauty as virtuous and respectability allows her to transgress social boundaries and access the role of upper-class Victorian woman.

Fear that a dangerous criminal aggregate lurked within the domestic realm of middle-class Victorian families, the nature of women was treated as misleading and unstable. Suggesting that the childlike innocent "appearance of girls could not be trusted," Mangham (2007, 15) claims that young women were suspect as they could spontaneously erupt into manic episodes of either melancholia or violent madness. Exemplified as the Victorian ideal of womanhood, described in detail by John Ruskin, Lady Audley's appearance and performance echoes the constructs of physical and behavioral femininity. Braddon introduces her heroine as *the* embodiment of upper-class perfection as she is "blessed with that magic power of fascination by which a woman can charm with a word or intoxicate with a smile. Everyone loved, admired, and praised her" (*Lady Audley*, 6). Braddon creates the illusion of desirable traits using "Lucy's" charm, beauty, and domestic skill. Although she is initially depicted as a vision of Victorian womanhood, "Lucy" is the duplicitous configuration of traditional values and social degradation as she represents both the angel and the wicked Other. Likewise, Braddon's portrayal of female protagonists challenges social ideologies by transgressive ontological boundaries. This subversion, or in this case introversion, disregards and challenges gendered traditions placed upon women during the early-to-mid-Victorian period. Braddon's protagonist transgresses between two identities: the quintessential angel of the house and the deviant, destructive Other. Her visual aesthetic coordinates with the Victorian gender ideology of feminine perfection; she is blonde-haired, blue-eyed, fair-skinned, and childish. "Lucy" is admired by society for her sweet disposition and skill in the female domestic arts. However, her depiction of the ideal Victorian woman transitions rapidly into the wicked criminal.

Lady Audley disguises her latent monstrous criminal behavior through performative identity shifts. Acting as a monstrous figuration of nature-culture, Braddon's "Lucy" insists on an ecoGothic approach that entangles the "material and discursive, natural and cultural, biological and textual" (Alaimo 2010, 12). As a material-semiotic monstrosity, "Lucy's" figuration operates as a threshold of intersecting signifiers that allow transgression of restrictive boundaries through environmental affects. The transitional shift between angel and demon occurs frequently as she consciously assimilates into a new environment. Throughout the novel, "Lucy" shifts her identity and behavior according to the situation(s) she encounters, and the affects imposed upon her. These transitions are conscious decisions made by Lady Audley's direct affective experiences that motivate her actions. Affect, in Lady Audley's case, is a visceral force that drives her to react accordingly and allows assimilation and survival within specific environments. This process of affect, as Gregory J. Seigworth and Melissa Gregg (2010, 2) identify, is "vital force" that inherently "marks a body's belonging to a world of encounters." Functioning in conjunction with Bladow and Ladino's explication of the body being the salient site for processing and expression, Lady Audley's mind-body is a [re]creation according to this affective force. "Lucy's" transformative ability, then, centers on her environmental appropriation. For example, she displays her recreative technique in discussion with Sir Michael. Lady Audley attempts to convince her husband of Robert's mania and contorts her composure from "a frivolous childish beauty into a woman, strong to argue her own cause and plead her own defence" (*Lady Audley*, 283). A common deception practiced by "Lucy" throughout the novel, she situationally reconstructs her behavior and appearance. The powerful projection of environmental affect impacts Lady Audley's precognitive emotions, thus allowing the residual traces to activate conscious thought and extension for physical and ontological transformation. "Lucy's" behaviors are determined by a conscious manipulation technique and neural mapping of the consciousness by habitual influences. Mobilizing these methods for her criminal deceptions, she mimetically assumes conventional femininity for personal gain.

Mimetic Sublimation: Becoming, Criminality, and Sexual Repression

The most obvious dynamic change occurs with the reconfiguration of "Lucy's" name and behavior through a process of becoming. This subject of embodiment, as Braidotti (2010, 44) argues, is acknowledged as "neither a biological nor a sociological category" but is, however, a juxtaposition of the material, physical, and immaterial symbols in social constructs. As a product of Victorian society, the figuration of "Lucy" is an amalgamated response that inverts social expectations of women and differs in her process of becoming. While the subjective figure of becoming transgresses social constructions of these conditions, and is repositioned as the feminine Other, not under the ontological direction of phallogocentric guidance, "Lucy" intentionally positions herself within the limits of conventional Victorian boundaries. Instead of trying to escape the culture and nature conflict, "Lucy" blurs the boundaries between the two and operates as a mimic to infiltrate upper-class society. In possession of a childlike innocence, she uses mimicry and becoming as a subversive technique that functions to invert the social traditions of Victorian womanhood and the institutions responsible for the creation of these constructs. Strategically placing herself within the discursive conventions of upper-class Victorian women, "Lucy," as a criminal infiltrator, occupies the position as Lady of Audley Court through learned habitual influences and mimicry.

"Lucy," then, challenges the authority of society by mimicking the role of upper-class Victorian womanhood. In her mimetic approach to upper-class becoming, "Lucy" strategically functions from within the feminine construct "to open up an enclosed system" (Alaimo 2000, 7). As a woman from a lower-class background, "Lucy," originally Helen Maldon, is the daughter of an impoverished social manipulator restricted from the upper classes. During this stage of her life, Helen is surrounded by the hardships of poverty and is used as a strategic pawn for her father's deceptions. With Lieutenant Maldon's "fine talks of the grandeur of his family," he exploits Helen's idealistic beauty and uses "shallow tricks" to attract suitors for his "his pretty daughter" (*Lady Audley*, 17). The Lieutenant instructs Helen to wear her femininity as a disguise in order to captivate the middle-and upper-class audience. "Lucy's" father's manipulation training affects the re-entrant process in her cortical regions, thereby evoking sensory input that creates a neuronal remapping. As a result, "Lucy's" behavior is cultivated through these habitual affective experiences as an impoverished woman raised by a mendacious parent. The habituation of repetitive instruction is an integrative process "of collective neuronal activity" that encourages an intricate interlaced "pattern of responses" singular to the specific subject and event (Edelman, Gally, Baars 2011, 3). Thereby, the neural remapping process through the Dynamic Core is what allows Lady Audley to consciously mimic the necessary situational behaviors based upon her environment. The brain remaps the consciousness to respond to appropriate affectations. These global mappings, then, create a dynamic spatiotemporal influx of events and actions. It is through this guidance and experience that Helen aligns herself with the Victorian expectations of middle- and upper-class ideologies. Educated by her father, Helen consciously assimilates into the necessary role and projects the learned manipulations through sweet smiles and a flirtatious attitude. Although her father leads the verbal deceit and instructive lessons, Helen is solely responsible for adapting to these expectations and ensnaring a husband, George Talboys, with her physical appearance and allure. After she is later abandoned by her husband, "Lucy" transforms her enticing sexuality into criminal tendencies.

"Lucy's" sublimation of sexual desires into that of self-adoration ultimately transitions into aggressive, criminal, behavior. In *Speculum of the Other Woman*, Irigaray argues that sublimation, as a defense mechanism that transforms impulses into typically acceptable behaviors, occurs through the "construction of narcissistic monuments," when the libido is pulled back from the desired object and desexualized "so it can carry out more sublimated activities" (1985, 54). From this perspective, Braddon's character represses her sexual instincts and utilizes the harnessed energy for mimetic performances. "Lucy's" sublimation is most visible during her declaration of love to Lord Audley when she proclaims that she "loved [George] as much as it was in my power to love anybody" but not as much as she loves Audley (*Lady Audley*, 279). Although she professes her love for Sir Michael, the situation renders it inauthentic and hollow. Reflecting the alleged "defects" of female criminality, "Lucy" displays a "morbid activity" of "sexual coldness," which is suspected to intensify the negative traits in women and "induces them to seek relief in evil deeds" (Lombroso and Ferrero 1895, 151). This coldness and calculative approach are presented in Lady Audley's response to Sir Michael, which is planned and worded strategically. Her well-structured declaration of love to Sir Michael is void of emotional outbursts and echoes Irigaray, Lombroso, and Ferrero's sublimation of sexuality. While married and comfortably enjoying George's inheritance, she assumed the role of blissful wedlock and complacency as a middle-class wife. When neglected and abandoned by her first husband, "her instincts are, in a way, in abeyance, in limbo, in vacuo, not cathected," thereby "Lucy" chooses to sublimate her passions (*Speculum* 1985, 71). In a transitive stage of overcoming this rejection, she denounces her instinctual drive for intimacy, which she declares later as "the common temptations that assail and shipwreck some women had no terror" for her (*Lady Audley*, 281). This repudiation of "a legion of tempters" suggests that deviance supplanted "Lucy's" sexual passion and desire for intimacy (*Lady Audley*, 281). What may have been passion for George turns to criminal calculation and desire for social ascendance.

Though the titular Lady Audley is often theorized as a madwoman with psychologically corrupt inclinations, she expertly navigates through the pages of the novel using logic and decisive manipulation. In Braddon's criminal figuration, there is no separation of madness and criminality from the perspective of Victorian society. Illustrated in the criminal analysis of Lombroso and Ferrero (1895, xvi), they argue that mental anomalies in offenders are a reoccurrence of moral instability observed through such actions as "excessive vanity." Female criminals, then, operate in methods akin to their inherent pleasures, which are claimed as deficient in their moral codes. This connection between criminal women and mental instability, echoes the medical rationale of James Cowles Prichard (1835, 109), who coined the term "moral insanity." Redefining madness as "not a loss of reason, but as deviance from social accepted behavior," Prichard's concept of moral insanity claims that individuals who act rationally, but immorally "should *still* be classified as insane" because their moral dispositions are inherently perverted (Showalter 1985, 29). Since Lady Audley transgresses social boundaries, attempts murder, and commits bigamy, she consciously performs according to immoral decisions, therefore necessitating punishment. This chastisement is bound up in the medicalization of her condition as a madwoman. Requested for analysis by Robert, Dr. Mosgrave arrives at Audley Court for Lucy's medical diagnosis. In conversation, Mosgrave explains to Robert that "madness is not necessarily transmitted from mother to daughter," which is the first implication that "Lucy" is in fact a criminal, not a madwoman as she claims (*Lady Audley*, 300). Also, unaware of her assaults, Dr. Mosgrave claims that "because there is no evidence" of her actions, he does "not believe that she is mad" (*Lady Audley*, 281). Leading into her evaluation, Mosgrave determines (based on his conversation with Robert) that "Lucy" is essentially undiagnosable.

Women who do not adhere to the social norms and traditions, whether through psychological or criminal acts, are designated as hereditarily insane. "Lucy," a woman who uses logic to manipulate and redefine her identity, claims she is inherently mad and is dismissed by Dr. Mosgrave as dangerous instead. After evaluating Lady Audley for ten minutes, he returns to Robert and declares that:

> there is latent insanity! Insanity which might never appear; or which might appear only once or twice in a lifetime. It would be dementia in its worst phase perhaps: acute mania, but its duration would be very brief, and it would only arise under extreme pressure. The lady is not mad; but she has the hereditary taint in her blood. She has the cunning of madness, with the prudence of intelligence. I will tell you what she is, Mr. Audley, she is dangerous! (*Lady Audley*, 301)

Mosgrave's immediate diagnosis of "Lucy" is a prelude to the claim that a perfectly normal woman who carries the taint of criminal deception can be discovered through her slight excitability. Prior to their session, "Lucy's" interactions with both Robert and Sir Michael present her as a frantic madwoman. However, up until the moment Robert confronts her on the criminal activity, she maintained a perspicacious and calm disposition. "Lucy's" criminal behavior and offensive actions do not provide the diagnosis of madwoman, however, her threatening intellect and excessive energy grant her this label. Dr. Mosgrave suggests that Robert would do society a service by sending her away to the madhouse. Within the walls of the *Maison de sante*, all of her secrets will remain as such.

Lady Audley's arrival to the dismal madhouse grounds is a direct reflection of her eventual demise. While on her journey to Villebrumese in Belgium, "Lucy" is presented with characteristic gothic elements such as "wild shrieks and whoops that had a demonic sound in the darkness," coupled with a building located in a "dreary courtyard" (*Lady Audley*, 303). The tones enacted by this dark imagery offer an antagonistic antithesis to "Lucy's" bright and angelic aesthetic. Still portraying a stoic guise, she envelops herself within finery and proceeds through the gateway, past "an enormous lamp" that encapsulates "one poor little shivering flame" that struggles against the wind (*Lady Audley*, 306). The representation of the obscure flame trapped within the larger structure offers foreshadowing to Lady Audley's future events and her lost fight against society. While the *Maison de sante* is presented as a safe haven, albeit possessing a "funereal splendor" for mentally unstable patients, Monsieur Val's introduction and tour of the facility alludes to its true intent to hide, and forget, unsavory people (*Lady Audley*, 306). With the introduction to her new setting, "Lucy" is denied access to her previous identity and is forcibly cast into the role of Madame Taylor.

Lady Audley's new environment negatively affects her consciousness and creates psychosomatic weakening. Drawing from Darwin's theory, nineteenth-century criminologists explain that women and children share similar traits and mental characteristics. Since women are portrayed as having brains somewhere between men and children, it is suggested that they lack in moral structure and are controlled by violent emotions of jealousy and vengeance. While "Lucy's" vociferations against Robert suggest a juvenile immaturity, her aggressions are a result of neuronal remapping. Furthermore, excessive neuronal influences can create "selective strengthening or weakening of particular populations of synapses," therefore, toward the end of the novel, "Lucy's" overexerted synapses weaken as a result of negative influences and affectations, leading to actions of aggression (Edelman 1989, 45). Since "Lucy" demonstrates strong passions, both Monsieur Val and Robert Audley deem it necessary to confine her and treat her like a misbehaved child. By assigning "Lucy" a new name, they also provide her with a new anonymous identity created by their own standards. Cast into this new role by male authorities of both the madhouse and the Audley family, "Lucy" is forcibly stripped of her carefully constructed agency.

Discovery of "Lucy's" criminality results in removal of agency and a newly prescribed role. While "Lucy" provides the illusion of conformity to Victorian womanhood, she functions as a transgressive mimic to ultimately disrupt institutional boundaries. Throughout the novel, "Lucy" deceives and commits heinous crimes to achieve desired success, however, she faces repercussions when discovered and is seemingly hidden, or banished, from society. Although appropriate, and authentic, female conformity to the Victorian stereotype is rewarded, artificiality or deviance is punished and shrouded by obscurity. With her forcible assignment to the role of Madame Taylor, "Lucy's" resolve disappears, and she presents the "beautiful devil," as hinted at by Monsieur Val (*Lady Audley*, 310). Her claim to inherent insanity dissolves and her criminal nature becomes apparent when she confronts Robert with:

> Has my beauty brought me to *this*? Have I plotted and schemed to shield myself and lain awake in the long deadly nights trembling to think of my dangers for this? You see, I do not fear to make my confession to you . . . for two reasons. The first is that you dare not use it against me, because you know it would kill your uncle to see me in a criminal dock; the second is, that law could pronounce no worse sentence than this, a life-long imprisonment in a madhouse. (*Lady Audley*, 313)

The disclosure of intentions and challenge to Robert's punishment results in "Lucy's" identity reassignment and secretive imprisonment. In recognition of her potential for familial destruction, she is forcibly removed from the Audley family by way of name and association. Prescribed a new identity by a patriarchal institution, "Lucy's" agency is removed, and she is concealed from society.

Lady Audley's dishonesty and criminal deception results in her imprisonment and constant state of becoming. Whereas "Lucy" is a self-proclaimed, and later diagnosed, madwoman, she presents a manipulative cunning and intellect to define her as an occasional criminal. However, due to the variations of external influences and assigned identities, "Lucy" struggles with obtaining a fixed role. While the affective experiences with the environment mark her as belonging to her surroundings, the conflictual interactions create a detrimental incurrence of questionable identity. Similar to the Dark Woman, "Lucy" does not obtain personal resolution, instead she succumbs to a *maladie de langueur*, or languorous malady, approximately one year after her incarceration. In her stages of lethargy, "Lucy," now Madame Taylor, is confined within the singular setting of the *Maison de sante*. Without the affectations of varied surroundings, she is restricted to the prescribed agency assigned by Monsieur Val. Denied access to her own freedoms, "Lucy's" actions are limited as she faces isolation and obscurity under the artificiality of Madame Taylor.

During the early-to-mid-Victorian period, women were labelled as emotional, irrational, and susceptible to corruption. Female actions such as promiscuity, rebellion, or criminal manipulation were designated as functions involuntarily caused by psychological and biological reactions. Women who yielded to their inherent instincts were viewed as unfeminine, mad, monstrous, and responsible for destroying patriarchal ideologies. While Victorians claimed that these criminal women possessed mental and physical disorders, their material-semiotic representations in gothic literature established how they rationally manipulated a society that rejected, abused, and neglected them.

NOTES

1. See Mina Murray Harker in Bram Stoker's *Dracula* (1897), Elizabeth Lavenza in Mary Shelley's *Frankenstein* (1818), Hetty Sorrel in George Eliot's *Adam Bede* (1859), Lydia Gwilt in Wilkie Collins's *Armadale* (1864–1866).

2. Tomkins was one of the first theorists to analyze affect theory. In his research, he used a psychological approach to address emotions and categorize affect. He segmented affect into three broad sections: Negative, Neutral, and Positive, while subcategorizing into nine distinctions of expressed affect.

3. See Jean-Baptiste de Monet de Lamarck, *Système Des Animaux Sans Vertèbres* (Charleston: Nabu Press, 1801/2011). Arguing that adaptive changes to organisms could occur throughout its lifetime, Lamarck notes that nature functions on the principles of time and favorable conditions to succeed. These evolutionary changes are replicated directly by the individual's progeny. Alterations of characteristics and traits occur because of environmental necessitation while consciousness, habit, and adaptation are all responsible for evolutionary change. Modified behavior in the individual occurs out of a desire for assimilative survival, therefore leading to either additional or lesser usage of the organ. Lamarck suggests that evolutionary changes and adaptive characteristics are predetermined by environmental conditions and the desires or striving of organisms in these conditions, which are then reproduced in offspring. While Lamarck's theory was later disproven by Mendel's research in genetics, it still set the stage for early Victorian fear of degenerative characteristics. Derived from Lamarckian theory, but diverging in important aspects, Charles Darwin's *The Origin of Species* (1859) argues that predetermination is not part of the evolutionary process. Whereas Lamarck suggests that characteristics are produced within the lifetimes of beings and passed directly to offspring, Darwin refutes this theory and declares that offspring mutations are random and those who survived, passed on the gene, perpetuating that mutated trait. Setting up the evolutionary process, coined as natural selection, Darwin's theory, informed by Lamarck, proliferated through reductive Victorian medical and scientific discourses.

4. While the title I am discussing here establishes James Malcolm Rymer as its primary author, experts are still unsure whether the penny was written by him or Thomas Peckett Prest. Therefore, whenever I refer to the text in discussion, I will address the author as James Malcolm Rymer.

5. *The Man from Ironbark* is an Australian poem by a bush poet named Banjo Paterson published in 1892. The poem references a mischievous barber who echoes that of Sweeney Todd. Also refer to George Dibdin Pitt's 1847 melodrama, *The String of Pearls*, Stephen Sondheim's *Sweeney Todd: The Demon Barber of Fleet Street. A Musical Thriller* from 1979, or Tim Burton's Gothic rendition *Sweeney Todd: The Demon Barber of Fleet Street* from 2007.

6. Located within a façade of the middle-class, Lovett performs within the boundaries of the middle- and upper-classes or replicate the necessary behavior and appearance to allow their infiltration. In the Victorian social hierarchy, lower-working-class citizens were subjected to unsanitary urban conditions, had sparse education and medical attention, and limited access to nourishment. These environmental conditions, of course, render lower-working-class women prime candidates for fears of degeneration and monstrosity. On the contrary, middle- and upper-class women, resided in cleaner conditions, had access to healthcare, education, and limited access to political or public events. Women of these classes were subjected to a sanitized environment informed by morals and forced ignorance. While middle- and upper-class women were not influenced by the same daily stressors of lower- and working-class citizens, their relatively easier existence forcefully repressed their instincts and held them to a higher standard. This is not to say that there is not an intense class-based critique available, of course. I am mindful of this context, though it lays beyond the scope of what I consider; it is, however, from the middle- and upper-class ideologies of womanhood that the monstrous female emerges for the sake of this research.

7. Malcolm J. Errym is the pseudonym for James Malcolm Rymer. Also see Malcolm J. Merry. In light of this information, I will be referring to Rymer as Errym since his pseudonym maintains authorship on this text.

8. George IV's title of the Prince Regent is between the years 1811 and 1820. The plot of the penny is loosely based around the Prince's illegitimate marriage to Maria Fitzherbert and his extramarital involvements.

9. Sixteen-String Jack is a popular character in penny blood and penny dreadfuls. Based off of John (Jack) Rann in the eighteenth century, a notable criminal and highway man, the characterization of Sixteen-String Jack became prolific in fiction.

10. RMA established in 1772 was an act of Parliament that states members of the British royal family could contract a valid marriage. This act protected against marriages that could diminish the status of the royal family. Thereby the right to veto by the sovereign of the house was enacted.

11. Throughout the chapter I put "Lucy" in quotes to draw attention to the voluntary artificiality of the name. The protagonist's birth name is Helen, but she later adopts "Lucy" as a sign of rebellion against social placement. Placing her chosen

name in quotes emphasizes her rejection against social binds and reiterates the artificial role she assumes.

12. See such sensation novels as Mary Elizabeth Braddon's *Aurora Floyd*, *Lady Audley's Secret*, and Wilkie Collins's *The Woman in White*.

Chapter Four

Monstrous Transformations and Victorian She-Wolves

> Cruelty may remain latent till, by some accident, it is aroused, and then it will break forth in a devouring flame.
>
> —Sabine Baring-Gould 1865, 93

Lycanthropic women in the Victorian Gothic are figured from a desire to return to nature and their rejection of repression, which, in turn, affects the mind-body. These monstrous figurations of women in the Gothic are caused by their desires to return to nature and the corporeal representation of the repression of instincts affecting the mind-body. Progressing the discussion of performative identity shifts as rejections of social confines, this chapter identifies the behavioral and physical transformations of Victorian Gothic characters into lycanthropic manifestations. The focus for this chapter is shifted, then, from angels, madwomen, and criminals to hybrid figures of she-wolves to emphasize the severity of psychosomatic reactions against instinctual repression. Cleaving to the theme of ontological transgressions, this investigation of the gothic she-wolf figuration exposes how the mind-body-woman monistic figuration unites with nature. Werewolves, or in this case she-wolves, as beings of chaos and impulse, are hyperbolic figures used to accentuate the power of female sexuality in ways that both inscribe and resist patriarchal discourses about their supposed intrinsic monstrosity. This monstrosity, as Jeffrey Jerome Cohen (1996, ix) postulates, is a "doubleness" condensed within an object of uncertainty that commands to have its fragmented self "restore[d]" and to have its "pieces put back together." Condensed within an object of uncertainty, the gothic she-wolf commands to have its fragmented self restored to its whole unified form. As singular representations of both inherent passions and bestial modes of nature, the shapeshifting women in this chapter are figurations of social rejection and personal desire.[1]

Nature, in this chapter, functions as a method, and space, for feminist resistance in the transformative she-wolves. The affective connection between the heroines and external influences in such gothic-style texts as Frederick Marryat's "The White Wolf of the Hartz Mountains" (1837–1839), George W. M. Reynolds's *Wagner the Wehr-Wolf* (1846–1847), and George MacDonald's "The Gray Wolf" (1871) demonstrate the embodiment of wild characteristics through female transformations into bestial monstrosities. Marryat's Christina, as the most monstrous figuration of the three, appears as a woman; however, she is only Nature's wolfish visual representation of one. As the embodiment of the patriarchy's worst fears, Christina's abuse and murder of Krantz's children opposes conventions of Victorian womanhood. Although Christina is eventually punished for her transgressions, her actions throughout the story figure as retribution against Krantz—the wife murderer, the man who thought to utilize nature for his own protection and to obtain another wife as a domestic resource. On the other hand, Reynolds's representation of monstrous femininity is exhibited by Nisida's relationship to Nature through her intimate partnership with Wagner, the wehr-wolf. As a monstrous woman, she spends an undisclosed amount of time in the natural world, free of inhibitions, detached from the social repression of an upper-class station. Nisida's eventual rejection of nature and return to civilization results in her imminent destruction. Finally, MacDonald's tale highlights monstrosity in its transformative, and nameless, young woman who operates in a natural environment and exhibits a dynamic hybrid state that causes the man to flee and allows the woman to live. These narratives present expressions of early discursive degeneration, manifestations of fear, and stories that enact the repressive elements of Victorian discourse, while monism recuperates women's connection to their natural instincts.

FULL MOON RISING: VICTORIAN SHE-WOLVES

Arising from a reductive sense of the woman-nature connection, she-wolves in the Gothic are embodiments of female sexuality and enactments of rebellion against oppressive social positions who express their desires to return to nature. As shapeshifters, werewolves are utilized in narratives to identify the intricacies of human nature. Furthermore, as transformative beings, werewolves, as Sam George and William Hughes consider in their informative text, *In the Company of Wolves: Werewolves, Wolves and Wild Children* (2020, 5), "question what humanity is." In doing so, they illustrate the dynamic and complex composition of their socio-political forms that speak to such conceptions as culture, language, psychology, physiology, instincts, and sexuality. Therefore, the figuration of the shapeshifting she-wolf is determined as a transgressive material-semiotic coalescence of nature and culture, male and female, and animal and human. Werewolves, or she-wolves, are influenced by cultural discourses and their propagation of values about societal expectations and beliefs by combining myths and discourses about women. In all three of the following texts, women are figured as these gothic material-semiotic responses to Victorian perplexities of degeneration and independence. Whereas two characters are fully transformative she-wolves, one demonstrates her monstrous nature through intimacy with a male werewolf. In these particular stories of female monstrosity, environmental affectations inform the consciousness and the coalescence of the mind-body, resulting in the material expulsion of Victorian restrictions. Building on the Victorian anxieties of corruptive female nature informed by such monsters as madwomen and female criminals, these figurations of she-wolves are the embodiments of untamed nature and rationale.

Female monstrosity in the Victorian Gothic represents ontological fragmentation resulting in disrupted ideologies and social anxiety. The Gothic notably constructs women into divisive categories emphasizing either mind *or* body, as demonstrated in the representation of Cathy in *Wuthering Heights*, whereby their monstrous behaviors are explicated through periods of mania. This gendered monstrosity in the Gothic also accentuates Victorian anxieties of degenerative sexuality, which is apparent in Bertha Mason of *Jane Eyre*. Commonly analyzed by their psyche or corporeal forms, women in the Gothic are figured into fragmented pieces. Women, most notably their bodies, have historically been associated with monstrosity. For example, Marie Mulvey-Roberts (2016, 106) argues that since women's bodies have always been marked by anatomical differences, they have proven "troublesome," historically. Therein, female sexuality and reproductivity, as the assumed origin of animality, were the cause to identify women's bodies as a stigma for institutional and systematic surveillance and regulation. In gothic literature, this anamorphic perspective of carnality and desire is visible through monstrous figurations and their direct correlations to Nature. While embodying misogynistic Victorian stereotypes, these women not only represent distorted images of social concerns, they also hyperbolically critique and retaliate against repressive injustices. Whereas some scholars focus on the behavioral aspect of monstrous women or their corporeal forms, here it's elucidated as the monistic gothic mind-body and women-as-nature. This rejection of a dualistic approach is particularly useful for the discussion of she-wolf fiction with its focus on the wild female body. Therefore, she-wolf monstrosities in Victorian Gothic fiction, then, are monistic material-semiotic representations of conflicting female expectations. As figurations of rejected repression, they are material beings created from anxiety and desire.

Monstrous women challenge social structures and stability through their inherent connections to Nature. As transgressive and natural figures, women become, what Stacy Alaimo (2001, 292) refers to as "a threat," one in which society must "defend" itself and "distance" itself from. As liminal figures, women are denounced as threatening borderline primitive creatures that patriarchal institutions must protect themselves and their culture, against. Thus, she-wolf figures are more than only a re-inscription of patriarchal dictates and repression through the punishment and expulsion of monstrous women. As hyperbolic exhibitions of fear, werewolves cast them in an ironic light. In these stories, too, monstrous women strike blows against representations of patriarchy and the machinery of their domination, even if the stories do end with their deaths or banishment. Furthermore, the hyperbole might also go some way to recuperating the woman-nature connection evoked in particularly reductionist ways by some Victorian discourses. In the early-to-mid-Victorian period, women were depicted as monstrous embodiments of nature driven by sexual excess, controlled by instincts, and subjected to degenerative primitivity. Popular Victorian literature constructed these women as hybrids of nature and monstrosity that reflected fears of this corruption and instability. Therefore, this hybridization of humanity with animality not only signified the implicit otherness, but the innate corruption embodied within the monistic female figuration. Situated in a transitional space between culture and nature, monstrous Victorian women were assumed as ontologically and biologically inferior to their male counterparts.

From Mind and Body to Mind-Body: Gothic Transformations and Women's Nature

Criticisms about the Victorian Gothic are known for analyzing women's ontologies according to binaries such as mind/body and culture/nature. Women operate within the marginalized space between nature and culture, therefore segregating nature from culture to ensure the safety and minimize the corruption of male humanity. This popular dualist approach was formed from a society that was notorious for its exclusion and utilization of "indigenous peoples, enslaved Africans, nearly all women, and even many white-skinned men (Slavs, Jews, the Irish)" as resources (Moore 2016, 12). Drawing from Bruno Latour's (1993) theory of the Great Divide, this nature/culture dualism perpetuates the violent fantasy that nature is a resource for extraction. As beings aligned with Nature, "along with trees and soil and rivers," women in these stories resent their repressive positioning as another of these resources that result in the fragmentation of identities and creation of social roles (Moore 2016, 79). Repression is expressed in the following stories in this particular way, a method that removes women from nature and forces them into socially appropriate positions. It is through this repressive state that a monist unification of the mind-body and consciousness return to the natural self.

To reclaim nature for women, feminism historically challenged the relationship between women and nature. However, while some feminist scholars attempt to remove women from this interconnection, it is imperative that nature is conceived as a space, or substance, of power and agency. Although nature, Alaimo (2000, 2) argues, is embedded in a "bedrock of oppressive ideologies," it is also a "space of feminist possibility." Denying the woman-nature connection simply re-inscribes the dualism, and further, leaves other beings on the wrong side of it. Rejecting Victorian standards, these transgressive, and assumedly monstrous, women who represent both animal and human, collapse the borders of nature and culture and mind and body. It is in this untamed space that women, as figurations of she-wolves, operate to access freedom and gain agency. Their rebellions reject the notion that men cannot be separated from nature even if they place women there as an intermediary to guarantee their own humanity as distinct from nature. It is this relationship with nature that women have the potential to heal and reject restrictive conventions.

The mind-body transition to nature in the form of the werewolf demonstrates how women are not constructs of culture. Drawing from the Gothic trope, shapeshifters, according to Brendan C. Walsh (2020, 2) are the "merger of species," established from the fear that the Other was a construct predicated on "humanity's inherent connectedness to the animal world." These amalgamated monstrosities are, however, confined by constructive institutions that inform specific roles to regulate undesired behavior. As a result, external affectations influence monstrous responses to retaliate against a suffocating society. Likewise, women in these Victorian Gothic tales reject prohibitive boundaries and return to their natural state. This female reclamation of nature rejects restrictive confines of society but also faces devastating results. Therefore, early-to-mid-Victorian women's repression results in social transgressions and monstrous representations. Eschewing the Cartesian tradition, she-wolves illustrate how the mind-body unifies and aligns women with the "natural" realm without reducing them to bodies alone. Operating in the gothic mode of transgression, these lycanthropic tales use monstrous women as material-semiotic responses to symbolize rejection of society and reclamation of the self. While in previous chapters these transformations of monstrosity were exhibited as figurations of madwomen as Bertha Mason, Catherine Earnshaw, and Agatha Jeffreys, and female criminals as Mrs. Lovett, Linda Mowbray, and "Lucy" Audley, the following characterizations of monstrous women transcend the divide between nature and society, thus presenting the repressed passions of restrained female instincts of assumed animality under the surface. Marryat's "White Wolf" transitions from wolf to woman to punish Krantz and his family for transgressions against his wife. Reynolds's *Wehr-Wolf* aligns intelligently devious women with nature, and MacDonald's "Gray Wolf" illustrates women's return to nature through full wolf transformation. Women were represented in social practice and popular fiction as beings of psychological or physiological excess. Therefore, their perpetuation of the species and potential for self-corruption, or that of their offspring, induced tensions in Victorian society. It is through this conception of perpetual instability and matrilineal degeneration that women are associated with destructive monstrosity.

FEAR OF DESCENT: VICTORIAN SCIENCE AND FEMALE MONSTROSITY

The nineteenth-century theories of evolution contributed to the patriarchal oppression of women by establishing a natural biological elucidation of the social order. To maintain social hierarchies, familial lineages, and distinctions between private and public spheres, women faced repression of behavior and instincts. In order to understand the response to this suppression expressed in werewolf stories, social contexts must be considered from a contemporaneous, not anachronistic approach. The following medical professionals correlate female monstrosity to reproductive functions including puberty, menstruation, and pregnancy. All implied markers of destructive female nature, these are the biological phases when women were considered susceptible and inimical to their prescribed roles. Therefore, she-wolves as exhibited in Victorian Gothic texts, consider the ways in which the regulation of female behavior was informed by developments of scientific narratives and evolutionary theory that evoked fears of regression and genealogical degeneration. These conclusions are not Darwin's per se, but applications of his theory to Victorian society and gender relations therein.

In the Victorian period, evolutionary theory joined the conversation of biological uncertainty and promoted the belief that higher life forms were derived from primitive figures. In his studies on speciesism and evolution, Darwin examines the evolutionary mechanisms that enable the descending traits that produce variabilities in progenitorial outcomes. Pushing back against the evolutionary theory expressed in terms of devolution/degeneration and inscription of monstrosity on female sexuality, Darwin's explications of biological differences provide feminist studies with a detailed analysis of nature's evolution and its temporal progress. Regarding this evolutionary advancement, there are specific principles which are the foundation for natural selection: "individual variation, the struggle for existence and the inheritance of variation, is the postulate for natural selection" (Grosz 1999, 35). These processes determine the outcome for future progeny. All inclusive of the repetitious performance of assigned to roles (i.e., societal, biological, institutional), these principles result in the future traits of the species. As theorized by Darwin, new characteristics randomly emerge in offspring in order for survival of the species in new conditions. This information about evolutionary and repetitive manipulation of the species informed society about the "new generation of a productive monstrosity" and the transgressions and overall dismantling of societal constructs (Grosz 1999, 43). As demonstrated in earlier chapters, psychological instability or felonious activity led institutions to fear deviations from proper moral conduct. Therefore, evolutionary theory coupled with these discourses, indoctrinated society to believe that repetitive female transgressions would result in devolution and destruction of the Victorian family.

Following such interpretations of evolutionary theory, discourses of genealogical corruption circulated in Victorian society. The introduction of Jean-Baptiste Lamarck (1801) and later, Darwin's theories, were to support the Victorian beliefs of idealistic hereditary succession, as Victoria Margree and Bryony Randall (2012, 218) posit, "by suggesting the perfectibility of species." However, while society recognized the forward directionality of evolutionary theory, they also believed that evolution could follow the course of devolution and offer a degenerative property to humanity, resulting in reversion of advancement and civilization. Identifying those changes in the species that could result in devolution ending in barbarity created fears of human degeneration. This fear of primitive regression of human nature and deviant behavior emerged as the destructive threat in Victorian families. It is this regression, or fear of humanity's return to an "archaic or primitive" state that is reflected in studies of physiognomy with special focus on characteristics of abnormalities or deviances (Botting 2014, 88). Supposedly degenerated individuals with abnormal and deviant characteristics, presented distinct criminal or sexual tendencies antagonistic to Victorian domestic standards. Scientific studies, as theorized by such experts as Darwin, Lamarck, and Laycock, suggested that this degenerative threat was not only located in the affective natural environment, but embodied within women. The inherent traits rooted within humanity, especially vulnerable women, provided institutions with troublesome notions about humanity, behavior, and ultimately human biology, coupled with reasons to enforce processes of identification, exclusion, and eradication of such aberrant individuals. Although prominent in the late Victorian period with the New Woman, fear of possible degeneration appeared earlier in the century. These implications of female devolution and atavistic primitivity flourished in medical journals and popular literature alike.

In the early-to-mid-Victorian period, science and medical treatises implicated women's reproductive stages in physiological and psychological abnormalities. Female reproductive development and correlative dysfunctions were problematic for social stability. Atavism and recidivism were discussed through psychotherapeutic theories of female hysteria and phrenological criminality. This correlates with reflex theories by Thomas Laycock (1840), who argues that the brain is affected by the nervous system, and physiognomic expressivity by Forbes Winslow (1851, 21), who claims that stages of female developmental reproductivity possess "faculties of the lower animals." The female system, as discussed by Victorian medical men, is a microcosm compiled of susceptible faculties and uncontrolled behaviors with potential for systematic retrograde. While Winslow recognizes evolutionary progress, he also argues that regression of human faculties is not only possible, but probable unless identified and restrained. This observational development was considered necessary and applied in searching for abnormalities and anomalies in the female mind-body structure that were argued as being parallel with beasts. Derived from Laycock's psychological studies of women, these analytical considerations were suggested to identify eccentricities that are possible through stages of reproductive development. In agreement with this panoptical approach of observation, Winslow an arbiter of Victorian morals, suggests that once puberty commences, it is the duty and honor of women to enter the martial state and populate the household with children. Like the promotion of the "married state" by Sarah Stickney Ellis (1842, 337), Winslow identifies these tasks as a necessary fulfillment for women's destiny. While such discourse characterizes the role of wife-mother as *the* ideal position for Victorian womanhood, it is a social restriction enacted to regulate women's desires and avoid procreative impairment.

Early-to-mid-Victorian medical experts theorized that biological stages of menstruation and pregnancy were responsible for primal regression and devolution. For instance, G. F. Girdwood (1843, 222), a notable London surgeon, claims that during menstruation, women's "sexual appetite" is "slightly developed" and rivals that of animals in "heat." Whereas Girdwood associates all explicit sexual desires to moments of menstruation, he dismisses all women's continuous animal passions. Only during the menstrual cycle were women believed to submit to their carnal passions and overt excitations—as illustrated in Bertha Mason and Agatha Jeffreys—however, upon cessation, these attitudes subside, and typical behavior resumes. Girdwood claims that women, unlike animals, are not hindered by these needs to the extent that lower animals are. In *The Making of Victorian Sexuality* (1995), Michael Mason argues that according to most nineteenth-century institutional discourses, women's increased fertility and passions at the time of menstruation were analogous with lower form animals. It was believed that the monthly cycle of menstruation, while monitored and regulated, was a "safe release of animal impulses" (Mason 1995, 196). Some medical writers also promoted the concept that women felt desire at all reproductive phases and faced arousal by such things as men's dress or smell, which is similar to the instincts found in zoological beings. Women, when placed under the moral restriction of Victorian society, were viewed as controllable and capable of functioning as closer to humans and not as byproducts of an animalistic nature.

To reject instinctual desire, some Victorian men of science align women with morality and domesticity. For example, Winslow argues that once women decide to marry and procreate, mental conditions change and become more focused on their offspring. Therefore, it was widely assumed that the instinctual desire for stimuli was diminished and any shifts in the nervous system resulted in behavioral changes in Victorian women. Whereas pubescent women demonstrate passions for intimacy, pregnant women were perceived as displaying tempers relative to their primitive counterparts. In such a case, as Laycock observes, all wives, whether strictly moral or not, possess longings during pregnancy. Claiming that some desire items such as furniture and dresses, Laycock (1840, 255) argues that "these 'longings' are spurious" and illusionary. Referring to *Bartholomew Fair* by Ben Jonson (1614), Laycock claims that these morbid longings belong exclusively to the appetite for food.[2] Basing his medical observations on a seventeenth-century play, Laycock posits the notion that uninhibited pregnant women can progress to abnormal gastric cravings and even speculates about their desire for flesh consumption. Quoting directly from John Elliotson (1839), a notable professor and physician, Laycock claims that pregnancy can transform women into cannibals who kill and eat raw flesh, if unregulated. While Elliotson's (1839, 337) lectures ascertain that it is "an absolute fact" that pregnant women "longed for raw flesh, and even for live flesh," such as "live kittens and rats," he explicitly states that he did not experience these patients but "heard cases'" of this disorder. Presenting this behavior of anthropophagy, medical institutions, informed by evolutionary theory, influenced societal anxieties of monstrously feral women.

In a period that promoted female morality, medical, legal, and cultural institutions labeled monstrous women as paradigmatic of typical and atypical, where the threat was real and quite possible. Designated as posing a fatal admonition to progressive lineage, women faced restrictive behaviors of subordination. As supposedly unstable beings, they were argued to present bodily indifferences through occurrences as puberty, menstruation, pregnancy, and menopause, hysterical disorders, and exhibitions of dysmorphia. Driven by inherent appetites for over-indulgence in passions and sexual excess, women were labeled by medical science as potentially destructive. Victorian institutions believed that while women were controlled and contained in prolific reproductive relationships, they were passive and glorified as ideals of pure womanhood. Whereas, when unrestrained by such a union, excessive sexuality and violence, as noted by Margrit Shildrick (2002, 30), "lay beneath the civilised veneer of every woman" and threatened both the familial reputation and future progeny. This contamination of social integrity and health casts unruly women as hyperbolic monstrous figurations of excessive desire in gothic fiction, or in this case, tales of female lycanthropes.

Victorian Wolves: The Beast within the Woman

Fear of primitive regression and female monstrosity proliferate in tales of lycanthropy. In the early-to-mid-Victorian era, the female werewolf re-emerged to reflect women's intrinsic association with nature through material representations of monstrous forms. In one of the first popular publications of lycanthropic lore and theory, Sabine Baring-Gould's *The Book of Werewolves: Being an Account of a Terrible Superstition* (1865) discusses folkloric accounts of human-animal admixtures. Exploring over a millennia of wolf lore, he offers information on mythologies, psychology, and lore of lycanthropy. Baring-Gould (1865, 9) defines lycanthropy, or werewolfism, as a man or woman who shapeshifts "into the form of a wolf" by way of magic or psychological means to enable the gratification of the hunt, or as punished by the gods. While Baring-Gould labels this as the popular definition of fictional representations, he also suggests that lycanthropic traits correspond to legitimate madness. In psychology, individuals with lycanthropy, or those who possess lycanthropic tendencies, believe that they are werewolves who enact animalistic behaviors. Superstitions surrounding historical implications of lycanthropy originated with the human assumption of animal skin.[3] Later, the definition expanded to incorporate such troubled individuals "afflicted with paroxysms of madness or demonic possession" (Baring-Gould 1865, 34). Whereas the were-creature was a historically global phenomenon, English folklore, prior to the mid-Victorian period, is relatively void of werewolf tales.[4] Revivifying the literary werewolf in a period that introduced evolutionary theory provided a gothic literary figuration of terror, degeneration, and female carnality embodied in the monstrous forms.

The signifiers of psychosomatic degeneration are inclusive of cannibalism and insanity and informed the construction of the she-wolf monstrosity. Coupled with Lamarck and Darwin's evolutionary processes and popular literary discourses, werewolves exhibited the potential for degeneration into barbarism and "catapulted" this significant threat "directly into the middle-class drawing room" (Bourgault du Coudray 2002, 10). Although Baring-Gould refers to historical folklore about female wolf tales, it is during the Victorian era that she-wolves became popular signifiers to warn society against the dangers of women. While Victorian women were sculpted into preferable roles, werewolf literature was used to demonstrate their potential for resistance and rejection of prescriptive sublimation. Thus, werewolves and women were exhibited as ambiguous figures harboring transgressive identities, trapped in a liminal space between nature and culture. These fears of devolution and female sexuality resulted in gothic literature about feral female monstrosities.

Throughout the Victorian era, werewolves represented conflicts of identity. Initially associated with folkloric tales, mythologies, and early-modern witchcraft, werewolves, in the nineteenth century, as Alexis Easley and Shannon Scott (2013, ix) indicate, became "crucial figure[s] in the history of Victorian fiction because [they] embodied cultural anxieties about social change." While in human form, the figure continues to exhibit beastlike traits such as high intellect, maliciousness, and savage aggression. Following these tropes, scientific and fictional representations of "the beast within," identify cultural transformations responsible for the re-emergence of the werewolf (Bourgault du Coudray 2006, 6). Examining this inner beast as part of the Freudian unconscious state it is clear that it refers to such psychical concepts as the uncontrolled id: the primal, chaotic, and drive for instant gratification. The werewolf, then, with its bestial guise, is a visual expression of these so-called female inhibitions displayed as wolfish characteristics. Prior to the Enlightenment, lycanthropic tropes were considered as occult-related or elements of superstition. In the late eighteenth century, these phenomena were rejected for reasonable and logical explanations. Scholars in the field of nineteenth-century science and medicine looked for scientific or medical explanations for lycanthropy. Manifestations of characteristics pertaining to what Chantal Bourgault du Coudray (2006, 2) refers to as "crimes of sociopaths, an atavistic craving for blood or human flesh," werewolves are reflective of atavistic criminality and excessive sexuality, related to degenerative properties or devolution. A hybrid figure of monstrosity, half wolf, half human, the werewolf embodies the concerns of Lamarckian and Darwinian psychosomatic evolution, degeneration, and Victorian society's fear of uncontrolled female agency.

Victorian she-wolves are symbolic representations of transgressive women. While tales of male and female lycanthropy comprise similar cultural traditions and values, female narratives focus on different aspects of representation. Surveying burgeoning female werewolf literature, attitudes toward precocious women are palpable. Indeed, she-wolf narratives, as Hannah

Priest (2015, 5) so succinctly notes in *She-Wolf: A Cultural History of Female Werewolves*, combine elements of the "lycanthropic origin myth" with historical and "cultural narratives" about female nature. This combination of different folklores with societal perspectives on women results in the depiction of Otherness. Furthermore, she-wolves are an admixture of monstrosity signifying contradictions and challenges to societal ideologies. This deviation from the hegemonic structure of the white Victorian male provided a symbolic representation about such concerns of female sexuality, human degeneration, Otherness, and a connectivity to nature. Similarly, George and Hughes (2020, 3) suggest that wolves, as "ambiguous social animals yet savage outsiders," blur the boundaries between humanity and animality. Thereby, she-wolf narratives reflect bestial spectacles of female desires and ambiguity. Male werewolves, on one hand, are exhibited as similar to wolves in behavior and purpose; however, she-wolves function as emotional and chaotic, reflective of the internal threat trapped within the social constructs of womanhood. Confined by the parameters of a suppressive patriarchal structure, female lycanthropes pose "a more insidious threat" as their narratives depict violence against domesticity and a necessity for escape (Priest 2015, 14). Assumed as more feral monsters than male werewolves, she-wolves in literature correlate to the characteristics of natural female instincts. However, the mind-body is not a social construct, but a mode of Nature affected by society, therefore monstrous women reject these influences and present their innate desires through material-semiotic figurations in gothic fiction.

Embodiments of Monstrosity

The mind-body as a singular mode, as defined in Spinozian monism, is informed by society as an equally affective mode. When consciously rejecting the modal influence, women's mind-body returns to the natural state exhibiting behavioral and corporeal monstrosity. Social institutions and popular discourses designate women as inherently unstable thereby creating roles to suppress female behaviors. Thereby, monstrous women, as embodiments of the immaterial-material, deviate from social normativity and consciously transition into something other.

While the immaterial and material are unified under a singular substance, the centrality of immateriality (most notably sexual subjectivity) is presented through reconfigured bodies. Female subjectivity and the repression of sexuality results in visual exhibitions of the corporeal form. Since bodies "have all the explanatory power of minds," as Grosz notes (1994, vii) in *Volatile Bodies: Toward a Corporeal Feminism*, they are used to identify inversive concepts relative to the mind-body with representations of the figure and the overall corporeal figuration. Deviating from the popular Cartesian dualism, the effects of bodily inscriptions and metamorphic transitions are elucidated as visualizations of internal sexual and neurological affects of psychical events. Therefore, sexuality is identified through four varied notions of the term. First, it is a drive, mostly discussed in psychology as a motivating impulse. Second, sexuality is a performative act that involves "bodies, organs, and pleasures" (Grosz 1994, viii). Third, it is an identity, affiliated with oppositional genders of binary male and female. Like Michel Foucault's (1976) view, sexuality became the part of discourse which locates individuals in positions relative to authoritative institutions. Finally, it is determined by desires and preferences; elements that drive the individual to obtain the optimal pleasure for their sexual orientations. In all of these identifiers of sexuality bodies are allies of the differences. It is because of this alliance that phallogocentric assumptions are created to enforce the regulation of women. This association of female sexuality in relation to biology and physical form faced subjectivity throughout history in both behaviors and roles. Whereas, these roles are instilled for intellectual or agentic elimination, female bodies and sexualities, however, resist dualist subjectivity.

Societal roles for women's bodies and behaviors are based on biological reductionism and evolutionary theory. Although not social constructs, female mind-bodies define conceptions of regulatory roles. Women's bodies, Grosz (1994, x) argues, "provide a neurologic locus" for the projection of identity. She believes that women's forms should be the corporeal sites that display desired internal reactions from the peripheral nervous system. However, while women exhibit agency through mind-body functions, social objectification of, and connections to, female bio-psychology result in the "denigration and containment of the female body" (Grosz 1994, xiv). Victorian women, as promoted by medical discourse, faced social inferiority as a result of discourses of biological reductionism. Presumed as weaker, women are implied as being more susceptible to biological functions and their irregularities, therefore socially and economically restricted. Due to an assumed corporeality and natural primitivism, constructed roles of sexuality and sociality are implemented based on male somatophobic (fear of the body) reactions. Coded by nature/culture and apprehensions of female mind-bodies, Victorian women were confined into social roles under patriarchal control.

Women present their rejection of socially prescribed roles through mind-body formations informed by affectations. In her exploration of rejection of social ideals, Grosz looks to the psychological and neurological approach related to the ego. The ego, as an agentic part of the psyche is a collection of mental processes. Whereas the id is responsible for the passions or instincts, the ego constitutes that of common sense, practicality, or reason. The ego ensures that any impulses issuing from the id are acceptable. While acting as a regulator for the id, the ego, Freud (1911) argues, is predominantly that of a bodily projection; a representation of surface conflict.[5] It is the filter for interpreting stimuli through affectations or internal regulation of identity. Similarly, ego, Grosz (1994, 37) notes, is the "mapping of the body's inner surface" and is a personalized experience of affects, bodily influences, and consciousness. It is responsible for controlling social and environmental affectations and determining the proper bodily, or behavioral response. The unbounded ego and the natural body, then, is dynamically modified by ever-progressing societal, or cultural, affectations. As a map of the body, the ego simultaneously reflects bodily subjectivity and trauma while projecting, or rechanneling, instinctual impulses onto the body, or into behavioral responses. Ergo, the ego, as a meeting point of corporeal and incorporeal, personal and social operates as a regulator of external influences and neuronal impulses, as identified by Gerald Edelman and Elizabeth A. Wilson. It is through the ego that affectations are filtered and applied to the consciousness, thus resulting in bodily responses of either social acceptance or rejection.[6] Whereas the body is realistically limited by biological boundaries, the mind-body formation in gothic figurations of monstrosity transgresses these shackles through depictions of animalistic transformations. While these scholars employ a realistic approach to mind-body rebellion, this rejection of Victorian social ideals is exhibited as hyperbolic in gothic fiction through the presentation of monstrous women as she-wolves.

Women's monstrosity is the gothic display of evolutionary transfiguration and psychosomatic transgressions. In her examination of identity in the Gothic, Kelly Hurley's *The Gothic Body: Sexuality, Materialism, and Degeneration at the Fin de Siècle* (1996) proposes abhumanity as one such transfiguration.[7] Whereas the abhuman is located in relation to *fin-de-siècle* Gothic, it has not been linked to werewolf stories before the 1870s. Initially using the term to identify the separation of an individual from humanity, the abhuman is redefined as a transformative figure. In the gothic mode, the abhuman subject is determined to be something that is not entirely human, although not quite inhuman but a figure with metamorphic dynamics. Characterized as chaotic, in a state of continuous fluctuation, the subject is "in danger of becoming not-itself, becoming other" (Hurley 1996, 3–4). Whereas this movement away from the self is a loss, it is also a progression toward something else. Therefore, the morphic capability of the gothic figure represents both the positive and negative. Representative of the devolutionary fear attached to women, on the one hand, the abhuman is reflective of female monstrosity. On the other hand, similar to the mutability accorded the possibilities for progression and regression of a species in evolutionary discourse, the abhuman is not fixed in a definitive state. The evolutionary integrity of the human species, then, is dismantled and reconstructed in order to adapt and assimilate to each situation. Psychosomatic transfigurations are perceived as possible through habituation, therefore the gothic plot "seized upon this logic as a device" to portray "monstrous embodiments" of admixture (Hurley 1996, 7). Using this concept of the abhuman, the Gothic presents humans as between human and nonhuman, in constant threat of becoming something other. Locked in a liminal state of perpetual indifference, the modifications present in the abhuman are informed by its environmental or cultural surroundings. In this way, authors of the following Gothic texts use their literature as a space to join the conversation about evolutionary degeneration, corruptible nature, and animalistic behavior through figurations of rebellious women and female lycanthropes.

NATURE'S RETALIATION IN "THE WHITE WOLF OF THE HARTZ MOUNTAINS" (1837–1839)

Frederick Marryat's "The White Wolf of the Hartz Mountains" is an extracted tale from his gothic novel *The Phantom Ship*. Originally released in serial format in *New Monthly Magazine* and *Humorist* between 1837 and 1839, the short story was published independently in 1839. Displaying characteristics of adultery and marital disturbances, "The White Wolf," hints at potential influences from his personal life.[8] Marryat's popular tale also introduces the female wolf-human shapeshifter to the Victorian era. As an early narrative of she-wolf literature, "The White Wolf" exhibits the monstrous woman as a signifier of Victorian anxieties. Introduced as an attractive female outsider, Christina is an amalgamation of fears relevant to feral female sexuality and unregulated behavior. Following the trope that werewolves are outsiders to civilization, usually discovered in remote locations. For example, Christina, is what Max Fincher (2016, 733) calls a "marginalized outsider," however, she infiltrates and threatens the social status quo. Marryat's she-wolf, then, is a material-semiotic figure who embodies cultural fear of female devolution and vehement retaliation against traditional Victorian gender restrictions.

The story begins with Krantz, whose first wife rejects Victorian marital traditions of monogamy and virtue. Krantz's wife is portrayed as an adulterous woman who provokes her husband's rage, resulting in his separation from society. Krantz's nameless wife, who is "more beautiful than virtuous," functions as a signifier of the corruption of female sexuality ("White Wolf," 25). Frequently "admired by the lord of the soil," she succumbs to seduction and participates in an affair with a nobleman ("White Wolf," 25). Upon his unexpected return, Krantz discovers the "intrigue" as he witnesses his wife in "the company of her seducer" ("White Wolf," 25). Overcome by rage, Krantz murders both his wife and the nobleman. For fear of discovery, Krantz disappears with his children to nature in "the confines of one of those vast forests which cover the northern part of Germany" ("White Wolf," 26). An antithesis to civilized society, the landscape of the Hartz Mountains offers a dichotomous imagery of the sublime and isolation:

> the tall pines which rose up on the mountain above us, and the wide expanse of forest beneath, on the topmost boughs and heads of whose trees we looked down from our cottage, as the mountain below us rapidly descended into the distant valley. In summer-time the prospect was beautiful; but during the severe winter, a more desolate scene could not well be imagined. ("White Wolf," 26)

Though this description evokes beauty and grandeur, the elements of the natural realm are threatening for those sequestered from society. In remote seclusion, Krantz and his family struggle to survive in the harsh environment. Living as, what the narrator labels a "savage sort of life," the family is under constant duress by feral wolves ("White Wolf," 27). In relation to earlier discussions of Darwin's limited scientific vocabulary, Victorian imperialism, and Lombroso and Ferrero's criminology, Marryat enters this conversation with language that refers to "savagery" as primitive or comparable to the supposedly "lower" races (Darwin 1871, 326–327). During one of his wolf hunts, Krantz meets a beautiful woman, Christina, and her father, Wilfred. Quick to fall in love with this young woman, Krantz marries her in an unorthodox ceremony professing his promises to Nature, not God. Unbeknownst to Krantz, Christina is a she-wolf who later murders two of his children, Caesar and Marcella. When her true identity is discovered, Krantz kills her, resulting in a curse on his family.

Christina, the eponymous white she-wolf of the Hartz Mountains, clearly exhibits the unification of women and nature. Marryat's depiction of Christina is a hyperbolic response to Victorian society's fear of women as monstrous beings. Exhibited as flawlessly beautiful, radiantly angelic, and charming, Christina disguises her true form, infiltrates the private sphere, and following the role of the monster typical in the Gothic, attempts to destroy and devour the patriarchal family. This transgressive shapeshifting figuration of Christina presents Spinoza's monistic approach of the mind-body, thus her monstrosity is a distinct attribute of the substance, Nature. As this attribute, Christina is the visual embodiment of Nature's rage and rejection of patriarchal society.

Christina's monstrosity is a direct presentation of the mind-body alignment with nature. Signifying societal fears of female biological complexities, Christina's behavior and body are inscribed with sociosexual implications. Christina's monstrosity is an indeterminate hybrid form of responsive retaliation against subjectivity. Her transgressive body reflects what Grosz (1994, 60) describes as an inscription of "desire and signification," that conjoins and functions "at the anatomical, physiological, and neurological levels."

This perspective of bodily inscriptions is found within the concepts of psychoanalytic theory and the monism of the mind-body. Christina's mind-body, then, operates under the desires and *conatus* of Nature. Defined by Spinoza as the element of persistence, the *conatus* is a tendency of a being to continue and enhance its existence; it performs as the drive to all elements in Nature. Nature's essence, or *conatus*, is exhibited by Christina's monstrous form. This *conatus* is the basic fundamental drive, that appears when a being seeks to preserve itself. In this case, it appears through Christina's animality against gender restrictions and the social mistreatment of women. Nature, as a singular infinite substance, Spinoza argues, holds domain over all derivative modes. Since society, as a finite mode, is inferior to Nature, it cannot restrain other modes. Christina, similarly, operates under the affectations of the infinite Nature. Therein, her wolf-woman hybridity depicts both a return to nature and embodiment of societal rejection.

Whereas depictions of female monstrosity, as evaluated in theories of hysteria and criminality, are centered in society, the she-wolf is derived from Nature. Early-to-mid-Victorian perspectives, as seen through Winslow and Laycock's popular medical opinions, demonstrate a fear of women's inherent nature. Unlike other gothic narratives centered on "monstrous" women, Marryat's Christina is not seeking an escape from society, but to destroy it from within. The monstrous white wolf is not specifically a figure outside of, or separate from, nature but a fearful creation of it. The monster, in this sense, is an epitomical example of Nature's ability "to produce alien forms [from] within," as nature, in its multiple facets, is assumed to manufacture beings of "ontological uncertainty" (Shildrick 2002, 10). With this in mind, Marryat's she-wolf, a figuration of abhumanity, also functions as a reflection of corrupt humanity symbolizing both the neglect and abuse of Victorian women. Christina's transgressive shapeshifting results in the notion that she is never truly a woman or a wolf but is like a being whose corporeal body transgresses its limitations and reconfigures itself accordingly. Christina uses her morphic abilities to operate within both the natural and cultural realm, thereby subjecting her mind-body to the consistent movement both from and towards being. As an exhibition of Hurley's abhuman subject, Christina's state of moving away from herself and becoming something other, is a figuration of both instability and capability. As a figuration of monstrosity, the she-wolf is a construct of ambiguity and contradictions that signify the struggles of female power. Functioning as a visual and material site where mind-body connect, the white wolf becomes a distinct delineation of female rejection of Victorian cultural values and ideologies. Embodying these social contradictions and repressed rage of Victorian women, Marryat's gothic monster is constructed with an alluring countenance and eroticism to infiltrate society.

"The White Wolf of the Hartz Mountains," a gothic tale infused with monstrous elements, is responsible for establishing the Victorian female werewolf. Marryat's tale establishes a pattern and variations for nineteenth-century werewolf stories. Two innovative features about this tale are established from Christina's transformation and what Brian J. Frost (2003, 62) refers to as the "introduction of an erotic element," by presenting the wolf as a young and enchanting woman. This portrayal became an imitative trope of the she-wolf genre, which can be seen in Clemence Housman's (1896) popular *fin-de-siècle* tale, *The Were-Wolf*, an allegorical tale about White Fell, a beautiful woman/she-wolf who infiltrates the home of twin brothers. Following similar characteristics of Marryat's Christina, White Fell consumes a child and is later destroyed by the martyred twin, Christian. As a late-Victorian tale of female monstrosity, Housman's she-wolf reflects social anxieties of women's suffrage and the New Woman movement. This depiction of a beautiful and radiant woman, as a disguise for a malicious wolf spirit, not only offers an opportunity for familial infiltration but alludes to the inherent evil nature of deceptive femininity.

Fear of female carnality and inherent primitivity is demonstrated in hypersexuality of the she-wolf. This overt-sexualization is a common trope found in female werewolf fiction. As sexuality is often feared in early-to-mid-Victorian women, their sexuality is portrayed in gothic werewolves as dominating and aggressive. In the she-wolf, conventional traits of femininity and sexuality are exaggerated, becoming aberrant bestial configurations of monstrosity. Following this ideal, Marryat's Christina is the embodiment of sexuality, reproductivity, and rebellion in a monstrous female form. Bourgault du Coudray's (2002, 6) examination of Housman's she-wolf, for instance, emphasizes that for an outsider to infiltrate the domestic household, "physical beauty" must disguise their "corrupt femininity." Likewise, Christina's angelic and desirable beauty encapsulates Victorian anxieties about the dichotomous identities of women. Depicting Krantz as suspicious of, and hostile toward, "the sex," Marryat creates Christina as the physical embodiment of the Victorian "angel." Described as "young," around twenty years of age, Christina's features are notably "very beautiful" and appealing to the narrator and to Krantz ("White Wolf," 31). With "glossy and shining" blonde hair "bright as a mirror," Christina's appearance is reminiscent of Braddon's "Lucy" Audley ("White Wolf," 31). Similar to "Lucy," Christina also harbors an underlying mystery. Emblazoned with distinct femininity and exhibiting an accentuated attractiveness, Christina idealizes enigmatic exoticness and womanly charm. While enamored by her beauty, the narrator observes that she flaunts a "somewhat large" mouth and there is "something about her eyes" ("White Wolf," 31). Marryat references Christina's eyes throughout the narrative as an indication of her animalistic ferocity and danger.

Used to depict the dichotomy of women's nature, female werewolves are epitomized as both monstrous and intriguing. As affectations previously demonstrated by Kyle Bladow and Jennifer Ladino (2018), inform the psyche, the internal conflict results in the material expulsion of Victorian restrictions. The werewolf identity mirrors the rupture that results from trying to embody conflicting roles. For example, during Christina's aggressions, "her eyes would flash fire" demonstrating a vehement internal passion and ferocity ("White Wolf," 35). Although a depiction of Winslow's (1851, 41) standard of *"moral* [and] *physical fitness,"* Christina cannot shroud the restlessness and furtivity of her eyes, which makes the "children afraid" ("White Wolf," 31). As monstrous beings of hyperbolic corporeality and repressive Victorian ideals of neutered female sexuality, werewolves are exhibitory embodiments of hypersexuality, as presented in the subtlety of Christina's expressive eyes. The narrator remarks that despite her incredulous beauty, there is a "cruelty in her eye" ("White Wolf," 31). Therefore, Christina's depiction of enigmatic ferality is Marryat's response to Victorian fears of monstrous infiltration into familial lineage. For example, Priest (2015, 7) notes that by the time Marryat's feral Christina was introduced as "a seductive, homicidal and ultimately doomed female lycanthrope," the wolf became a signifier of cultural contradictions and difference. Simultaneously a wolf and a human woman, Christina is the embodiment of unrestrained nature, an infiltrator into the Victorian home. As an ideal figure of both beauty and lycanthropy, Christina, is the ideal embodiment of female corruption within the Victorian home. Supporting the argument that she-wolves are internally malignant, Marryat's Christina destroys the domestic sphere and Krantz's legacy. Playing to Krantz's desire for attractive women, Christina manipulates her way into their remote household.

The spirits of nature, embodied in a beautiful human female form, seduce Krantz and enact revenge from within his family home. During a period when women, albeit restricted by moral standards and domesticity, were suspected as dangerous, it was necessary for male protagonists to overcome the threat. While Christina is portrayed as a beauty who "performed all the household duties," she is still an outcast to the social structure ("White Wolf," 31). As outsiders, or Others, werewolves, Easley and Scott (2013, xiii) posit, are considered inherently "dangerous" women who prey "upon widowers and bachelors," who purposefully distract them "from their paternal and fraternal responsibilities" with their sexualities. Christina, as a monster in the Gothic, is not only unconsciously repulsive and desirable, a seductive figure that demands attention. Initially hesitant, and disdainful toward women, Krantz demonstrates "a great change," conquers his "aversion to the sex" and becomes increasingly "attentive" to Christina ("White Wolf," 31). With this newly placed trust, Krantz allows his second wife to take control of the domestic sphere. Creating the illusion that she is "kind to [the] children" and fulfills her role as mother and wife, Christina is deceptively monstrous ("White Wolf," 35). Krantz's daily hunting excursions expose Christina's double-life to the children. Left in charge of the household, she does not "show any kindness" and "often beats" the children ("White Wolf," 35). Described by Baring-Gould (1865, 92) as targets of the most savage of crimes, women and children are often the primary victims of werewolves, an acted listed as one of the monster's "most atrocious cruelties." As a figuration that rejects the Victorian temperament and, as Stickney Ellis (1839, 94) states, aligns the home with women's "affection" and "love," Christina inverts social expectations of Victorian femininity. Assuming the position, not the role, of Krantz's wife, she creates an uneasiness, and "unusual" feeling in the children ("White Wolf," 32). For example, when Christina approaches Krantz's daughter, and "caresse[s] her," little Marcella "burst into tears, and sobbed as if her heart would break" ("White Wolf," 33). An antithesis to such morality and domestication, as advertised by Ruskin, Stickney Ellis, and Winslow, Christina embodies the atrocities resulting in the "dreadful[ly] mangled" bodies of her stepchildren, Caesar and Marcella ("White Wolf," 38). Cleaving to the role of deadly outsider, Christina, instead of nurturing their childhood development, threatens their lives and consumes them. Rejecting the conventions of Victorian domesticity, Christina's behavior hints at her agency through an animalistic disposition and connection to Nature.

The EcoGothic and Christina

Marryat constructs Christina as a material-semiotic figure of environmental and female crisis. Nature, used in context with women and domination, Val Plumwood (1993, 4) suggests, "is to be defined as passive, as non-agent and non-subject," as a "resource empty of its own purposes or meanings" and a place to be shaped or molded. Depicted as an absence of information, the blankness of nature is constructed as a screen for crisis. Here, nature is not just a resource for Krantz's extraction, a place where he can take refuge for his crimes, nor a resource for his hunting, it is agentic and retaliates against intrusion. Presenting its agency through the "large, white she-wolf," Nature rejects the imposition of artificial domestic order in the sense that it is not blank but teeming with life and agency ("White Wolf," 40). According to Richard Dyer's (1997, 127) *White: Essays on Race and Culture*, he suggests that the "glowing" whiteness of women hyperbolized symbol of a moral "idealization." However, while Marryat's figuration of Christina exhibits a visualization of angelic purity, he inverts her behavior to demonstrate her very connection to nature through the manipulation of social constructs. Marryat constructs her as a figuration of virginesque purity and a blank slate, however,

Christina's façade is a performative gesture for assimilation into Krantz's domestic realm. The prominent illustration of whiteness demonstrates a mutability characteristic of the relationship between dominant culture and subordinate nature. White, as a blank canvas of unsullied purity, promotes the notion that nature can be shaped by culture. However, Christina, as the white she-wolf, eschews this imbalance of power and rejects the authority of society. Derived from nature, Christina's visage of whiteness from her dress "deeply bordered with white fur," a "cap of white ermine," "flaxen" hair, and "brilliant teeth" signifies her embodiment of crisis ("White Wolf," 31). A corrupted antithesis to the white model of the Virgin Mary, Christina's enclosure in "white clothing," then, acts as a "fall from whiteness," not a representation of it (Dyer 1997, 123). Presented as a cultured picturesque exhibition of Victorian femininity and virtue, Christina is truly the embodiment of nature who rejects the purity of traditional womanhood and challenges society.

Operating as a gothic amalgamation of the nonhuman, human, and environment, Christina portrays a notion that identifies the social apprehension to acknowledge and accept their association to what Davide Del Principe (2014, 1) refers to as "their nonhuman ancestry and the common, biological origins of life." As a figuration of nature and its *conatus*, Christina presents these characteristics through her predatory "nocturnal wanderings" and desire for outdoor activities ("White Wolf," 37). Under constant surveillance by all three Krantz children, Christina's mysterious outings result in suspicion. As observed by the narrator, on "many [nights], and always at about the same hour" Christina would "leave the cottage—and after she was gone, [they] invariably heard the growl of a wolf under our window, and always saw her, on her return, wash herself before she retired to bed" ("White Wolf," 35). Purposefully rejecting the role as the mother figure content to reside within the boundaries of the home, Christina escapes domestication into the natural sphere. Continuing this transgression of Victorian gender ideologies, Christina "seldom [sits] down to meals, and when she [does], she appear[s] to eat with dislike" ("White Wolf," 35). As a gothic figuration, Christina, then, reminds the reader that she is not only shaped by her ancestral roots and the interactive affectation of the environment. Dismissing the perpetuation of discursive domestic femininity, Marryat's figuration of Christina as a material-semiotic monstrosity allows her to own the language of nature and functions as a reminder of women's capabilities. The rejection of domestic fulfillment and subservience removes Christina from the confines of social constructs and promotes her agency as a being of nature. As a destructive admixture of woman-animal, she embodies the social crisis about dichotomous female identities.

Christina's feral animality mirrors early-to-mid-Victorian fears of female nature. The condemnation of such monstrous forms results from the abject reaction, or the fear of underlying female imperfection. Furthermore, Baring-Gould (1865, 93) suggests that the most virtuously refined individual can face violent episodes, and that innate "cruelty may remain latent" until enticed, at which time it will "break forth in a devouring flame." Demonstrating similar perspectives of Victorian systematic and institutional ideologies, the werewolves' innate appetite for destruction disregards class and gender. Created as figurations where meaning is lost and boundaries of nature-culture and mind-body are amalgamated, female monsters are viewed as abhorrent and destructive. In this assessment of the werewolf, it is suggested their motivations are driven by an impulse to feed, kill, or by an inherent love of destruction. With this assumption of their monstrous behavior, lycanthropic passions for violence and blood are synonymous to those of hate and love and the circumstances are enigmatic until provoked. As instinctual expressions, these passions of love, hate, and "bloodthirstiness," then, Baring-Gould (1865, 93–94) argues, "may lurk in the deeps of some heart" and "a word, glance, a touch" are sufficient enough to foment a reaction. Therefore, passions are repressed by any individual and exposition of lycanthropic violence is possible. Marryat's she-wolf is a disjointed embodiment of anxieties which has the potential for societal disturbance and corruption, therefore viewed as abject. Operating in a liminal space, Christina is visually enticing but, similar to Mrs. Lovett in James Malcolm Rymer's *The String of Pearls*, she produces sensations of revulsion in the children, thus presenting underlying abnormalities of Victorian women. Christina, as fully aligned with her natural self, is considered dangerous and must be destroyed to ensure the safety and success of society.

Christina, as a material-semiotic figure, reflects social fears of primitive devolution and the predatory nature of Victorian women. While later trends in werewolf literature portray women transitioning into animals, Marryat depicts Christina as a manifestation of nature who devours flesh in human form. Folklore dictates that because of their "innate savageness," wolves consume the innocent, such as children, which Marryat incorporates as a characteristic of Christina (Baring-Gould 1865, 172). Synonymous with Elliotson's predilections of rumored cannibalism and consumption of corpses, Christina's role as a she-wolf incorporates these tropes. Aligning with the Victorian concerns that pregnant women, or women with menstrual irregularities, long for "things out of season," Christina embodies the monstrous speculations of female reproductivity, as promoted by Laycock and Elliotson, through her cannibalistic behavior (Elliotson 1839, 937). However, Marryat inverts these werewolf characteristics while depicting Victorian anxieties about feral women. Unlike comparable werewolf texts by Housman, Reynolds, and MacDonald, when Christina violates Marcella's grave, she is discovered in human form. In this feral event, Christina's explicit wildness opposes her initial attack on Krantz's eldest son. Caesar's destruction is made implicit by Marryat through the fallible narration of Hermann, Krantz's middle child. In the night-time observations of his "mother-in-law," Caesar's curiosity drives the pursuit, however, it results in Christina covered in blood with a "gun-shot wound" ("White Wolf," 36). Operating in secrecy, she "threw the garments she had worn into the fire" and bandaged her leg ("White Wolf," 36). Unbeknownst to the Krantz family, Christina destroys the suspecting Caesar and attributes his death to a "wolf" ("White Wolf," 37). Christina's explicit destruction of Marcella's grave, however, exhibits her distorted femininity. Dressed in a "white night-dress" with the full moon shining on her, Christina digs at the grave and "throw[s] away the stones . . . with all the ferocity of a wild beast" ("White Wolf," 39). Once again, shrouded in the mutability of whiteness, Christina eschews social boundaries and acts as a monstrous expression for Nature. Her display of wild animality, while operating under the full moon, parallels Victorian medical discourse of the female menstrual cycle and madness. This transformation of the feminized she-wolf under the exposure to the full moon is a direct parallel to the cycles of menstruation perpetuated in Victorian discourses. Demonstrating similar characteristics as Bertha Mason and Agatha Jeffreys, Christina's wildness mirrors the full moon exhibition of gothic madwomen and biological instability.

An image of feral primitivity and masculine strength, Christina epitomizes the biological degeneration of Victorian women. Demonstrating werewolf characteristics of basking (unchanged) in the moonlight while "tearing off large pieces" of Marcella's flesh and "devouring them," Christina assumes a human form but maintains the "avidity of a wolf" ("White Wolf," 39–40). In this moment, Christina's femininity, coupled with the ferocity of a beast, alludes to early Victorian's pseudo-medical perspectives of menstruating, or pregnant, women. It is only when Krantz kills Christina that she assumes her true form of a "large, white she-wolf" ("White Wolf," 40). This cannibalistic act and transformation from woman to wolf, speaks to the gender politics of the time and the corrupt nature of women. While it is too early in the Victorian period for the arrival of the New Woman, Marryat's Christina is the antecedent that encapsulates similar characteristics of later tales. For example, Easley and Scott (2013, xiii) argue that in later werewolf texts, independent shapeshifting women demonstrate "masculine" characteristics of intellect and strength, therefore they "must be vanquished to restore social stability." Indeed, this destruction of feral women and their perpetuation of instability and violence is addressed in Christina's death. With the discovery of Christina's animalistic behavior, Krantz in his "concentrated rage . . . levelled his piece" and shot the "wretch who he fostered in his bosom" ("White Wolf," 40). Marryat's destruction of the she-wolf by the patriarchal male responds to cultural concerns about female corruption in the Victorian family.

Christina, in her position as mother, destroys Krantz's lineage and transforms from woman to wolf upon death, thereby joining popular Victorian discourses that demonstrate pernicious female influences on society. Marryat ends this narrative of feral womanhood with Krantz striking "the head of the dead animal with the heel of his boot" ("White Wolf," 40). By obliterating his literary monstrous woman, Marryat attempts to alleviate readers' anxieties of invasive female sexuality in the traditional home. Following this pattern of destruction of female deviance and monstrosity, the following narrative demonstrates the rejection of women's acceptance of Nature.

LAYING WITH WOLVES: DESIRE AND DEGENERATION IN *WAGNER, THE WEHR-WOLF* (1846–1847)

First serialized as a penny blood from 1846–1847, George William MacArthur Reynolds's *Wagner, the Wehr-Wolf* was published in *Reynolds' Magazine of Romance, General Literature, Science and Art*.[9] As expected from its genre, Reynolds's *Wagner* echoes notable literary sources, including other pennys narratives. Reflecting the title of James Malcolm Rymer's *Varney, the Vampire* (1845–1847), Reynolds's *Wagner, the Wehr-Wolf* approaches gothic monstrosities using lycanthropic transformations. As a popular author of nineteenth-century urban mysteries (a genre with sensational attributes), Reynolds incorporates images of intelligent women with malicious intents, as anti-heroines. For example, in this novel, his figuration of the anti-heroine, Nisida of Riverola, is an embodiment of malicious intent and violence informed by an intimate relationship with a werewolf. Reynolds's novel of lycanthropy, Joseph Crawford (2020, 107) notes, provides "the blueprint" for future English werewolf literature. In all preceding tales, the werewolf demonstrated variability in transformations, presenting both voluntary and involuntary figures with differences in their transgressive cycles. However, *Wagner, the Wehr-Wolf* was responsible for introducing the trope of the uncontrollable, emergent lycanthropic transformation that occurs "each month at the full moon" (Crawford 2020, 107). Previously, reference to the full moon connected the bestial curse to degenerative psychological affectation, which was theorized as a provocation for madness. As demonstrated in the interpretations of Marryat's Christina, Brontë's Bertha Mason, and Urban's Agatha Jeffreys, the full moon in Reynolds's narrative also results in affectations of animalistic tendencies. While Reynolds's figuration of the monstrous Nisida of Riverola exhibits similar tendencies, her monstrosity is truly informed by nature and an explicit intimate alliance with a werewolf.

Wagner is set in the early sixteenth century. It begins in the Black Forest of Germany with Wagner and Faust, and concludes in Florence, Italy with the death of Wagner and Nisida. The narrative introduces the reader to Fernand Wagner, a ninety-year-old shepherd who is abandoned by his beloved granddaughter, and caretaker. Derived from the Faustian legend, Wagner succumbs to loneliness and agrees to a pact with the Devil.[10] For a year of servitude, Wagner is promised wealth, eternal youth and rejuvenation, and increased intelligence. Under this pact, Wagner must also transform into a werewolf once a month at the full moon. Agreeing to this contract, Wagner eventually travels to Florence and meets Nisida, the maliciously deceptive daughter of a noble family. After developing an intimate relationship with Nisida, Wagner, unaware of her true nature, is imprisoned for a murder that Nisida commits. In the meantime, Nisida is abducted by brigands and shipwrecked on an uninhabited island. Once Wagner escapes from prison, he locates and joins Nisida in their new "habitat" (*Wagner*, 132). As habitat is defined as an environment for the occupation of animals or plants, Reynolds's use of the term hints at Nisida's process of becoming-animal while detached from restrictive societal spaces. The couple spends an undisclosed amount of time in the natural realm, indulging in their unrestrictive passions. Eventually, when influenced by the Devil, they return to society. Unable to assimilate and thrive in civilization, both Wagner and Nisida die.

In Reynolds's tale, Wagner is the werewolf but Nisida, the reticent lady, is the true monster. While she does not transition into an animal, Nisida does align with Nature and takes on bestial characteristics. As a liminal figure, Nisida is trapped between the responsibilities to her noble family and a desire to return to nature. Maliciously navigating through society by way of murder and deceit, Nisida maintains an appropriate façade of social femininity. When relocated to the "natural" realm with Wagner, Nisida indulges in her inhibitions and becomes a physical and psychical embodiment of Nature. This is presented in her actions such as living off the land, removal of clothing and redressing in flowers, and sexual engagement with a wehr-wolf. Living without restrictions imposed by social boundaries, Nisida returns to a natural state. Viewed as favorable by her father and granted an authoritative position, "there was consequently no spy upon Nisida's actions" (*Wagner*, 13). Upon her father's death, Nisida would "bec[o]me possessed of the estates" and would "enjoy . . . the title of 'Countess,'" while her brother Francisco would los[e] that of 'Count'" (*Wagner*, 13). Owing to these familial obligations Nisida is forced to return to the confines of society, thereby causing her destruction. Behaviorally debased, Nisida murders, lies, and corrupts her lineage. Unknowingly aligned with the wehr-wolf, Nisida marries Wagner and becomes impregnated, thus prohibiting her re-admission to the cultural/social sphere. Thus, Nisida's rejection of both nature and society results in her isolation in a non-operative liminal state facing extinction.

In this narrative, there is a distinct overlap between criminal women and enigmatic violence. While Nisida of Riverola is reminiscent of such criminal women as Linda Mowbray or Mrs. Lovett in chapter 3, she finds a place in this chapter because of her direct affiliation to Nature. The recidivistic women, as discussed previously, use affectations and mimicry to appropriate behaviors and identities. Whereas Nisida demonstrates similarities through deceptions and homicide, she is inherently monstrous because of her atavistic desires. Although not a she-wolf herself, she accepts her innate connection to Nature, rejects society, and becomes impregnated by a male wehr-wolf. Unable to reorient into civilized society, under the Victorian prescription of conventional women, Nisida is eradicated.

Affected by the ideals of high society, Nisida appropriates the conventional behavior of upper-class femininity and exhibits an attractive guise. Her initial inability to access nature and instincts result from a repression or redirection of "the libidinal impulses," created by societal repression (Grosz 1994, 32). Nisida's ego, unimpaired by Nature's affectations, configures to social expectations of femininity. The ego, then, functions as a site of confluence for the mind and the body, and, in the case of Nisida, operates under the influence of nobility and feminine conduct. When the reader is introduced to Nisida, Reynolds offers intricate details emphasizing her physical presentation, demeanor, and lifestyle. Located in a "magnificently-furnished chamber," in "one of the largest mansions of Florence," Nisida is presented as a captivating fixture within the residence (*Wagner*, 7). Identified as twenty-five years of age, Nisida is a statuesque figure, described as "tall, graceful, and elegant," of which Reynolds compares her "fine proportion[s]" with those of the Sylph and Hebe (*Wagner*, 7).[11] With these correlations to mythological beings, Reynolds offers his own perspective on the Victorian angel with considerable variances.

Nisida is a spectacle of both Victorian femininity and malicious deceit. Although illustrated under the visual guise of mythological spirituality and grace, Nisida is figured as an embodiment of the dichotomies of both angel and devil. Indeed, her role of enigmatic malefactor is suggested by her features. Portrayed as "eminently beautiful" and, albeit a bit disheveled, Nisida "dazzle[s]" with the "whiteness" of her skin contrasted by "long, black, glossy hair" (*Wagner*, 7). While Reynolds emphasizes how his anti-heroine is aesthetically pleasing to both the reader and surrounding characters, his descriptions align with Lombroso and Ferrero's later description of occasional female offenders. These particular appearances conceal any behavioral deviance and deter suspicion "when the hair is black and plentiful . . . and the eyes are bright, a not unpleasing appearance is presented" (Lombroso and Ferrero 1895, 97). Echoing Nisida's appearance, this rhetoric of criminology suggests that, albeit pleasing, the beauty of the criminal shrouds the underlying sexual instinct and misleads observers to ignore the overt passions, allowing for social deception. As previously ascertained in chapter 3, it was scientifically believed that physically unblemished criminals possess the attributes to assimilate and navigate, unsuspected, through society. Reynolds displays Nisida as a projection of elegant beauty and intertwines her desire for sexual freedom and independence with a forced demeanor of complacency. As reflective of Grosz's perspective, Nisida's sexuality cannot be contained, hence it transgresses restrictive boundaries to express her desires. Therefore sexuality, as a desire for instinctual expression, refuses confinement and permeates through the mind-body. As a drive, derived from Nature's *conatus*, Nisida's sexuality infests all parts of the individual and makes its presence known. Reynolds's construction of Nisida as the anti-heroine responds to fears of female sexual ambiguity and treachery. A behavioral antithesis to the Victorian angel of the house, Nisida's pleasing countenance is "expressive of intellectuality and strong passions" (*Wagner*, 7). Presenting "large black eyes" that are "full of fire," Nisida's glance is suggested to "penetrate the soul" (*Wagner*, 7). Whereas Reynolds previously aligned her to mythological beings of serenity and innocence, Nisida's countenance, like Marryat's Christina, suggests concealment of destructive monstrosity.

In Cohen's (1996, 13) seven theses of monstrosity, he asserts that each monster's origin is compiled of "a double narrative." As an amalgamation, or hybrid, of discourses, beliefs, and prejudices, the monstrous form provides testimony of its origin and its cultural use. In the case of women, female monstrosity is driven by the restrictive discourses on sexuality. The figuration of the monster, then, is an embodiment of repressed sexual desires that must remain concealed while also performing as a warning of cultural regulation (Cohen 1996). Nisida of Riverola is the definitive Victorian monstrosity. One story provides the *origin* of her monstrous becoming, and the other describes the *reason* for her monstrosity. Whereas Wagner is the visual monster in Reynolds's tale, it is Nisida who is the cultural monstrosity, to which Cohen refers. Represented as a dark angel, Nisida harbors two secrets relevant to her transgressive ontologies. Referred to as "the deaf and dumb daughter" of the House Riverola, Nisida displays an affliction which results in the social treatment of fragility (*Wagner*, 7). Intentionally assuming these characteristics, Nisida exaggerates the idiosyncratic expectations of Victorian docility and repression. At the age of fifteen she witnessed the mysterious death of her mother, and Nisida's formerly outspoken attitude transitioned into watchful silence. Unbeknownst to the reader at this time, Nisida's affliction is a voluntary act that allows her to obtain information from her surroundings. Sharing similarities with Christina's response to Krantz's uxoricide, Nisida utilizes the death of her mother to respond against the violence perpetuated on women by men. As the only individual familiar with the cause of her mother's death, she uses her silence as a manipulative technique for revenge.

Nisida is the stereotypical embodiment of sin concealed by refinement and beauty. In Barbara Creed's (1993, 42) *The Monstrous-Feminine Film, Feminism, Psychoanalysis*, she suggests that the concept of abjection, or sin, resides deep within and acts to "position women as deceptively treacherous." Like Reynolds's Nisida, the monster may appear superficially virtuous and beautiful but harbors villainous intent. It is this stereotypical representation of wicked femininity that proliferates through popular discourses that targets women as dominated by nature. Abiding by this stereotype, Reynolds creates Nisida as the monstrosity, while aligning his werewolf, Wagner, with the desire for family and personal absolution. Prior to Wagner's primitive influence, Nisida embodied hidden passions and sinful intent. However, it is through his relationship with Nisida, that she openly embraces her natural self and rejects social confines to become the depiction of female monstrosity.

A monster divided between institutional and instinctual impulses, the lycanthropic outsider poses a threat to the social order. The werewolf is an affective figure of ambivalence and controversy. In Reynolds's novel, he uses the werewolf as a plot device to motivate and impair the anti-heroine. A construction of veiled implications and impulsivity, the werewolf is an informative figure compiled of taboo characteristics. Authors in the Victorian period use the monstrously primitive figure to symbolize sexual instincts and desires of feral animality. Translating carnal passions and "forbidden desires" into aggressive monstrosity, the werewolf's brutality is equated to a "self-indulgent form of sexual gratification" (Frost 2003, xi). Through its societal incursion, the werewolf's hybridity allows it to communicate with the natural environs while inhabiting the social domain. Therefore, the lycanthropic figure's enigmatic and duplicitous composition is used in Reynolds's narrative to affect and influence susceptible individuals through the adaptation of Nature's *conatus*.

Transformations: Nisida's Re-alignment into Nature

Reynolds uses the werewolf Wagner to influence Nisida's monstrosity. As a mode of Nature, Wagner's bestial connection enigmatically affects Nisida, influencing her return to the natural self. Operating as the essence of Nature, Wagner is used to inform Nisida's *conatus* and awaken her instincts. The essence and *conatus*, as per Beth Lord's (2010) interpretation, function as a method of ensuring the perseverance of its being. As determined by the essence, instincts act to ensure the survivability and promote the ability to thrive. These experiences, then, as Grosz (1994, 95) points out, "can only be understood between mind and body" through the conjunction of other mind-bodies. As an embodiment of Nature's essence, Nisida is easily influenced by the primitivity of Wagner's essence. Unbeknownst to Nisida, Wagner is a dichotomous figure of civilized humanity and bestial savagery. It is by his primitive side that Nisida is affected. When first introduced to Nisida, she becomes "ardent and impassioned" and exclaims that "she experiences the kindling of all the fierce passions and sensuality in her breast" (*Wagner*, 21). As a werewolf, Wagner is a hypersexualized being whose carnality emanates through affectation, therefore inducing Nisida's desire for a return to Nature. An immediate affectation from Wagner influences Nisida and causes her to claim a "passion capable of every extreme" (*Wagner*, 24). The linkage between Nisida and Wagner as modes are established and affectations of social confines are eradicated. In her rejection of social conventions, Nisida's mind-body aligns with Nature.

As a place "where" and "how" events occur, the natural world is a prominent feature for gothic settings. Nature, in *Wagner, the Wehr-Wolf*, not only operates as a realm for escape but blurs the distinctions and destroys the dualism of Nisida's identity. As both a singular substance and space, Nature, as an undomesticated space, is used for female expression and reclamation of the true self. Nature allows for Nisida's rejection of social artificiality. Therefore, Nisida's full return to Nature occurs when shipwrecked on the Mediterranean island. It is only through her full integration into nature that Nisida can identify and reclaim her agency. This submersion in the natural world functions to make humans better than if they were in city spaces. On the island Nisida casts off the constriction of social boundaries and demonstrates instinctual inhibition. Acclimating to her new environment, she observes that there are "no signs of the presence of man" and that "Nature appear[s] to be the undisputed Empress of the land" (*Wagner*, 65). The environment, according to Lisa Kröger (2013, 18), "acts as a kind of conduit of emotions, a way to experience feelings and sometimes to purge them." Unified with Nature, Nisida rejects social restrictions and transforms her mind-body to reflect the emotions of the surrounding environs. Designating herself, "Queen of the Mediterranean isle," Nisida is temporally healed in the natural realm (*Wagner*, 107). No longer depicted as a Greek goddess surrounded by material extravagance, Reynolds now portrays Nisida as a mythological creature of Nature. His presentation of Nisida as a "mermaid" while she "disport[s] in the water" and "wander[s]" the shore "like a naiad," demonstrates a fantastical, yet appropriate perspective of her character (*Wagner*, 107). While encapsulated within societal boundaries, Nisida shrouds herself in dark elegance and silence. Now, free of restrictions, nature, as an antithetical space to society, allows for her exhibition of instincts. Echoing the wildness of Catherine Earnshaw as a "wicked little soul," Nisida in her new habitat, evokes the freedoms of nature (*Wuthering Heights*, 346).

Nisida's full immersion into nature results in her rejection from social re-assimilation. Traditionally assumed as beings from nature, women are restricted as proxies for behavioral and instinctual regulation. Positioned as intermediaries between the untamed sphere of nature and the structure of culture, women function to distance nature from the civilization of men. Responsible for moderating their sexual inhibitions, Victorian women are contained within the domestic boundaries of the home. Furthermore, women's primitivity was believed as not only the ability to transgress but blur the boundaries between human and nonhuman nature. These beliefs, or superstitions for monstrous women, as Bourgault du Coudray (2006, 2) states, originate in "an atavistic craving" for flesh or destruction is also created from "new mythological patterns brought about by mistaken word associations." Systematically portraying women as monstrous, nineteenth-century discourses transformed beliefs of women as witches who metamorphosed into she-wolves or as beings who "devoured their victims" (Baring-Gould 1865, 9, 54). While in these roles, monstrous women possess the potential for social and familial destruction. This transgression of the culture-nature boundary provides an infiltration of the household, which suggests that hereditary corruption is possible. It is through this fear of "savage" admixture into the Victorian family that Nisida becomes the quintessential monstrous woman.

The early-to-mid-Victorian fear of devolution and degenerative lineage results in ideas of female monstrosity. In patriarchal discourses, women are affiliated with the "abject face of nature" because of their reproductive roles as "mother[s] of the human species" (Creed 2015, 183). Monstrous women are created from the threat of female reproductivity and destruction of social stability. Likewise, women's access to male bodies and species' proliferation suggested the notion that there is a threat of potential human retrograde. Throughout Reynolds's narrative, Nisida shrouds evil behavior behind her agreeable disposition and attractive countenance. Unbeknownst to her relatives, Nisida is responsible for the harassment and death of Wagner's granddaughter and the imprisonment of Flora, her brother's betrothed. Whereas these concealed actions suggest Nisida's deviance it is actually her marriage to, and impregnation by, Wagner that labels her as a monstrous woman. Shortly after the marriage, Nisida announces that she "shall soon become a mother" (*Wagner*, 94). As women are harbingers of the human species, they are responsible for gestation and procreative development. Also considered unstable and susceptible to external influences, women have the potential to corrupt the patriarchal lineage. While women's primary objective is, arguably, the perpetuation of humankind, it is the duty of men "to regulate and rule over" the practice (Creed 2015, 183). Since Nisida rejects the regulations of traditional domesticity and marriage, her reproductive function is susceptible to Nature's involvement. "Espous[ing]" Wagner "with solemn vows plighted in the face of heaven," Nisida perverts the Victorian marital structure with her union to a werewolf (*Wagner*, 94). Thoroughly unified with Nature and responsible for introducing "uncivilized" relations into her noble lineage, Nisida is restricted from re-entering society.

Reynolds ends his narrative with Nisida and Wagner's rejection of civilized society. Nisida's declaration of pregnancy and Wagner's exposure as a primitive beast result in their destruction. Since women, as Darwin (1871, 372) postulates, "certainly transmit most of their characters . . . to their offspring of both sexes," it is assumed that any children of Nisida and the werewolf, Wagner, would be "modif[ied] in the same manner." Derived from the contaminated Nisida, there is potential to produce animalistic characteristics or deviant behavior. Victorian beliefs of natural selection and evolutionary theory not only reinforce the progression of the species, but suggest the possibility of degeneration, which perpetuates the belief that human evolution has the capacity for devolution. With this concept in mind, Reynolds's depiction of Nisida's pregnancy creates a discourse which exaggerates the potential for women's corruptive biological functions. As a perversion of traditional pregnancy and parentage, Nisida's figuration is an exaggeration reflective of women's capability for societal corruption. Antagonistic to traditional Victorian ideologies and procreation, Nisida is denied (re)access to her social position. Similar to Marryat's Christina, Nisida must be sacrificed to ensure social stability. Whereas Christina is a monstrosity seeking to purposefully destroy the Victorian family, Nisida unintentionally corrupts her ancestry.

Trapped within a liminal space, unable to access society or nature, Nisida is unfit to live. At the end of the narrative, Wagner discovers Nisida's deceptions and revokes his lycanthropic abilities. Presenting a "frightful change" in front of Nisida, Wagner transforms into a dying "old, old man, whose years are verging fast towards a century" (*Wagner*, 140). Succumbing to shock, Nisida, illustrates a "ghostly pallor" that "overspread her entire countenance" and issues "painful gaspings" and violent palpitations (*Wagner*, 140). Nisida claims that her observation of Wagner's "superhuman beauty which had changed to such revolting ugliness,—it was all this that had struck her down—paralysed her—inflicted a mortal, though not an instantaneous blow" (*Wagner*, 140). The acknowledgment of Wagner's true identity results in Nisida's death. In the conclusion of their relationship, Reynolds portrays Fernand Wagner and Nisida of Riverola laying "side by side . . . stiff, motionless, cold" (*Wagner*, 152). As a figuration driven by instincts and drawn to nature, Nisida is a semiotic response to the security of families and society. Reynolds implies that women, albeit figures of beauty and perfection, even Victorian "angels" possess the ability to destroy society through their reproductive functions. Reynolds uses Nisida's death to inform readers of the transgressive identities of women and the potential for corruption, while providing a lesson in morality and warning of the rejection of social obligations. In Nisida's demise, Reynolds closes down the possibilities present in the figuration of her wildness. The same closure is not so certain in the following and final story, where the potential and space for rebellion remains open.

ACCEPTANCE OF THE NATURAL SELF IN "THE GRAY WOLF" (1871)

George MacDonald's story focuses on the torment, and transgressive ontologies, of a liminal character. Trapped between nature and the desire for human/social interaction, the young woman struggles with her hybridity. In this story, the immaterial-material connection reflects in uncontrollable bodily transformations from human to wolf. MacDonald constructs the nameless she-wolf as a material-semiotic response to Victorian anxieties about female devolution and compliance with natural instincts. Published in 1871, the short story is part of MacDonald's ten-volume collection, *Works of Fancy and Imagination*. Predominantly an author of fantasy stories and children's literature, MacDonald combines the characteristics of fairy tales and the Gothic in "The Gray Wolf." Similar to Marryat's "The White Wolf," MacDonald's tale presents a Darwinian primitivity and carnality of Victorian women through a destructive and hypersexualized she-wolf. Published during the same time as Darwin's *Descent of Man*, MacDonald's tale of a she-wolf emphasizes explicit, uncontrolled feral characteristics, while Marryat and Reynolds's monstrous women focuses on social corruptors. Deviating from the other two texts in this chapter, MacDonald's story, appearing closer to the *fin-de-siècle* period, situates the young woman as primitive, uncivilized, and controlled by animalistic and degenerative functions. Interjecting the student as a representative of English society, the author demonstrates the conflict of influential affectations in the material form of the she-wolf. This transmogrification of the young woman's corporeal form from human into wolf exhibits how she is a material-semiotic representation of Victorian tensions. Juxtaposing the binary identities of women, as both angel and monster, MacDonald's alignment of the young woman with Nature presents her as the mid-Victorian exhibition of female degeneration.

The short story introduces the reader to an English student lost in the Shetland Islands. Separated from his friends, he finds temporary shelter in a cave during a tumultuous storm. Discovered by a young woman, the student is offered refuge at her family cottage. Upon arrival at the home, the student is introduced to the young woman's mother who provides him with food and a bed for the night. During his stay, he observes the young woman and develops a fascination with her. One night, while asleep, the student awakens to pain and discovers a creature whose claw is embedded in his shoulder and mouth closing in on his throat. The student grabs the wolf by its throat and forces it to retreat from the house. In the morning, the mother advises him to leave, and in return, the young woman transforms into a wolf and attacks her. Witnessing her transformation from woman to wolf, the student escapes and the tale ends with a mournful howl of the abandoned wolf.

MacDonald creates a setting familiar to past werewolf tales intertwined with folkloric characteristics. Gaelic folklore and traditional stories from the region claim that the Shetland Islands are home to the wulver. A mythical being that resides off the coast of the mainland, the wulver depicts a hybrid human-wolf. Jessie Saxby (1932), a folklorist from the region, claims that the wulver is a descendant from fairies who resides in peaceful isolation until otherwise disturbed. Unlike the traditional werewolf, the wulver is not a shapeshifter but a permanent hybrid beast. Presented as "a creature like a man with a wolf's head," the wulver lives in a "cave dug out of the side of a steep knowle, half-way up a hill" (Saxby 1932, 141). MacDonald, who resided in Aberdeenshire, was arguably familiar with the traditional lore of Scotland, therefore used the region to construct his own rendition of the wulver, its behavior, and habitation. The short story introduces the reader to an English student, lost in the Shetland Islands of Scotland. Separated from his friends, the young man finds himself in a sudden onset of "a storm of wind and hail" ("Gray Wolf," 114). As the storm becomes increasingly violent, the student takes shelter in a cave, halfway down the cliff, with "the bones of many small animals scattered about" ("Gray Wolf," 114). With direct correlation to Saxby's reference of the wulver's dwelling, MacDonald replicates this environment to create apprehension in the reader. Residing in the cave during a treacherous storm, the young student adds to this uneasiness by claiming to hear a "stealthy and light" footfall, "as that of a wild beast" ("Gray Wolf," 114). To both the student's surprise, and arguably that of the reader, a young woman appears at the cave entrance. MacDonald, therefore, inverts the traditional Scottish wulver from a male figure to that of a startled woman.

MacDonald's wulver is re-created as a she-wolf to represent concerns of Victorian uncertainty about female nature. The figuration of a *monster* is a typically pattern, or code, that unsettles the cultural moment. The monster, then, as Cohen (1996, ix) notes, is an unsettling "presence or absence" that is created as an illusion "to be received as natural, human." The early-to-mid-Victorian perception of sexualized women indeterminately positioned them between humanity and animality. With the introduction of sciences relevant to nature and biological functionality, women were viewed as destructively monstrous. Evolutionary theory and societal fears of devolution allowed MacDonald to create a wulver variant that incorporates Victorian ideas about potential female "savagery." The body of this particular monster, then, is a representation of cultural fears, created a symbolic juxtaposition of specific anxieties, where its form embodies terror, fear, speculation, and impulses. Since the Scottish wulver originated during the time of Norway's annexation of the Shetland Islands, it symbolizes the particular cultural anxieties of the ninth century. MacDonald's she-wolf, on the other hand, is indicative of the early-to-mid-Victorian fear of the dichotomous nature of women, angelic yet feral. As a fully assimilated character, MacDonald's young woman operates under the unified substance of Nature depicting both woman-wolf psychosomatic exhibitions. Utilizing her abhumanity as a transgressive method, the young woman shifts between society and woman, and nature and wolf. Mired in the contexts of repression and reductionism, the young woman, albeit connected to nature, is affected by social influence and struggles with her abhumanity.

Nature and the Monster: Material Transformations

The corporeality of the young woman is determined by environmental influences. Corporeal forms, as materialities, reject containment and structure, yet are affected by external sources. As discussed previously, the material form and immaterial mind are established as modes under Nature. Through this extension from a singular source, modes maintain the ability for communicative affectation. Furthermore, extraneous events leave traces on bodies, therefore the beliefs of these influences "affect and leave images" in the mind and impressions on the body (Lord 2010, 69). The essence of the body is displayed through affectations of other bodies-minds. The consciousness of the self, and the body is a dynamic map that outlines what was experienced in the world and what has impacted it. Therein the consciousness is not self-aware but is a repository of ideas about what happens to the immaterial-material figuration. Arguably, the young woman's mind-body is impacted by both Nature and the appearance of the student (as a representation of English society). Affected by an inherent desire for primitive expression and an expectation to remain socially amicable, the young woman becomes a conflux of corporeal instability. In an indeterminate state, the mind-body is an unrestricted source of symbolism and ideas. As an open-ended figuration the body is composed of significations, which allow the form to be inscribed upon and subjected to re-inscription. In the case of MacDonald's young woman, environmental and social affectations leave imprints in her consciousness, resulting in an interchangeable corporeal form.

Conflicting affectations create ambiguity and abhumanity in the young woman, causing a monstrous (re)presentation. Following Hurley's ideation, the young woman, while sharing similarities to Marryat's Christina, struggles with her transformations, marking her as a truly abhuman. Whereas Christina controls her abilities to shapeshift, MacDonald's young woman is perpetuated in a cycle of becoming and is "continually in danger of becoming not itself, becoming other" (Hurley 1996, 3). Although Marryat's she-wolf is a figuration of abhumanity, she consciously enters the phases of becoming, the young woman, on the other hand is characteristically more abhuman in her instability. Gothic monsters, as reflections of upsetting vulnerabilities, are duplicitous as they are both human and nonhuman, good and evil, mind and body. Primarily liminal figures, these monsters refuse stability and blur the boundaries resulting in transformations and transgressions. An embodiment of indeterminism who rejects normative identities, the young woman, as a figuration of monstrosity, transgresses the borders between woman and wolf. MacDonald, then, uses both micro-transgressions and full corporeal transformations to illustrate the young woman's inability to assimilate.

Throughout the narrative, the young woman demonstrates an inefficiency to fully function in either role. While she is a visual representation of monstrosity, her behavior suggests contrition. Her temperament coincides with a misalignment of neither fully human, nor fully animal. While under observation by the student, the young woman throws herself on a bench "in an unusual posture" and fixes him with a "craving" look ("Gray Wolf," 115). Although in a human form, she depicts feral characteristics that suggest an inability to control her transformations. As she takes a small drink from the bowl, the student notices that the young woman only tastes the beverage. Under the impression that the "drink must have been drugged," he observes visible changes in the young woman's appearance: her hair "smoothed itself back" while her forehead simultaneously drew backwards away from her other facial features ("Gray Wolf," 117). Projecting the lower part of her face towards the bowl, the student notes that "her dazzling teeth" become strangely prominent ("Gray Wolf," 117). In her semi-transformative state, the young woman visibly displays her abhumanity. The movement away from her human form moves her closer to the state of lycanthropy. The partial wolf-human metamorphosis identifies the young woman as distinctly Other. No longer identified by the student as a human being, the young woman becomes a visible embodiment of "the slavery to instinctual drives" (Bourgault du Coudray 2006, 49). These physical anomalies, or stigmatic markings of the lycanthropic incarnation of human features, exposes the repression of female rage and instincts. Reminiscent of nineteenth-century criminal phrenology, the female visage of "deep-seated physical anomalies" advertises animalistic characteristics (Lombroso and Ferrero 1895, xvi). As an embodiment of instability and potential female deviations, MacDonald's display of feral animalism suggests such degeneration.

MacDonald's monstrous young woman is a material-semiotic configuration of Victorian gender conflict. Therefore, the werewolf, or more particularly the she-wolf in Victorian literature, "became a useful device for expressing anxieties about the animal within" and a figurative exhibition of escape for repressed women (Easley and Scott 2013, xi). Depicted as a fictional representation of human atavism and devolution, the werewolf symbolizes fears about female sexuality and a return to primitivity. MacDonald constructs his literary monster as an uncontrollable transgressional damsel in distress without definitive agency. Throughout the short story, the she-wolf is referred to as a young woman, deficient in an identifiable family name. Although both her mother and the English student lack familial labels, they are granted agency through their roles and behaviors. Whereas the mother is the domestic hostess, offering hospitality and acting as guardian, the male student is a representative of cultured English society. The young woman, on the other hand, lacks a singular agency and a distinct identity. Fragmented between human and animal transitions, the young woman's mind-body demonstrates an inability to accept a singular role. Trapped in a perpetual state of abhumanity, MacDonald's woman-wolf hybrid reflects the social fear of female atavism and psychosomatic instability in early-to-mid Victorian women.

An image of feral beauty, the young woman represents nineteenth-century perspectives of women's nature. Following the tropes of werewolf stories, the young woman faces isolation in a savage environment. As a being different from the social norm, the monstrous Other must be evicted from and isolated outside the borders of society. Purposefully separated from culture, MacDonald demonstrates how acceptance of natural instincts result in banishment from society. The young woman exudes animalistic traits and epitomizes the fear of women's biological devolution into uncontrollable beings. As a monstrous hybrid capable of transgressing social boundaries, she transforms into a hypersexual and violent monster that exposes the "beast within" (Creed 2006, 6). Primarily in her human form, the young woman evokes a bestial presence replete with primitivity and inherent sexuality. Appearing to the student as "barefooted" with a bewitching smile that reveals "the whitest of teeth," the young woman shares similarities to Marryat's Christina ("Gray Wolf," 115). Both women are unnaturally enchanting but possess feral attributes. The student, after getting a "glimpse of her blue eyes," becomes bewitched and is unable to avert his gaze ("Gray Wolf," 115). Noticing his fascination, the young woman deliberately avoids his stare, however, when he does catch her glance, "his soul shatter[s] within him" ("Gray Wolf," 115). Entranced by the young woman's "lovely face and craving eyes," the student alternates between "fascination and repulsion," again, mirroring similarities to Mrs. Lovett ("Gray Wolf," 116). On the journey back to the cottage, the student correlates all of the young woman's characteristics to a state of undomesticated animality. He notes that she moves over the "sharp stones" in a "catlike" manner, her clothing is "scanty and torn," and her hair is unkempt and blows "untangled in the wind" ("Gray Wolf," 115). The young woman's sparse clothing, animal appeal, and disheveled hair suggests both primitivity and savage sexuality. The young woman's unkempt appearance and feral movement hints at an external representation of embodied affectations. In adherence to primitive depictions, the young woman's unification with nature offers solace and protection.

EcoGothic and MacDonald's Young Woman

The natural realm operates as a space for monstrous expression but also protection for non-conforming women. The hybrid state itself operates as the embodiment of both human and nature. This feature is prominent in the werewolf's affinity for the natural environment, in both the human and non-human form, the natural landscape is preferred (Hatter 2016). This alignment with the natural realm refers to an inherent instinctive state antithetical to social constructions. The natural environment, most notably the forest, Janine Hatter (2016, 10) claims, "promotes freedom from the restricting rules of civilization" and has "no religion, no social status, no governing body." But Hatter's argument does not take account of the direct connection between nature and the young woman. With acceptance, and full emergence in the natural realm, the young woman achieves her autonomy, albeit influenced by the presence of the English student. MacDonald's young woman finds freedom in this natural environment and lets her instincts take control which allows for full corporeal, and behavioral, transformation. Reflecting the attribute that werewolves possess an instinctual affinity with nature, the young woman prefers the forest habitat over the social order of humans. Since the unregulated environment is free of restrictions and boundaries, the hybrid human-animal is allowed to develop agency and independence. In this narrative, the natural landscape not only influences the progression of the story but acts as a guardian for the young woman.

MacDonald creates a direct connection between nature and the young woman. In the middle of the night, the student awakens to find claws in his shoulder and the "grinning teeth" of an animal reaching for his throat ("Gray Wolf," 117). For fear of its attack, he grapples it and wraps his fingers around the animal's neck while grabbing for his knife. When he attempts to stab the creature, the weather reacts as it lets out a mix of a "scream and a howl" ("Gray Wolf," 118). Seemingly related to the environmental responses of gothic madwomen: Catherine, Bertha, and Agatha, the young woman's vociferous call of terror results in the "wind blowing" the door open and dousing the student in "a sheet of spray" ("Gray Wolf," 118). This event allows the wolf to escape from destruction into the darkness of the cottage. As "gruesome sound[s] of "mingled weeping and howling" emerge from the depths, the night becomes "wild" with "raving" wind, pouring rain, and waves breaking near the cottage ("Gray Wolf," 118). As a derivative mode of Nature, the young woman demonstrates an unconditional connection with the surrounding environment. As she struggles for survival, Nature responds with a retaliatory strike against the societal threat. Echoing Marryat's Christina as a vengeful agent of nature, the environment and its relationship with the young woman offers protection and a source for personal expression. While the young woman demonstrates unification of mind-body under the protective substance of Nature, she struggles with assimilating the affectations of English society. The introduction of the student influences the young woman's behavior therefore unveiling a visual conflict of savage beast and vulnerable Victorian woman.

Femme animale: Victorian Exhibitions of Vulnerability and Monstrosity

The she-wolf is a material rejection of the early-to-mid-Victorian feminine role. The female hybrid creature, although abject and terrifying, functions as a figuration of "sympathy" as her struggle for agency involves her desertion of the "proper feminine role" (Creed 2015, 188). MacDonald's she-wolf appeals to the reader's sympathy through her visible illness and reflection of Victorian maladies. The young woman's depiction of sickness reflects a particular lycanthropic tendency that Victorian medical men suggested as a physiological anomaly or mental malady. This particular ailment results in the desire to draw blood and compels the individual "to commit the most horrible atrocities" (Baring-Gould 1865, 67). MacDonald enters this conversation as he demonstrates the young woman's rejection of food when her "nostrils and mouth quivered with disgust" and she flashes "strange look[s] of greed" at the student ("Gray Wolf," 115). Echoing Baring-Gould's description of bizarre cravings, MacDonald provides all evidence of the young woman's lycanthropic ailments. This connection to lycanthropic madness proliferates in MacDonald's short story. While the young woman illustrates a visible malady with a visage as sickly and "gray in complexion," it is not the same Victorian ailments presented in the pathological madwomen, Catherine Earnshaw, Bertha Mason, or Agatha Jeffreys ("Gray Wolf," 115). MacDonald's discourse presents her as a figure of fragility and instability who appears "lithe," small, "delicate," "smooth-skinned," and "worn" ("Gray Wolf," 115). Admiring her "faultless" curves, the student observes the young woman's nervousness through her "tremulous" nostrils and "her long fingers" as they "kept clutching and pulling" at her skirt ("Gray Wolf," 115). Although reminiscent of early-to-mid-Victorian female nervous conditions and mania, the young woman clearly illustrates lycanthropic traits and behavioral instability.

Operating within the mode of both the Gothic and the fairy tale, MacDonald's young woman refers to the distressed heroine trope of the Female Gothic. Similar to the Victorian attitude that women must be restricted for safekeeping, the young woman, as a she-wolf, must either be saved by the student, "shunned," or eradicated "to protect society" (Franck and Hatter 2016, 2). When the mother announces the necessary departure of the student, the young woman presents a "flash of wrath in her face" ("Gray Wolf," 119). Observing this look of animosity, the mother "approach[es] her daughter" and lifts a hand "to strike" ("Gray Wolf," 119). In her function to restrict the young woman, the mother is a representation of Victorian society and its reinforcement of feminine behavior. Perpetuating the beliefs of middle-class domesticity, the older woman offers the student shelter and food while simultaneously oppressing the animalistic instincts in the young woman. The student, on the other hand, represents the English male savior, and stops the attack but accidentally reveals the young woman's secretive hybridity as a "huge gray wolf" ("Gray Wolf," 119). Although the reader is not granted access to witness the human-to-wolf transformation, the conflated fear and pity is demonstrated through the student's reaction. Albeit offering a vociferous "cry of horror" at the presentation of the monstrous form, the student proclaims that his "inborn chivalry would never have allowed him to harm a woman even under the guise of a wolf" ("Gray Wolf," 119). Maintaining his English civility, the student refuses to physically impair the young woman during her lycanthropic transformation. Instead of attacking, she converts back into a woman, and falls "on his bosom," weeping and wrapping "her arms around his neck" ("Gray Wolf," 119). Transforming back into a wolf, she demonstrates her torment by howling and bounding up the cliff to the cave. Since the young woman is already exiled from civilized society, MacDonald alleviates her from punishment. Used as a demonstration of the instability of women, his figuration of the she-wolf is allowed to exist within its natural forest habitat. Rejecting submission to her monstrous ambush, the young man finds safety and escapes the island.

Female instability and acceptance of instincts result in rejection from civilized society. Arguably, transformations into she-wolves, as Kaja Franck and Janine Hatter (2016, 4) suggest, "evoke a fear of the loss of the human subject" while also "challenging the most problematic elements of being human." The young woman's transgressive, and unstable form is indicative of her "atavistic double self that had the potential to destroy" society if reincorporated (Easley and Scott 2013, xi). Therein, the English student's inability to destroy the young woman presents a societal rejection of her inverted female identity. Presenting "bestial aspects of humanity," notable transformations of monstrosity, and "violence and a vociferous appetite," the young woman faces continued isolation in the Shetland Islands (Franck and Hatter 2016, 2).

MacDonald ends the tale with "the girl" in human form, "standing on the edge of the cliff," while the student finds safety on the "opposite shore" ("Gray Wolf," 120). This closure that depicts a singular female form abandoned in isolation, suggests MacDonald's response to mid-Victorian women who seek independence and agency. As a material-semiotic figure in MacDonald's gothic tale, like Reynolds's Nisida, both women return to nature and accept their inherent instincts, which results in removal from civilized society. While Nisida's return resulted in her catastrophic social rejection, the acceptance of nature for MacDonald's young woman is beneficial. As a figuration of a she-wolf created at the end of the mid-Victorian period, MacDonald uses the young woman to promote a discourse of women's agency and independence from a restrictive society.

These variations of she-wolves, and relational werewolves exhibit how gothic monsters in the early-to-mid-Victorian period were embodiments of female desire and rejection of social confines. While monsters circulated through gothic texts as fragmented cultural embodiments reflective of social anxieties, these narratives created their monstrous women as unified mind-body figurations of passion and attempted reclamations of agency. From this perspective, women who rejected traditional roles are portrayed in the Gothic as material-semiotic figures of monstrosity. In all three stories, these monstrous women are created as hyperbolic embodiments of Victorian anxieties. Facing the fear of female reproductivity and sexual expression, these authors, operating in the gothic mode, construct hyperbolic female monstrosities to demonstrate the outcome of women's desire for independence. These narratives demonstrate how the female monsters are figurations of the subjective experience mapped onto the mind-body. As Victorian anxieties of female instincts and desires, these semiotic figures of monsters partake in consumption of flesh and attacks of men and children. In the narratives by Marryat, Reynolds, and MacDonald, figurations of female monsters are created to alleviate social tensions of destructive women. Therefore, she-wolf fiction of the early-to-mid-Victorian period fits in with the developing arguments that centralize madwomen and criminals at the intersection of women, nature, and the mind-body. Furthermore, these monstrous women in when considered under an ecocritical lens that dichotomizes them along the Great Divide between culture/nature, the perspectives of imperialist European history that informed the discursive biological subjugation of women clearly result in monstrous exhibitions of hysterical madwomen, manipulative criminals, and carnivorous she-wolves.

NOTES

1. Here I return to the philosophy of monism to highlight the effects of Nature's authoritative insurrection against artificial restrictions. Nature in this chapter is aligned to Spinozian concept of a singular substance, either God or Nature therefore, when referring to nature as a governing entity, it will be presented as a proper noun.

2. In Ben Jonson's play, the pregnant character Win feigns cravings for roast pork to obtain her real cravings for unusual activities. See Act III. Scene I.

3. See reference to Nordic mythologies and sagas. In the *Volsung Saga*, demi-gods and warriors transformed into wild beasts, or wore the skin to absorb the strength of the animal.

4. Wolves were expatriated in England by Anglo-Saxon kings; therefore, citizens were alleviated of their threatening presence. This absence was reflected in British folklore stories up until the Victorian period.

5. This concept of the body ego, as put forth by Freud asserts that forming of the consciousness during infancy is based on sensory experiences (and environmental affections). In this way the consciousness and construct of being is formed in cohesion with external influences, the internal id, ego, and superego. The superego is responsible for making moral decisions and judgments and interprets the results of behavior. Whereas the id is instinctual, the ego has the guidelines for rules and standards, and the superego, as found in the conscious, preconscious, and unconscious, aligns behaviors with civilized expectations.

6. Grosz uses anorexia as an ego-responsive, conscious form of social protest reflected on women's bodies. Subjugated to patriarchal ideals, the ego reconfigures cultural affectations into projections of defiance through extreme compliance, resulting in a disorder.

7. Hurley signals that the "ab" prefix in abhuman signifies the movement away while simultaneously asserting that is a "move towards" a place or state of being.

8. The Editors of Encyclopedia Britannica, "Frederick Marryat: English naval office and author," In *Encyclopedia Britannica* (Anad: Ria Press, 2016), 14. https://www.britannica.com/biography/Frederick-Marryat. As an officer in the Royal Navy, many of Marryat's tales reflect his nautical and travel experiences. Experiencing marital issues, Marryat sailed to North America, during which he filed for formal separation while writing his gothic tale.

9. Which later becomes *Reynolds's Miscellany* with James Malcolm Rymer as its lead novelist.

10. A German legend, Johann Faust is a successful, yet unsatisfied man who makes a pact with the Devil in exchange for his soul.

11. The Sylph is a mythological air spirit. Hebe is the Greek goddess of youth and the cupbearer to the Gods.

Conclusion

While the nineteenth-century Gothic was preoccupied with the division and examination of the singular immaterial female spirit or material corporeal form, the question of the unified mind-body in early-to-mid-Victorian Gothic was in desperate need of an answer. By integrating monism into studies of the Victorian Gothic, this text joined the conversation of transgressive ontologies and monstrosity and bridged the necessary void that defragments female identities. Accentuating the struggle and internal conflict of each gothic antiheroine, material-semiotic figurations of supposed monstrosity identifies how repression of human instincts and separation from nature resulted in catastrophic psychosomatic monstrous behaviors. The Victorian Gothic novel, and coinciding criticism of the Female Gothic, reflects a deeply embedded Cartesian dualism that transitions the identity of women into fragmented segments of mind *or* body and nature *or* culture. However, Victorian women, especially viewed through Spinoza's monistic lens, which argues for "the nature of the union between the mind and body," justifies violent women in the Gothic as complete figurations (Spinoza 2014, 7). Monism aligns nature-culture with the mind-body and so challenges the reductionism and essentialism that characterized much discourse in the period. The dichotomy of female monstrosity is a concept that has indeed been explored in gothic literature time and again, however, the focus of a unified mind-body, as a rejection of society and an acceptance of nature, offers a new reading of the mode. Women in the Gothic, then, function as monistic mind-body figurations through their direct connections with nature. Choosing to perform according to their natural instincts, these monstrous women represent the rejection of social confinement and repression. This has the further consequence of highlighting the ecoGothic encoding of these texts, by revealing what Dawn Keetley and Matthew Sivils (2017, 7) refer to as "the inevitability of humans intertwined with their natural environment." As embodiments of culture and nature, these monstrous women functioned as monistic paradigms of ecophobia and transgressive female behaviors to retaliate against a repressive society.

Female sexuality, as promoted by early-to-mid-Victorian medical and cultural discourses, was reduced to biological functionality, and associated with instability, excessiveness, irrationality, and social and psychological degeneration. The consequence of this rhetoric was the regulation of women's identities by social institutions, conduct books and culture, all of which urged women to focus on procreation and fulfilling the role of domestic caregiver. Through the self-governed roles of conventional femininity, early-to-mid-Victorian women's sexuality was subjected to discursive promotion of repression and sublimation. Regarding subjectivity and embodiment, as explained by Elizabeth Grosz (1994), sexuality is unable to be restricted by rigid constructs, as it fluidly transgresses boundaries and permeates all areas, self and other. As part of the instinctual drive, or female nature, desires for agency and expression in certain women rejected the repressive structure of gendered ideologies and manifested in exhibitions of vexatious or destructive dispositions. Women who displayed these characteristics, antagonistic to the social classification of the "high moral standards" of conventional Victorian womanhood, were stigmatized, pathologized, and criminalized by society (Ellis 1842, 219). Thereby, demonstrations of carnality, as lust or desire, were repudiated from social acceptance and characterized as monstrous.

Depictions of such monstrous women, while informed by the restrictive guides of Victorian gender ideologies, are visual exhibitions of the animus within. Strongly linked with female sexuality, nineteenth-century monstrosity was correlated to an innate connection to nature. This, then, articulates the challenges women experienced with repression in the early-to-mid-Victorian period. Furthermore, as discussed previously, the notion of women's instability was perpetuated by the oppressive discourse of patriarchal institutions such as medicine and science which connected women to their bodies. This classification of biological affiliation resulted in the restriction of women's social roles. To rely on reductionism and essentialism allowed misogynistic ideals to reduce women to their roles of biological functionality. Therefore, women were identified as solely physiological beings, which allows for metamorphic transformations because they were considered "more biological, more corporeal, and more natural than men" (Grosz 1994, 14). Demonstrated through investigations of medical discourse and cultural texts, women were discursively labeled as beings driven by their reproductive organs and desire for procreation. This designation falsified female identities and promoted artificial experiences and expectations through discourse as a method of behavioral regulation. This biological reductionism resulted in a constructivist approach that appropriated women's behaviors and identities as relevant to reproductive functionality. Therefore, ideas on corporeality and biological reductionism illustrate how corporeal excess was promoted as the cause for both psychological and physiological excess and evoked in support of the necessary creation of behavioral and social roles for women.

As Gina Wisker (2016, 154) has rightly argued, these contrasting binaries of female passivity and aggression are "the stuff of Gothic" and suggests that female readers and writers "celebrate the dualities" to cope with real terrors inflicted by male authorities. Female monsters in early-to-mid-Victorian Gothic texts and penny narratives are material-semiotic figurations of social perspectives of women's entanglement in nature. Informed by immaterial discourse and material conditions, monstrous women in the Gothic produce explicit outcomes as exhibitions of hysterical madwomen, deviant criminals, and shapeshifting she-wolves. Confined within a discursive feedback loop of reductive biology, these women both influenced, and were influenced by medical and cultural practices of the era. Social ideologies and gender expectations informed female identities with psychological and physiological restrictions. Behavioral restrictions in the nineteenth century required that women abide by the conventional role of passive complacency resulting in the struggle whereby, they attempted to repress such characteristics and behaviors that threatened their social status as idealistic angels. According to cultural and medical discourse women were expected to be embodiments of artificially created angels, and repressed figures of desire therefore, dichotomous binaries of angel/whore resulted in exhibitions of female monstrosity, such as madwomen, criminals, and she-wolves, in the gothic literature of the period. Whereas early-to-mid-Victorian institutions regarded women as bipartite constructs of desire and instability, the Gothic offered a place of freedom and self-expression. Speculations of women as uncontrollable "monsters" created a division of female identities as constructs of instability and societal corruption. This period arbitrated these female divisions and negotiated with gothic themes to exacerbate these issues of socially mandated repression and the expression of natural instincts.

When faced with neglect or abuse, the monistic mind-body of the material-semiotic female figure rejects socially prescribed roles and disrupts the process of ontology, transforming women into monstrous (re)presentations. To deter independence and restrain sexuality, society imposed upon women ideologies of artificiality, promoting virtue, repression of instincts, and a strict normative morality. As a result, women who operated outside of the prescriptive definition of middle- and upper-class femininity were labeled as monstrous. The boundaries of socially constructed and repressive Victorian identities determine the wild and monstrous figurations found in the Gothic. Following Lucie Armitt's (2016, 60) suggestion that monsters in the Gothic "give shape" to salient social concerns, the fear of women's biology, and in turn psychology, resulted in the promotion of female corruption and danger in popular discourse. This exhibition of antagonistic behaviors might, however, also be read as a repudiation of social confinement and an expression of women's desire to re-connect with nature. For example, Cathy of *Wuthering Heights*, instead of accepting the role of domestication with Edgar, demands her place in nature with Heathcliff, and succumbs to what doctors of the period labeled "hysteria." Linda Mowbray of *The Dark Woman*, in her rejection of repressive social boundaries, uses the environment to navigate between the façade of upper-class femininity and monstrous criminality. Christina, in the "White Wolf," ferociously retaliates against society and uses her position in the domestic sphere to destroy the family whose structures proved fatal to her predecessor. These figurations are not only, then, reflective of social anxieties informed by the misogyny Grosz and others identify, but also a way of negotiating and repudiating that misogyny.

The intertextual relationship between medical discourse, conduct books, theology, the Gothic, and penny narratives in the nineteenth century and their contextual variations of female aberrance, illustrates how monstrous women are capable of psychological and biological transformation, of which is typically compiled of defined psychosomatic figurations, thereby proving that they are "morphologically dubious" (Braidotti 1994, 90). Hence, the body is important in understanding female subjectivity without reducing bodily material to the essence of biology and nature that has been so detrimental to women, as demonstrated in the varied accounts of medical discourse in the nineteenth century. As identified by their bodies, women were considered sites of monstrosity and fragmentation therefore their classifications were determined by the reproductive body and misogynistic articulation of social fear. This representation occurs in Victorian Gothic fiction and, as Jack Halberstam (1995, 6) explains, used the monster figure as an amalgamation of "race, gender, and sexuality" to illustrate the complexity of their subjectivity and influence on society. Therefore, the Gothic, formulated by these discursive oppositions and fragmented identities, allowed the expression of repression of Victorian women through the polarization of opposing identities and behaviors.

Female monsters, while abhorrent, are also enticing figures of promises and threats, entrancing beings that demand attention. Following their vociferous calls and invitations for recognition, if we are daring enough to explore the depths of their monstrosity, we discover that what was labeled as monstrous, was really their plea for expression and freedom of agency.

Appendix

FOR FURTHER READING

Acker, Paul, and Thomas Rowland. "Basilisk." In the *Ashgate Encyclopedia of Literary and Cinematic Monsters*, edited by Jeffrey Andrew Weinstock, 29–31. Burlington: Ashgate Publishing Company, 2014.

Acton, William. *Prostitution Considered in its Moral, Social and Sanitary Aspects in London and Other Large Cities and Garrison Towns with Proposals for the Control and Prevention of its Attendant Evils*. London: J. Churchill and Sons, 1857/1870.

Adams, James Eli, Tom Pendergast, and Sara Pendergast. *Encyclopedia of the Victorian Era Volumes 1–4*. Danbury: Grolier Academic Reference, 2004.

Ahmed, Sarah. "Happy Objects." In *The Affect Theory Reader*, edited by Melissa Gregg and Gregory J. Seigworth, 29–51. Durham/London: Duke University Press, 2010.

———. "Orientations Matter." In *New Materialisms: Ontology, Agency, and Politics*, edited by Diana Coole and Samantha Frost, 234–257. Durham: Duke University Press, 2010.

Allan, Janice M. "Mrs. Robinson's 'Day-book of Iniquity': Reading Bodies of/and Evidence in the Context of the 1858 Medical Reform Act." In *The Female Body in Medicine and Literature*, edited by Andrew Mangham and Greta Depledge, 169–181. Liverpool: Liverpool University Press, 2011.

Allingham, Philip V. "The Victorian Sensation Novel, 1860–1880." *The Victorian Web: Literature, History, & Culture in the Age of Victoria*. Published October 2016. http://www.victorianweb.org/genre/sensation.html

American Psychiatric Association. *Diagnostic and Statistical Manual of Mental Disorders*, Fifth Edition. Arlington: American Psychiatry Publishing, 2013.

Anderson, Ben. "Modulating the Excess of Affect Morale in a State of 'Total War.'" In *The Affect Theory Reader*, edited by Melissa Gregg and Gregory J. Seigworth, 151–185. Durham/London: Duke University Press, 2010.

Anonymous, "Review of Wuthering Heights." In *Atlas* (January 1848). http://academic.brooklyn.cuny.edu/english/melani/novel_19c/wuthering/contemp_rev.html.

Anonymous, "Review of *Wuthering Heights*." In *Douglas Jerrold's Weekly Newspaper* (January 1848). http://academic.brooklyn.cuny.edu/english/melani/novel_19c/wuthering/contemp_rev.html.

Appignanesi, Lisa. *Mad, Bad & Sad: A History of Women and the Mind Doctors*. New York/London: W. W. Norton & Company, Inc, 2008.

Armitt, Lucie. "The Gothic Girl Child." In *Women and the Gothic: An Edinburgh Companion*, edited by Avril Horner and Sue Zlosnik, 60–73. Edinburgh: Edinburgh University Press, 2016.

Asma, Stephen T. *On Monsters: An Unnatural History of Our Worst Fears*. Oxford/New York: Oxford University Press, 2009.

Atkinson, Juliette. "To 'Serve God and Mammon' Braddon and Literary Transgression." *New Perspectives on Mary Elizabeth Braddon*, edited by Jessica Cox, 133–154. Amsterdam/New York: Rodopi B.V., 2012.

Austen, Jane. *Persuasion*. New York: Millennium Publications, 1818/2014.

Bagley, Benjamin. "Loving Someone in Particular." *The University of Chicago Press Journals* no. 2 (January 2015): 477–507.

Bailin, Miriam. *The Sickroom in Victorian Fiction: The Art of Being Ill*. Cambridge/New York: Cambridge University Press, 1994.

Baird, Jonathan David, and Coleman Eugene Trantham. *A Wolf in Petticoats: Essays Exploring Darwinism, Sexuality, and Gender in Late Victorian Gothic Horror*. Lenoir: Crosstime Publishing, 2016.

Bane, Theresa. *Encyclopedia of Fairies in World Folklore and Mythology*. Jefferson: MacFarland, 2013.

Barad, Karen. *Meeting the Universe Halfway: Quantum Physics and the Entanglement of Matter and Meaning*. Durham: Duke University Press, 2007.

Barger, Andrew. *The Best Werewolf Short Stories 1800–1849: A Classical Werewolf Anthology*. Loco Hills: Bottletree Books, 2010.

Barrow, Robin. "Braddon's Haunting Memories: Rape, Class, and the Victorian Popular Press." *Women's Writing* no. 13.3 (2006): 348–368.

Beller, Anne-Marie. "Sensational Bildung? Infantilization and Female Maturation in Braddon's 1860s Novels." In *New Perspectives on Mary Elizabeth Braddon*, edited by Jessica Cox, 113–132. Amsterdam/New York: Rodopi B. V., 2012.

Bennett, Jane. "A Vitalist Stopover on the Way to a New Materialism." In *New Materialisms: Ontology, Agency, and Politics*, edited by Diana Coole and Samantha Frost, 47–69. Durham: Duke University Press, 2016.

Bennett, Mark. "Generic Gothic and Unsettling Genre: Mary Elizabeth Braddon and the Penny Blood." *Gothic Studies* no. 13.1 (May 2011): 38–54.

———. "Reynolds, G. W. M. (George William MacArthur)." In *The Encyclopedia of the Gothic*, edited by William Hughes, David Punter, and Andrew Smith, 554–556. West Sussex/Hoboken: Wiley-Blackwell, 2016.

———. "Sensation Fiction." In *The Encyclopedia of the Gothic*, edited by William Hughes, David Punter, and Andrew Smith, 607–612. West Sussex/Hoboken: Wiley-Blackwell, 2016.

Berecz, John M. "Towards a Monistic Philosophy of Man." *Andrews University Seminary Studies (AUSS)* no. 14.2 (1976): 279–288.

Bernstein, Susan David. "Dirty Reading: Sensation Fiction, Women, and Primitivism." *Criticism: A Quarterly for Literature and the Arts* no. 36.2 (Spring 1994): 213–241. Periodical Archives Online.

Biehl, João, and Peter Locke. "Deleuze and the Anthropology of Becoming." *Current Anthropology* no. 51.3 (June 2010): 317–351.

Blaffer Hrdy, Sarah. "Raising Darwin's Consciousness: Female Sexuality and the Prehominid Origins of Patriarchy." *Human Nature* no 8.1 (July 1996): 1–49.

Bodichon Smith, Barbara Leigh. *A Brief Summary of the Laws in England Concerning Women: Together with a Few Observations Thereon*. London: John Chapman, 1856.

Boehm, Christopher. *Blood Revenge: The Anthropology of Feuding in Montenegro and Other Tribal Societies*. Lawrence: The University of Kansas, 1984.

Bohata, Kristi. "Unhomely Moments: Reading and Writing in Welsh Female Gothic." In *The Female Gothic: New Directions*, edited by Diane Wallace and Andrew Smith, 180–195. New York: Palgrave Macmillan, 2007.

Bondar, Alanna F. "Bodies on Earth: Exploring Sites of the Canadian Gothic." In *Ecogothic*, edited by Andrew Smith and William Hughes, 72–86. Manchester: Manchester University Press, 2013.

Braidotti, Rosi. *Metamorphoses: Towards a Materialistic Theory of Becoming*. Cambridge/Malden: Polity Press, 2002.

———. *Nomadic Subjects: Embodiment and Sexual Difference in Contemporary Feminist Theory*. New York: Columbia University Press, 1994.

Brantlinger, Patrick. "Imperial Gothic." In *Victorian Gothic: An Edinburgh Companion*, edited by Andrew Smith and William Hughes, 202–216. Edinburgh: Edinburgh University Press, 2012.

———. *Rule of Darkness: British Literature and Imperialism, 1830–1914*. Ithaca: Cornell University Press, 1990.

———. "What is 'Sensational' About the 'Sensational Novel'?" *Nineteenth-Century Fiction* no. 27.1 (June 1982): 1–28.

Brill, Dr. A. A. *The Basic Writings of Sigmund Freud*. New York: The Modern Library, 1995.

Buell, Lawrence. *The Environmental Imagination: Thoreau, Nature Writing, and the Formation of American Culture*. Cambridge/London: Harvard University Press, 1995.

Burney, Elizabeth. "Crime and Criminology in the Eye of the Novelist: Trends in Nineteenth Century Literature." *The Howard Journal of Criminal Justice* (May 2012): 160–172.

Burrows, George Man. *Commentaries on the Causes, Forms, Symptoms, and Treatment, Moral and Medical of Insanity*. London: Thomas and George Underwood, 1828.

Butler, Judith. *Bodies That Matter: On the Discursive Limits of Sex*. Abington/New York: Routledge, 1993.

———. *Gender Trouble: Feminism and the Subversion of Identity*. Abington/New York: Routledge, 1990.

Byron, Glennis, and Dale Townshend. *The Gothic World*. New York: Routledge, 2014.

Cameron, Ed. *The Psychopathology of the Gothic Romance: Perversion, Neuroses and Psychosis in Early Works of the Genre*. Jefferson/London: McFarland & Co., 2010.

Carey, Nessa. *The Epigenetics Revolution: How Modern Biology is Rewriting Our Understanding of Genetics, Disease, and Inheritance*. New York: Columbia University Press, 2012.

Carpenter, Ginette. "Mothers and Others." In *Women and the Gothic: An Edinburgh Companion*, edited by Avril Horner and Sue Zlosnik, 46–59. Edinburgh: Edinburgh University Press, 2016.

Carpenter, Mary. "On the Treatment of Female Convicts." In *Transactions of the National Association for the Promotion of Social Science 1858*, edited by George Woodyatt Hastings. London: Longmans, 1858.

———. "Reformatories for Convicted Girls." In *Transactions of the National Association for the Promotion of Social Science 1857*, edited by George Woodyatt Hastings. London: Longmans, 1857.

Carstens, Lisa. "Unbecoming Women: Sex Reversal in the Scientific Discourse on Female Deviance in Britain, 1880–1920." In *Journal of the History of Sexuality* no. 20.1 (January 2011): 62–94.

Cheah, Pheng, "Non-Dialectical Materialism." In *New Materialisms. Ontology, Agency, and Politics*, edited by Diana Coole and Samantha Frost, 70–91. Durham: Duke University Press, 2016.

Cherry, Kendra. "Studying the Brain and Behavior in Biopsychology." *VeryWellMind*, edited by Steven Gans M. D. Published August 2019. https://www.verywellmind.com/what-is-biopsychology-2794883.

Clark, Anna. "Female Sexuality." In *The Routledge History of Women in Europe Since 1770*, edited by Deborah Simonton, 54–92. Abingdon/New York: Routledge, 2006.

Cheyne, George. *The English Malady: Or a Treatise of Nervous Diseases of All Kinds, as Spleen, Vapours, Lowness of Spirits, Hypochondriacal and Hysterical Distempers, etc*. London: G. Strahan, 1733.

Chitham, Edward. *The Birth of Wuthering Heights: Emily Brontë at Work*. London/New York: Macmillan/St. Martin's Press, 1998.

Choat, Simon. "Science, Agency, and Ontology: A Historical-Materialist Response to New Materialism." *Political Studies Sage Journals* no. 66.4 (November 2018): 1027–1042.

Chow, Rey. "The Elusive Material, What the Dog Doesn't Understand." In *New Materialisms: Ontology, Agency, and Politics*, edited by Diana Coole and Samantha Frost, 221–233. Durham: Duke University Press, 2010.

Cininas, Jazmina. "Wicked Wolf-Women and Shaggy Suffragettes: Lycanthropic Femme Fatales in the Victorian and Edwardian Eras." In *Werewolves, Wolves, and the Gothic*, edited by Robert McKay and John Miller, 37–64. Cardiff: University of Wales Press, 2017.

Clemens, Valdine. *The Return of the Repressed: Gothic Horror from the "Castle of Otranto" to "Alien."* Albany: State University of New York Press, 1999.

Clough, Patricia T. "The Affective Turn: Political Economy, Biomedia, and Bodies." In *The Affect Theory Reader*, edited by Melissa Gregg and Gregory J. Seigworth, 206–228. Durham/London: Duke University Press, 2010

Cohen, Jeffrey Jerome. *Stone: An Ecology of the Inhuman*. Minneapolis: University of Minnesota Press, 2015.

Coleman, Carla E. "'The Stage! Oh, Flora, The Very Idea Frightens Me!': Representations of Victorian Professional Theatre in *Rupert Godwin* and *A Lost Eden*." In *New Perspectives of Mary Elizabeth Braddon*, edited by Jessica Cox, 231–250. Amsterdam/New York: Rodopi B. V., 2012.

Cominos, Peter T. "Innocent Femina Sensualis in Unconscious Conflict." In *Suffer and Be Still: Women in the Victorian Age*, edited by Martha Vicinus, 155–172. New York: Routledge, 1972/2013.

Connolly, William. "Materialities of Experience." In *New Materialisms: Ontology, Agency, and Politics*, edited by Diana Coole and Samantha Frost, 178–200. Durham: Duke University Press, 2010.

Conolly, John. *An Inquiry Concerning the Indications of Insanity with Suggestions for the Better Protection and Care of the Insane*. London: John Taylor, 1830.

Conway, Jill. "Stereotypes of Femininity in a Theory of Sexual Evolution." In *Suffer and Be Still: Women in the Victorian Age*, edited by Martha Vicinus, 140–154. New York: Routledge, 1972/2013.

Coole, Diana. "The Inertia of Matter and the Generativity of Flesh." In *New Materialisms: Ontology, Agency, and Politics*, edited by Diana Coole and Samantha Frost, 92–115. Durham: Duke University Press, 2010.

Coole, Diana, and Samantha Frost. *New Materialisms: Ontology, Agency, and Politics*. Durham: Duke University Press, 2010.

Cox, Jessica. *New Perspectives on Mary Elizabeth Braddon*. Amsterdam/New York: Rodopi B. V., 2012.

Cross, F. L. *The Oxford Dictionary of the Christian Church*. London: Oxford University Press, 1957.

Crossen, Carys. "'The Complex and Antagonistic Forces That Constitute One's Soul': Conflict Between Societal Expectations and Individual Desires in Clemence Housman's *The Werewolf* and Rosamund Marriott Watson's 'A Ballad of the Were-wolf.'" In *She-wolf: A Cultural History of Female Werewolves*, edited by Hannah Priest, 111–127. Manchester: Manchester University Press, 2015.

Crowe, Catherine. "A Story of a Weir-Wolf." In *Terrifying Transformations: An Anthology of Victorian Werewolf Fiction*, edited by Alexis Easley and Shannon Scott, 42–64. Valancourt Books, 2013.

Curran, Bob. Werewolves: *A Field Guide to Shapeshifters, Lycanthropes, and Man-Beasts*. Franklin Lakes: New Page Books, 2009.

Curtis, Jeni. "The 'Espaliered' Girl: Pruning the Docile Body in Aurora Floyd." In *Beyond Sensation: Mary Elizabeth Braddon in Context*, edited by Marlene Tromp,

Pamela K. Gilbert, and Aeron Haynie, 77–92. Albany: University of New York Press, 2000.

Cvetkovich, Ann. *Mixed Feelings: Feminism, Mass Culture, and Victorian Sensationalism*. New Brunswick: Rutgers University Press, 1992.

Darwin, Charles. *The Expression of the Emotions in Man and Animals*, edited by Joe Cain and Sharon Messenger. London/New York/Ontario: Penguin Classics, 1872/2009.

———. *Notebooks from the Voyage of the Beagle, 1831–1836*, edited by Richard Darwin Keynes. Cambridge/New York: Cambridge University Press, 2009.

———. *The Origin of Species: By Means of Natural Selection of the Preservation of Favoured Races in the Struggle for Life*, edited by Sir Julian Huxley, London/New York: Signet Classics, 2003.

de Beauvoir, Simone. *The Second Sex*, translated by Constance Borde. London/New York: Random House, Inc, 1949/2010.

de Sousa Correa, Delia. *George Eliot, Music, and Victorian Culture*. Hampshire/New York: Palgrave Macmillan, 2003.

Deacon, Terrence W. *Incomplete Nature: How Mind Emerged from Matter*. New York/London: W.W. Norton & Company, 2012.

Degler, Carl N. "What Ought To Be and What Was: Women's Sexuality in the Nineteenth Century." *The American Historical Review* 79 no. 5 (December 1974): 467–490.

Dennett, Daniel. *Consciousness Explained*. Boston/New York/London: Back Bay Books, Little Brown and Company, 1991.

DeRosa, Robin. "'To Save the Life of the Novel': Sadomasochism and Representation in *Wuthering Heights*." *Rocky Mountain Review of Language Literature, RMMLA* no. 52.1 (1998): 27–43.

Diedre, David. *The Cambridge Companion to the Victorian Novel*. Cambridge: Cambridge University Press, 2001.

Dittmer, Nicole C, and Sophie Raine. *Penny Dreadfuls and the Gothic: Investigations of Pernicious Tales of Terror*. Cardiff: University of Wales Press, 2022.

Donnelly, Michael. *Managing the Mind: A Study of Medical Psychology in Early Nineteenth-Century Britain*. London: Tavis-tock Press, 1983.

Drucker, Johanna. "The History of the Book." *UCLA* (January 2018). https://hob.gseis.ucla.edu/Resources/Rodgers_Reference.html#:~:text=Conduct%20books%20were%20in%20many,quo%22%20(Morrison%20205).

Durbach, Nadja. *Spectacles of Deformity: Freak Shows and Modern British Culture*. Berkeley/Los Angeles/London: University of California Press, 2010.

Dziemianowicz, Stefan. *Penny Dreadfuls: Sensational Tales of Terror*. New York: Fall River Press, 2014.

———. "The Werewolf." In *Icons of Horror and the Supernatural: An Encyclopedia of Our Worst Nightmares Volumes 1 & 2*, edited by S.T. Joshi, 653–688. Westport/London: Greenwood Press, 2007.

Editors of Encyclopedia Britannica, "Frederick Marryat: English naval office and author." In *Encyclopedia Britannica*. Anad: Ria Press, 2016. https://www.britannica.com/biography/Frederick-Marryat.

Edwards, Jason. "The Materialism of Historical Materialism." In *New Materialisms: Ontology, Agency, and Politics*, edited by Diana Coole and Samantha Frost, 281–298. Durham: Duke University Press, 2016.

Ellis, Havelock. *Studies in the Psychology of Sex: Volume 1*. London/Scotts Valley: CreateSpace Independent Publishing Platform Reprint, 2014.

———. *Studies in the Psychology of Sex: The Sexual Impulse in Women Volume 3*. London/Scotts Valley: CreateSpace Independent Publishing Platform Reprint, 2017.

Emsley, Professor Clive. "Crime and the Victorians." *BBC*. Published 2014. http://www.bbc.co.uk/history/british/victorians/crime_01.shtml.

Ernst, Waltraud, and Agnes Kovacs. "New Materialisms, Older Ones, and New Genderings." *New Materialism: How Life Comes to Matter* (2018): 1–12. http://newmaterialism.eu/content/5-working-groups/2-working-group2/position-papers/joint-position-paper-new-old-materialism.pdf.

Eron, Sarah. "Patmore's Religious Background and Conversions," *The Victorian Web* (June 2004). http://www.victorianweb.org/authors/patmore/eron8.html.

Farran, C. d'O. "The Royal Marriages Act, 1772." *The Modern Law Review* vol. 14 no.1 (January 1951), 53–63.

Favareau, Donald. *Essential Readings in Biosemiotics: Anthology and Commentary*. Heidelberg: Springer Netherlands, 2009.

Ferguson Ellis, Kate. "Can You Forgive Her? The Gothic Heroine and Her Critics." In *A New Companion to the Gothic*, edited by David Punter, 457–468. Oxford: Blackwell Publishing Ltd, 2012.

Fisk, Nicole. "'Lady Audley as Sacrifice': Curing Female Disadvantage in Lady Audley's Secret." *Victorian Newsletter* no. 105 (2004): 24–36.

Fletcher, Loraine. "Review: Murder and Moral Decay in Victorian Popular Literature by Beth Kalikoff." *English Literature in Translation, 1880–1920* (Winter 1988): 383–385.

Fraser, Robert. *Victorian Quest Romance*. Horndon/Tavistock/Devon. Northcote House Publishers, 1998.

Friedman, Sharon. *Feminist Theatrical Revisions of Classic Works*. Jefferson: McFarland & Company, Inc, 2009.

Frost, Samantha. "Fear and the Illusion of Autonomy." In *New Materialisms: Ontology, Agency, and Politics*, edited by Diana Coole and Samantha Frost, 158–177. Durham: Duke University Press, 2016.

———. "The Implications of the New Materialism for Feminist Epistemology." In *Feminist Epistemology and Philosophy of Science*, edited by Heidi E. Grasswick, 69–83. Berlin: Springer/Dordrecht, 2011.

Furneaux, Holly. "Victorian Sexualities." *The British Library*. Published May 2014. https://www.bl.uk/romantics-and-victorians/articles/victorian-sexualities.

Garrad, Greg, "Environment." In *The Encyclopedia of the Gothic*, edited by William Hughes, David Punter, and Andrew Smith, 217–219. West Sussex/Hoboken: Wiley-Blackwell, 2016.

Garrison, Laurie. "'She read on more eagerly, almost breathlessly': Mary Elizabeth Braddon's Challenge to Medical Depictions of Female Masturbation in *The Doctor's Wife*." In *The Female Body in Medicine and Literature*, edited by

Andrew Mangham and Greta Depledge, 148–168. Liverpool: Liverpool University Press, 2011.

Gaskell, Elizabeth. *North and South*. London: Wordsworth: 1854/1987.

Gasperini, Anna. *Nineteenth Century Popular Fiction, Medicine and Anatomy: The Victorian Penny Blood and the 1832 Anatomy Act*. Cham: Springer, 2019.

Geddes, Sir Patrick, and J. Arthur Thomson. *The Evolution of Sex Revised Edition*. New York: The Walter Scott Publishing Co. Ltd, 1889/1908.

George, Sam, and William Hughes. "Introduction: Werewolves and Wilderness." *Gothic Studies* no. 21.1 (May 2019): 1–9.

Germaine-Buckley, Chloé. "A Tale of Two Women: The Female Grotesque in Showtime's *Penny Dreadful*," *Feminist Media Studies* 20.3 (2020): 377.

Gilbert, Pamela K. *Disease, Desire, and the Body in Victorian Women's Popular Novels*. New York/Cambridge: Cambridge University Press, 1997.

Gilman, Sander, Helen King, Roy Porter, G.S. Rousseau, and Elaine Showalter. *Hysteria Beyond Freud*. Berkeley: University of California Press, 1997.

Gilman, Sander L. "Review: Figuring Madness in Nineteenth-Century Fiction." *Victorian Studies* no. 42.2 (2000): 309–310. JSTOR.

Good, John Mason. *The Study of Medicine*. New York: Harper and Brothers, 1829.

Grant, Barry Keith. *The Dread of Difference*. Austin: University of Texas Press, 1996.

Greg, William Rathbone. *Why Are Women Redundant?* London: N. Trubner & Co., 1869.

Griffin Wolff, Cynthia. "The Radcliffean Gothic Model: A Form for Feminine Sexuality." In *The Female Gothic*, edited by Julian Fleenor, 210–231. Montreal/London: Eden Press, 1983.

Groneman, Carol. "Nymphomania: The Historical Construction of Female Sexuality." *Signs* no. 19.2 (Winter 1994): 337–367.

Grosz, Elizabeth. "Feminism, Materialism, and Freedom." In *New Materialisms: Ontology, Agency, and Politics*, edited by Diana Coole and Samantha Frost, 239–257. Durham: Duke University Press, 2010.

———. *The Incorporeal: Ontology, Ethics, and the Limits of Materialism*. New York: Columbia University Press, 2017.

———. *The Nick of Time: Politics, Evolution and the Untimely*. Crow's Nest/Sydney: Allen & Unwin, 2004.

———. *Space, Time, and Perversion: Essays on the Politics of Bodies*. London/New York: Routledge, 1995.

Hall, Marshall. "On the Functions of the Medulla Oblongata and Medulla Spinalis, and on the Excito-motory System of Nerves." *The Royal Society of London* no. 3 (December 1837): 463–464.

Hamlett, Jane. *At Home in the Institution: Material Life in Asylums, Lodging Houses and Schools in Victorian and Edwardian England*. Hampshire/New York: Palgrave Macmillan, 2015.

Hanson, Helen, and Catherine O'Rawe. *The Femme Fatale: Images, Histories, Contexts*. Hampshire/New York, 2010.

Haraway, Donna. *Modest_Witness@Second_Millenium.FemaleMan©_Meets_ OncoMouse: Feminism and Technoscience*. New York/London: Routledge, 1997.

———. *Simians, Cyborgs, and Women: The Reinvention of Nature*. New York/Abington: Routledge, 1991.

———. *The Haraway Reader*. Abingdon/New York: Routledge, 2004.

Hare, John B. "The Book of Were-wolves by Sabine Baring-Gould." *Evinity*, last modified 2010. https://www.sacred-texts.com/goth/bow/index.htm.

Haugtvedt, Erica. "The Victorian Serial Novel and Transfictional Character." *Victorian Studies* no. 59.3 (Spring 2017): 409–418.

Haynie, Aeron. "'An Idle Handle That Was Never Turned, and a Lazy Rope so Rotten': The Decay of the Country Estate in *Lady Audley's Secret*." In *Beyond Sensation: Mary Elizabeth Braddon in Context*, edited by Marlene Tromp, Pamela K. Gilbert, and Aeron Haynie, 63–75. Albany: University of New York Press, 2000.

Heholt, Ruth, and Melissa Edmundson. *Gothic Animals: Uncanny Otherness and the Animal With-Out*. Cham: Palgrave Macmillan, 2020.

Hogle, Jerrod E. "Monstrosity." In *The Encyclopedia of the Gothic*, edited by William Hughes, David Punter, and Andrew Smith, 455–457. West Sussex/Hoboken: Wiley-Blackwell, 2016.

Höing, Anja. "A Retreat on the 'River Bank': Perpetuating Patriarchal Myths in Animal Stories." In *Women and Nature? Beyond Dualism in Gender, Body, and Environment*, edited by Douglas A. Vakoch and Sam Mickey, 27–42. Abington/New York: 2018.

Holcombe, Lee. *Victorian Ladies at Work: Middle-Class Working Women in England and Wales, 1850–1914*. North Haven: Archon Books, 1973.

Horner, Avril. "Victorian Gothic and National Identity: Cross-Channel 'Mysteries.'" In *Victorian Gothic: An Edinburgh Companion*, edited by Andrew Smith and William Hughes, 108–123. Edinburgh: Edinburgh University Press, 2012.

Houston, Gail Turley. "Mary Braddon's Commentaries on the Trials and Legal Secrets of Audley Court." In *Beyond Sensation: Mary Elizabeth Braddon in Context*, edited by Marlene Tromp, Pamela K. Gilbert, and Aeron Haynie, 17–30. Albany: University of New York Press, 2000.

Howard, Jaqueline. *Reading Gothic Fiction: A Bakhtinian Approach*. Oxford: Clarendon Press, 1994.

Hughes, William. "Victorian Medicine and the Gothic." In *Victorian Gothic: An Edinburgh Companion*, edited by Andrew Smith and William Hughes, 186–201. Edinburgh: Edinburgh University Press, 2012.

Hughes, William, David Punter, and Andrew Smith. *The Encyclopedia of the Gothic*. West Sussex/Hoboken: Blackwell Publishing, 2016.

Hunt, Aeron. "Married Women's Property Acts." *Encyclopedia of the Victorian Era Volume 3*, edited by James Eli Adams, Tom Pendergast, and Sara Pendergast, 7. Danbury: Grolier Academic Reference, 2004.

Hurley, Kelly. "Science and the Gothic." In *Victorian Gothic: An Edinburgh Companion*, edited by Andrew Smith and William Hughes, 170–185. Edinburgh: Edinburgh University Press, 2012.

Huyssen, Andreas. *After the Great Divide: Modernism, Mass Culture, Postmodernism*. Bloomington: Indiana University Press, 1986.

Ioannou, Maria. "'A brilliancy of their own': Female Art, Beauty and Sexuality in Charlotte Brontë's Jane Eyre." In *Brontë Studies* no. 43.4 (2018): 323–334.

Johnson, Patricia E. *Hidden Hands: Working-Class Women & Social-Problem Fiction*. Athens: Ohio University Press 2001.

Johnson-Woods, Toni. "Mary Elizabeth Braddon in Australia: Queen of the Colonies." In *Beyond Sensation: Mary Elizabeth Braddon in Context*, edited by Marlene Tromp, Pamela K. Gilbert, and Aeron Haynie, 111–126. Albany: University of New York Press, 2000.

Jones, Ernest. *The Life and Work of Sigmund Freud*. New York: Basic Books, 1961.

Jordan, H.W., E.W. Lockert, M. Johnson-Warren, C. Cabell, T. Cooke, W. Greer, and G. Howe. "Erotomania Revisited: Thirty-Four Years Later." *Journal of the National Medical Association* no. 98 (2006): 787–793.

Jordanova, Ludmilla J. *Sexual Visions: Images of Gender in Science and Medicine Between the Eighteenth and Twentieth Centuries*. Madison: University of Wisconsin, 1989.

Joshi, S. T. *Icons of Horror and the Supernatural: An Encyclopedia of Our Worst Nightmares Volumes 1 & 2*. Westport/London: Greenwood Press, 2007.

Kalikoff, Beth. *Murder and Moral Decay in Victorian Popular Literature*. Rochester: University of Rochester Press, 1986.

Karschay, Stephen. *Degeneration, Normativity and the Gothic at the Fin de Siècle*. London:
Palgrave Macmillan, 2015.

Killeen, Jarlath. "Victorian Gothic Pulp Fiction." In *Victorian Gothic: An Edinburgh Companion*, edited by Andrew Smith and William Hughes, 45–56. Edinburgh: Edinburgh University Press, 2012.

King, Helen. "Once Upon a Text: Hysteria from Hippocrates." In *Hysteria Beyond Freud*, edited by Sander L. Gilman, Helen King, Roy Porter, G. S. Rousseau, and Elaine Showalter. University of California Press, 1993.

King, Jeannette. *The Victorian Woman Question in Contemporary Feminist Fiction*. London/New York: Palgrave Macmillan, 2005.

King, Kenneth. "Obsession—Beginning with the Brontës: A Revisitation." In *The Antioch Review* no. 73.2 (2015): 225–241.

Kinsbourne, Dr. Marcel. "Mind and Brain, The Remembered Present: A Biological Theory of Consciousness." *The American Journal of Psychiatry* no. 149.3 (Spring 1992): 3.

Kisch, Heinrich E. *Die Sterilität des Weibes: ihre Ursachen und ihre Behandlung*. San Francisco: Forgotten Books Reprint 2017.

Kleges, Mary. *Literary Theory: A Guide for the Perplexed*. London/New York: Continuum International Publishing Group, 2006.

Knight, Mark. "Figuring Out the Fascination: Recent Trends in Criticism on Victorian Sensation and Crime Fiction." *Victorian Literature and Culture* no. 37.1 (2009): 323–333.

Knowles, Nancy, and Katherine Hall. "Imperial Attitudes in *Lady Audley's Secret*." In *New Perspectives of Mary Elizabeth Braddon*, edited by Jessica Cox, 155–174. Amsterdam/New York: Rodopi B. V., 2012.

Koven, Seth. *Slumming: Sexual and Social Politics in Victorian London*. Princeton: Princeton University Press, 2006.
Kozel, Susan. "The Diabolical Strategy of Mimesis: Luce Irigaray's Reading of Maurice Merleau-Ponty." *Hypatia* no. 11.3 (Summer 1996): 114–129.
Kruks, Sonia. "Simone de Beauvoir: Engaging Discrepant Materialisms." In *New Materialisms: Ontology, Agency, and Politics*, edited by Diana Coole and Samantha Frost, 258–280. Durham: Duke University Press, 2010.
Kuhl, Sarah. "*The Angel in the House* and Fallen Women: Assigning Women their Places in Victorian Society." *Department for Continuing Education* (July 2016): 171–176.
Laing, Ronald Davis. *The Divided Self: An Existential Study in Sanity and Madness*. London: Penguin Press, 1960/2010.
Langland, Elizabeth. "Enclosure Acts: Framing Women's Bodies in Braddon's *Lady Audley's Secret*." In *Beyond Sensation: Mary Elizabeth Braddon in Context*, edited by Marlene Tromp, Pamela K. Gilbert, and Aeron Haynie, 3–16. Albany: University of New York Press, 2000.
Law, John. "Material Semiotics." *The Open University, Milton Keynes, UK and Sami Allaskulva* (Winter 2019): 1–19.
Laycock, Thomas. *An Essay on Hysteria: Being and Analysis of its Irregular and Aggravated Forms; Including Hysterical Hemorrhage, and Hysterical Ischuria*. Philadelphia: Haswell, Barrington, and Haswell, 1840.
Lee, Sidney, "Smith, William Tyler," In Dictionary of National Biography, edited by Leslie Stephen, 53. London: Smith, Elder & Co., 1885.
Lewis, Matthew. *The Monk*. London/New York: Penguin Books, 1796/1999.
Liggins, Emma. "Review of Domestic Murder in Nineteenth-Century England: Literary and Cultural Representations by Bridget Walsh." *Journal of Victorian Culture* no. 201.1 (2014): 141–143.
Lim, Erle C. H. and Raymond C. S. Seet. "What is the place for placebo in the management of psychogenic disease?" *Journal of the Royal Society of Medicine* no. 100.2 (February 2007): 60–61.
Lin, Michelle. "'To Go Boldly Where No Woman Has Gone Before: Alicia Audley and the New Woman." In *New Perspectives of Mary Elizabeth Braddon*, edited by Jessica Cox, 59–74. Amsterdam/New York: Rodopi B. V., 2012.
Long Hoeveler, Diane. "Victorian Gothic Drama." In *Victorian Gothic: An Edinburgh Companion*, edited by Andrew Smith and William Hughes, 57–71. Edinburgh: Edinburgh University Press, 2012.
Macaluso, Elizabeth D. *Gender, the New Woman, and the Monster*. Cham: Palgrave Macmillan, 2019.
Maines, Rachel P. *The Technology of Orgasm: "Hysteria," The Vibrator and Women's Sexual Satisfaction*. Baltimore: Johns Hopkins University Press, 1999.
Mangham, Andrew. "'Drink it Up Dear; It Will Do You Good': Crime, Toxicology, and the Trail of the Serpent." In *New Perspectives of Mary Elizabeth Braddon*, edited by Jessica Cox, 95–112. Amsterdam/New York: Rodopi B. V., 2012.
Mangham, Andrew, and Greta Depledge. *The Female Body in Medicine and Literature*. Liverpool: Liverpool University Press, 2011.

Marino, Elisabetta. "'The Devil in the House': The Character of Lucy in *Lady Audley's Secret.*" *B.A.S* no. xx (2014): 15–20.

Marks, Sylvia Kasey. "'Clarissa' as Conduct Book." In *South Atlantic Review* no. 51.4 (November 1986): 3–16.

Massumi, Brian. "The Future Birth of the Affective Fact: The Political Ontology of Threat." In *The Affect Theory Reader*, edited by Melissa Gregg and Gregory J. Seigworth, 52–70. Durham/London: Duke University Press, 2010.

Mattacks, Kate. "Sensationalism on Trial: Courtroom Drama and the Image of Respectability in His Darling Sin." In *New Perspectives of Mary Elizabeth Braddon*, edited by Jessica Cox, 211–230. Amsterdam/New York: Rodopi B. V., 2012.

Matus, Jill M. "Disclosure as 'Cover-up': The Discourse of Madness in *Lady Audley's Secret.*" *University of Toronto Quarterly* no. 62.3 (Spring 1993): 334–355.

———. *Unstable Bodies: Sexuality and Maternity in Victorian Culture*. Manchester: Manchester University Press, 1995.

Maudsley M. D., Henry. *Sex in Mind and Education*. Syracuse: C. W. Bardeen Publisher, 1884.

Mazzoni, Cristina. *She-Wolf: The Story of a Roman Icon*. Cambridge/New York: Cambridge University Press, 2010.

McDowell, Stacey. "Penny Dreadfuls." In *The Encyclopedia of the Gothic*, edited by William Hughes, David Punter, and Andrew Smith, 489–490. West Sussex/Hoboken: Wiley-Blackwell, 2016.

McKay, Robert, and John Miller. *Werewolves, Wolves, and the Gothic*. Cardiff: University of Wales Press, 2017.

McMillen Conger, Syndy. "The Reconstruction of the Gothic Feminine Ideal in Emily Brontë's *Wuthering Heights.*" In *The Female Gothic*, edited by Julian Fleenor, 91–106. Montreal/London: Eden Press, 1983.

Merchant, Carolyn. "The Scientific Revolution and the Death of Nature." *Isis* no. 97 (2006): 513–533.

Merriam-Webster. "Dark." In *Merriam-Webster Dictionary* (2020). www.merriam-webster.com/dictionary/dark.

Metsvahi, Merili. "Estonian Werewolf Legends Collected from the Island of Saaremaa." In *She-wolf: A Cultural History of Female Werewolves*, edited by Hannah Priest, 24–40. Manchester: Manchester University Press, 2015.

Midgley, David. *The Essential Mary Midgley*. London/New York: Routledge, 2005.

Miller, Adams. "A Material Semiotics?" *The Other Journal: An Intersection of Theology & Culture*. Published August 2010. https://theotherjournal.com/2010/08/05/a-material-semiotics/.

Millet, Kate. "The Debate Over Women: Ruskin vs. Mill." In *Suffer and Be Still: Women in the Victorian Age*, edited by Martha Vicinus, 121–139. New York: Routledge, 1972/2013.

Mitchell, Silas Weir. *Fat and Blood: An Essay on the Treatment of Certain Forms of Neurasthenia and Hysteria*. Philadelphia: J. B. Lippincott Company, 1877.

Mitten, Diane, and Chiana D'Amore. "The Nature of Body Image: the Relationship Between Women's Body Image and Physical Activity in Natural Environments."

In Women and Nature? Beyond Dualism in Gender, Body, and Environment, edited by Douglas A. Vakoch and Sam Mickey, 96–116. Abington/New York: Routledge, 2018.

Moers, Ellen. *Literary Women: The Great Writers*. New York/Oxford: Doubleday/Oxford University Press, 1976/1985.

Montweiler, Katherine. "Marketing Sensation: *Lady Audley's Secret* and Consumer Culture." In *Beyond Sensation: Mary Elizabeth Braddon in Context*, edited by Marlene Tromp, Pamela K. Gilbert, and Aeron Haynie, 43–62. Albany: University of New York Press, 2000.

Moqari, Shaqayq. "Representations of Mad Woman in *Lady Audley's Secret* by Mary Elizabeth Braddon." *World Scientific News, WSN* no. 22 (2015): 76–90.

Morton, Timothy. *Ecology Without Nature: Rethinking Environmental Aesthetics*. Cambridge: Harvard University Press, 2007.

Mulvey-Roberts, Marie "'Dracula and the Doctors": Bad Blood, Menstrual Taboo and the New Woman," In *Bram Stoker: History, Psychoanalysis, and the Gothic*, edited by William Hughes and Andrew Smith, 75–95. New York: St. Martin's, 1998.

———. "The Female Gothic Body." In *Women and the Gothic: An Edinburgh Companion*, edited by Avril Horner and Sue Zlosnik, 106–119. Edinburgh: Edinburgh University Press, 2016.

Nayder, Lilith. "Rebellious Sepoys and Bigamous Wives: The Indian Mutiny and Marriage Law Reform in *Lady Audley's Secret*." In *Beyond Sensation: Mary Elizabeth Braddon in Context*, edited by Marlene Tromp, Pamela K. Gilbert, and Aeron Haynie, 31–42. Albany: University of New York Press, 2000.

Newman, Beth. "Review: The Birth of *Wuthering Heights*: Emily Brontë at Work." *Victorian Studies* no. 42.2 (2000): 310–312.

Nightingale, Florence. *Suggestions for Thought by Florence Nightingale: Selections and Commentaries*, edited by Michael D. Calabria and Janet A. Macrae. Philadelphia: University of Pennsylvania Press, 1994.

Nunokawa, Jeff. "Sexuality in the Victorian Novel." In *The Cambridge Companion to the Victorian Novel*, edited by Diedre David, 125–148. Cambridge: Cambridge University Press, 2001.

Orlie, Melissa A. "Impersonal Matter." In *New Materialisms: Ontology, Agency, and Politics*, edited by Diana Coole and Samantha Frost, 116–138. Durham: Duke University Press, 2010.

Ortner, Sherry B. "Is Female to Male as Nature Is to Culture." In *Women, Culture, and Society*, edited by M.Z. Rosaldo and L. Lamphere, 68–87. Stanford: Stanford University Press, 1974.

Otten, Charlotte F. *A Lycanthropy Reader: Werewolves in Western Culture*. Syracuse: Syracuse University Press, 1986.

Packard, Alpheus S. *Lamarck the Founder of Evolution His Life and Work*. New York/London/Bombay: Longmans, Green, and Co., 1901/2008.

Panksepp, Jaak. *Affective Neuroscience: The Foundations of Human and Animal Emotions*. Oxford/New York: Oxford University Press, 1998.

Paris, Bernard J. "Wuthering Heights." *Imagined Human Beings: A Psychological Approach to Character and Conflict in Literature*. New York: New York University Press, 1997.

Parker, Elizabeth. *The Forest and the EcoGothic: The Deep Dark Woods in the Popular Imagination*. London: Palgrave Macmillan, 2020.

Pegg, Samantha. "'Madness is a Woman': Constance Kent and Victorian Constructions of Female Insanity." *Liverpool Law Rev* (2009): 207–223.

Pike, Judith. "'My name was Isabella Linton': Coverture, Domestic Violence, and Mrs. Heathcliff's Narrative in *Wuthering Heights*." *Nineteenth-Century Literature* no. 64.3 (December 2009): 347–383.

Piper, Alana Jayne. "'Woman's Special Enemy': Female Enmity in Criminal Discourse during the Long Nineteenth Century." *Journal of Social History* no. 49.3 (2016): 671–692.

Pope, Anne-Marie. "American Dime Novels, 1860–1915." *Historical Association: The Voice for History* (2020).https://www.history.org.uk/student/resource/4512/american-dime-novels-1860-1915.

Porter, Roy. "The Body and the Mind, The Doctor and the Patient: Negotiating Hysteria." In *Hysteria Beyond Freud*, edited by Helen King, Roy Porter, G. S. Rousseau, and Elaine Showalter, 225–285. Berkeley: University of California Press, 1997.

Powell, Anna, and Andrew Smith. *Teaching the Gothic*. New York: Palgrave Macmillan, 2006.

Pugh, Evelyn L. "Florence Nightingale and J.S. Mill Debate Women's Rights." *Journal of British Studies* no 21.2 (Spring 1982): 118–138.

Punter, David. *A New Companion to the Gothic*. West Sussex: Blackwell Publishing, 2012.

———. *Gothic Pathologies: The Text, the Body, and the Law*. Hampshire/New York: Palgrave Macmillan, 1998.

Pykett, Lyn. "Sensation and the Fantastic in the Victorian Novel." In *The Cambridge Companion to the Victorian Novel*, edited by Diedre David, 192–211. Cambridge: Cambridge University Press, 2001.

Radcliffe, Ann. *The Mysteries of Udolpho*. Oxford/New York: Oxford University Press, 1794/2008.

Ransom, Amy J. "Werewolves." In the *Ashgate Encyclopedia of Literary and Cinematic Monsters*, edited by Jeffrey Andrew Weinstock, 577–587. Burlington: Ashgate Publishing Company, 2014.

Reed, Edward S. *From Soul to Mind: The Emergence of Psychology from Erasmus Darwin to William James*. New Haven: Yale University Press, 1997.

Rees, Emma L. E. "Narrating the Victorian Vagina: Charlotte Brontë and the Masturbating Woman." In *The Female Body in Medicine and Literature*, edited by Andrew Mangham and Greta Depledge, 119–134. Liverpool: Liverpool University Press, 2011.

Reyes, Xavier Aldana. *Horror Film and Affect: Towards a Corporeal Model of Viewership*. New York/Abington: Routledge, 2016.

Rhys, Jean. *Good Morning, Midnight*. New York/London: W.W. Norton & Company, 1938/2000.

Riley, Denise. "Am I That Name?": *Feminism and the Category of "Women" in History*. London: The Macmillan Press, 1988.

Robbins, Ruth, and Julian Wolfreys. *Victorian Gothic: Literary and Cultural Manifestations in the Nineteenth Century*. New York: Palgrave, 2000.

Roberts, Helene E. "Marriage, Redundancy or Sin: The Painter's View of Women in the First Twenty-Five Years of Victoria's Reign." In *Suffer and Be Still: Women in the Victorian Age*, edited by Martha Vicinus, 45–76. New York: Routledge, 1972/2013.

Rodensky, Lisa. *The Crime in Mind: Criminal Responsibility and the Victorian Novel*. Oxford/New York: Oxford University Press, 2003.

Rosenman, Ellen Bajuk. "'Virtue of Illegitimacy': Inheritance and Belonging in *The Dark Woman* and *Mary Price*." In *GWM Reynolds: Nineteenth-Century Fiction, Politics, and the Press*, edited by Anne Humphreys, 211–224. New York: Routledge, 2016.

Rousseau, G. S. "'A Strange Pathology': Hysteria in the Early Modern World, 1500–1800." In *Hysteria Beyond Freud*, edited by Helen King, Roy Porter, G. S. Rousseau, and Elaine Showalter, 91–221. Berkeley: University of California Press, 1997.

Rubinow Gorsky, Susan. "'I'll Cry Myself Sick': Illness in *Wuthering Heights*." *Literature and Medicine* no. 18.2 (Fall 1999): 173–188.

Rylance, Rick. *Victorian Psychology and British Culture 1850–1880*. Oxford: Oxford University Press, 2000.

Sanzo, Kameron. "New Materialism(s)." *Genealogy of the Posthuman*. Published April 2018. https://criticalposthumanism.net/new-materialisms/.

Saxey, Esther. "Introduction." In *Lady Audley's Secret*, edited by Esther Saxey. Hertfordshire: Wordsworth Classics Edition, 2007.

Schroeder, Natalie. "Feminine Sensationalism, Eroticism, and Self-Assertion: M. E. Braddon and Ouida." *Tulsa Studies in Women's Literature* no. 7.1 (Spring 1988): 87–103.

Schwartz, Laura. "Freethinking Feminists: Women in the Freethought Movement." In *Infidel Feminism: Secularism, Religion and Women's Emancipation, England 1830–1914*, edited by Laura Schwartz, 41–72. Manchester: Manchester University Press, 2013.

Scott, Sir Walter. *The Bride of Lammermoor*. Mineola: Dover Publications, 1819/2017.

Scull, Andrew. "In the Social History of Psychiatry in the Victorian Era." *Madhouses, Mad-Doctors, and Madmen: The Social History of Psychiatry in the Victorian Era*, edited by Andrew Scull, 5–33. Philadelphia: University of Philadelphia Press, 1981.

———. *Madhouses, Mad-Doctors, and Madmen: The Social History of Psychiatry in the Victorian Era*. Philadelphia: University of Philadelphia Press, 1981.

Sedgwick, Eve Kosofsky. *The Coherence of Gothic Conventions*. London: Routledge, 1986.

Shaefer, Donovan O. *Religious Affects: Animality, Evolution, and Power*. Durham: Duke University Press, 2015.

Shakespeare, William. *Hamlet* Folger Edition. Delran: Simon and Schuster, 1609/1992.

Shea, Victor. "Penny Dreadfuls." In *Encyclopedia of the Victorian Era*, edited by James Eli Adams, Tom Pendergast, and Sara Pendergast, 185–186. Danbury: Grolier Academic Reference, 2004.

Showalter, Elaine. "Florence Nightingale's Feminist Complaint: Women, Religion, and *Suggestions for Thought*." *Signs* no 6.3 (Spring 1981): 395–412.

———. "Hysteria, Feminism, and Gender." In *Hysteria Beyond Freud*, edited by Helen King, Roy Porter, G. S. Rousseau, and Elaine Showalter, 286–344. Berkeley: University of California Press, 1997.

Sigsworth, E. M., and T. J. Wyke. "A Study of Victorian Prostitution and Venereal Disease." In *Suffer and Be Still: Women in the Victorian Age*, edited by Martha Vicinus, 77–99. New York: Routledge, 1972/2013.

Simpson, Philip L. "Review: The Essential Guide to Werewolf Fiction." *The Journal of American Culture* no. 27.4 (December 2004): 443–445.

Smith, Andrew. *Gothic Literature: Edinburgh Critical Guide*. Edinburgh: Edinburgh University Press, 2013.

———. "Victorian Gothic Death." In *Victorian Gothic: An Edinburgh Companion*, edited by Andrew Smith and William Hughes, 156–169. Edinburgh: Edinburgh University Press, 2012.

Smith, Andrew, and Diane Wallace. "The Female Gothic: Then and Now." *Gothic Studies* no. 6.1 (May 2004): 1–7.

Smith, H. R. *New Light on Sweeney Todd, Thomas Peckett Prest, James Malcolm Rymer, and Elizabeth Caroline Grey*. London: Jarndyce, 2002.

Smith, Tyler W. "The Climacteric Disease: A Paroxysmal Affection Occurring at the Decline of the Catamenia." *Journal of Medicine: A Monthly Record of the Medical Sciences* no. VII (July 1849): 601–609.

Spink, Amanda. *Information Behavior: An Evolutionary Instinct*. London/New York: Springer, 2010.

Spivak, Gayatri Chakravorty. "Three Women's Texts and a Critique of Imperialism." *Critical Inquiry* no. 12.1 (Autumn 1985): 243–261.

Springhall, John. "'A Life Story for the People?' Edwin J. Brett and the London 'Low-Life' Penny Dreadfuls of the 1860s." *Victorian Studies* no. 33.2 (Winter 1990): 223–246.

———. "'Pernicious Reading'? The Penny Dreadful as Scapegoat for Late-Victorian Juvenile Crime." *Victorian Periodical Review* no. 27.4 (Winter 1994): 362–349.

Steere, Elizabeth Lee. "'I Thought You Was an Evil Spirit': The Hidden Villain of *Lady Audley's Secret*." *Women's Writing* no. 15.3 (December 2008): 300–319.

Stott, Rebecca. *The Fabrication of the Late-Victorian Femme Fatale: The Kiss of Death*. London: Palgrave Macmillan, 1992.

Suglia, Joseph. "It's not what you think: Affect Theory and Power Take to the Stage." Duke University Press. Published February 2016. https://dukeupress.wordpress.com/2016/02/15/its-not-what-you-think-affect-theory-and-power-take-to-the-stage/.

Summerscale, Kate. *Mrs. Robinson's Disgrace: The Private Diary of a Victorian Lady*. London/New York: Bloomsbury Publishing, 2012.

Talairach-Vielmas, Laurence. *Moulding the Female Body in Victorian Fairy Tales and Sensation Novels*. New York: Routledge, 2007.

———. "Sensation Fiction: A Peep Behind the Veil." In *Victorian Gothic: An Edinburgh Companion*, edited by Andrew Smith and William Hughes, 29–42. Edinburgh: Edinburgh University Press, 2012.

Talbot, James Beard. "The Miseries of Prostitution." *The Making of the Modern Law*. London: J. Madden, 1844: 142.

Tarr, Clayton Carlyle. *Gothic Stories Within Stories: Frame Narratives and Realism in the Genre, 1790–1900*. Jefferson: McFarland & Company, Inc, 2017.

Thomas, Ardel. "Queer Victorian Gothic." In *Victorian Gothic: An Edinburgh Companion*, edited by Andrew Smith and William Hughes, 142–155. Edinburgh: Edinburgh University Press, 2012.

Thormahlen, Marianne. "The Lunatic and Devil's Discipline: The 'Lover's' in *Wuthering Heights*." *The Review of English Studies* no. 48.190 (March 1997): 183–197.

Tomaiuolo, Saverio. *In Lady Audley's Shadows: Mary Elizabeth Braddon and Victorian Genres*. Edinburgh: Edinburgh University Press, 2010.

Tomkins, Silvan A. *Affect Imagery Consciousness: The Complete Edition*. New York: Springer Publishing Company, 2008.

Tromp, Marlene. "The Dangerous Woman: M.E. Braddon's Sensational (En)gendering of Domestic Law." In *Beyond Sensation: Mary Elizabeth Braddon in Context*, edited by Marlene Tromp, Pamela K. Gilbert, and Aeron Haynie, 93–110. Albany: University of New York Press, 2000.

Tromp, Marlene, Pamela K. Gilbert, and Aeron Haynie. *Beyond Sensation: Mary Elizabeth Braddon in Context*. Albany: University of New York Press, 2000.

Tyler, Melissa. "Performativity." *SAGE Research Methods Foundation* (2019). https://doi.org/10.4135/9781526421036798814.

Ussa, Riikka. "Representations of the Female in Mary Elizabeth Braddon's *Lady Audley's Secret* and Wilkie Collins's *The Woman in White*." MA Thesis. University of Tempere, 2009.

Vakoch, Douglas A., and Sam Mickey. *Women and Nature?: Beyond Dualism in Gender, Body, and Environment*. New York: Routledge, 2018.

Valera, Luca. "Francoise d'Eaubonne and EcoFeminism: Rediscovering the Link between Women and Nature." In *Women and Nature? Beyond Dualism in Gender, Body, and Environment*, edited by Douglas A. Vakoch and Sam Mickey, 10–25. Abington/New York: 2018.

Van de Vijver, Gertrudis, and Filip Geerardyn. *The Pre-Psychoanalytic Writings of Sigmund Freud*. Abingdon/New York: Routledge, 2018.

Van De Warker M. D., Ely. "Impotency in Women." *American Journal of Obstetrics and Diseases of Women and Children* no. XI.I (January 1878): 1–21.

Vicinus, Martha. *Suffer and Be Still: Women in the Victorian Age*. New York: Routledge Reprint, 2013.

Voskuil, Lynn M. "Acts of Madness: Lady Audley and the Meanings of Victorian Femininity." *Feminist Studies*, no. 27.3 (Autumn 2001): 611–639.

Wagner, Tamara S. "Re-plotting Inheritance: The Triangulation of Legacies and Affinities in the Fatal Three." In *New Perspectives of Mary Elizabeth Braddon*, edited by Jessica Cox, 175–194. Amsterdam/New York: Rodopi B.V., 2012.

Wallace, Diane. "'A Woman's Place.'" In *Women and the Gothic: An Edinburgh Companion*, edited by Avril Horner and Sue Zlosnik, 74–88. Edinburgh: Edinburgh University Press, 2016.

———. "The Female Gothic." In *The Encyclopedia of the Gothic*, edited by William Hughes, David Punter, and Andrew Smith, 231. Hoboken: Wiley-Blackwell Publishing, 2016. Macmillan, 2009.

Waller, Jason. "Benedict de Spinoza: Metaphysics." *Internet Encyclopedia of Philosophy*, 507–523 (2009). https://www.iep.utm.edu/spinoz-m/.

Walpole, Horace. *The Castle of Otranto*. New York: Dover Publications, 1764/2004.

Walsh, Brendan C. "'Like a Madd Dogge': Demonic Animals and Animal Narratives in Early Modern Possession Narratives." In *Gothic Animal: Uncanny Otherness and the Animal With-Out*, edited by Ruth Heholt and Melissa Edmundson, 21–41. Cham: Palgrave Macmillan, 2020.

Watley, John. "Crime." In *The Encyclopedia of the Gothic*, edited by William Hughes, David Punter, and Andrew Smith, 149–151. West Sussex/Hoboken: Blackwell Publishing, 2016.

Weliver, Phyllis. *Women Musicians in Victorian Fiction, 1860–1900: Representations of Music, Science and Gender in the Leisured Home*. Oxon/New York: Routledge, 2016.

Wetzel, Grace. "Homeless in the Home: Invention, Instability, and Insanity in the Domestic Spaces of M. E. Braddon and L. M. Alcott." In *New Perspectives of Mary Elizabeth Braddon*, edited by Jessica Cox, 75–94. Amsterdam/New York: Rodopi B.V., 2012.

Wiener, Martin J. *Reconstructing the Criminal: Culture, Law, and Policy in England, 1830–1914*. Cambridge/New York/Victoria: Cambridge University Press, 1990.

Wiesenthal, Chris. *Figuring Madness in Nineteenth-Century Fiction*. Hampshire/New York: Macmillan/St. Martin's Press, 1997.

Williams, Anne. "Review: *The Gothic Psyche: Disintegration and Growth in Nineteenth-Century English Literature*." *Victorian Studies* no. 42.4 (Summer 1999): 674–675.

Wilson, Glenn. *Love and Instinct: The Sociobiological Theory that Separates Instinct from Social Convention and Gives a Provocative View of the Basic Difference Between the Sexes*. New York/Abington: Maurice Temple Smith, 2014.

Wilson Carpenter, Mary. *Health, Medicine, and Society in Victorian England*. Santa Barbara: Praeger, 2010.

Wise, Sarah. *Inconvenient People: Lunacy, Liberty and the Mad-Doctors in Victorian England*. London: The Bodley Head, 2014.

Wojtczak, Helena. *Women of Victorian Sussex: Their Status, Occupations and Dealings with the Law 1830–1870*. Hastings: The Hastings Press, 2003.

Wolfreys, Julian. "The Victorian Gothic." In *Teaching the Gothic (Teaching the New English)*, edited by Anna Powell and Andrew Smith, 62–77. Hampshire/New York: Palgrave Macmillan. 2006.

Woolston, Jennifer M. "Lady Audley as the Cunning 'Other': An Economic, Sexual, and Criminal Attack on the Victorian Patriarchal Mindset." *EAPSU Online: A Journal of Critical and Creative Work* no. 5 (2008): 156–168.

Youngson, A. J. *The Scientific Revolution in Victorian Medicine*. New York: Routledge, 1979.

Zedner, Lucia. *Women, Crime, and Custody in Victorian England*. Oxford: Oxford University Press, 1994.

Zisowitz Stearns, Carol, and Peter N. Stearns. "Victorian Sexuality: Can Historians Do It Better?" *Journal of Social History* no. 18.4 (Summer 1985): 625–634. JSTOR.

References

Acton, William. *The Functions and Disorders of the Reproductive Organs in Childhood, Youth, Adult Ages, and Advanced Life: Considered in Their Psychological, Social, and Moral Relations* sixth edition. London: J&A Churchill, 1862/1875.

Alaimo, Stacy. *Bodily Natures: Science, Environment, and the Material Self.* Bloomington: Indiana University Press, 2010.

———. "Discomforting Creatures: Monstrous Natures in Recent Films." In *Beyond Nature Writing: Expanding the Boundaries of Ecocriticism*, edited by Karla Armbruster and Kathleen R. Wallace, 279–296. Charlottesville: The University Press of Virginia, 2001.

———. *Undomesticated Ground: Recasting Nature as Feminist Space*. Ithaca: Cornell University Press, 2000.

Alaimo, Stacy, and Susan Hekman. *Material Feminisms*. Bloomington: Indiana University Press, 2008.

Alexander, Christine, and Margaret Smith. *The Oxford Companion to the Brontës*. Oxford/New York: Oxford University Press, 2006.

Anderson, Vicki. *The Dime Novel in Children's Literature*. Jefferson: McFarland & Company, Inc, 2005.

Armstrong, Nancy. *Desire and Domestic Fiction: A Political History of the Novel*. Oxford/New York: Oxford University Press, 1987.

Baker Brown, Isaac. *On the Curability of Certain Forms of Insanity, Epilepsy, Catalepsy, and Hysteria in Females*. London: Robert Hardwicke, 1866.

Barad, Karen. "Posthumanist Performativity: Toward an Understanding of How Comes to Matter." *Signs* no. 28.3 (Spring 2003): 801–831.

Baring-Gould, Sabine. *The Book of Werewolves: Being an Account of a Terrible Superstition*. Smith, Elder and Co., 1865.

Barker-Benfield, Ben. "The Spermatic Economy: A Nineteenth Century View of Sexuality." *Feminist Studies* no. 1 (Summer 1972): 45–74.

Beard, George. "Neurasthenia or Nervous Exhaustion." *Boston Medical and Surgical Journal* no. 80 (1869): 217–221.

Beer, Gillian. *Darwin's Plots: Evolutionary Narrative in Darwin, George Eliot and Nineteenth-Century Fiction*. Third edition. Cambridge/New York: Cambridge University Press, 2009.

Bladow, Kyle, and Jennifer Ladino. *Affective Ecocriticism: Emotion, Embodiment, Environment*. Lincoln: University of Nebraska Press, 2018.

Bodichon Smith, Barbara Leigh. *Reasons for the Enfranchisement of Women*. London: McCorquodale & Co., 1866/1872. http://webapp1.dlib.indiana.edu/vwwp/view?docId=VAB7059&doc.view=print.

Botting, Fred. *Gothic: The New Critical Idiom*. New York: Routledge, 2014.

Bourgault du Coudray, Chantal. *The Curse of the Werewolf: Fantasy, Horror, and the Beast Within*. London/New York: I.B. Tauris & Co., 2006.

———. "Upright Citizens on All Fours: Nineteenth-Century Identity and the Image of the Werewolf." *Nineteenth-Century Contexts* no. 24.1 (2002): 1–16.

Braddon, Mary Elizabeth. *Lady Audley's Secret*, ed. Esther Saxey. Hertfordshire: Wordsworth Classics Edition, 2007.

Braidotti, Rosi. "Becoming Woman: or Sexual Difference Revisited." *Theory, Culture, and Society SAGE* no. 20.3 (2003): 43–64.

———. "The Politics of 'Life Itself' and New Ways of Dying." In *New Materialisms: Ontology, Agency, and Politics*, edited by Diana Coole and Samantha Frost, 201–220. Durham: Duke University Press, 2010.

Breuer, Josef, and Sigmund Freud. *Studies on Hysteria*, trans. James Strachey. New York: Basic Books, 1895/2000.

Brontë, Charlotte. "Jane Eyre." In *The Brontë Sisters*, 1–328. London/New York: Penguin Books, 2009.

Brontë, Emily. "Wuthering Heights." In *The Brontë Sisters*, 329–533. London/New York: Penguin Books, 1847/2009.

Carpenter, Mary. *Our Convicts*. London: Longman, Green, Longman, Roberts & Green, 1864.

Carter, Robert Brudenell. *On the Pathology and Treatment of Hysteria*. London: John Churchill, 1853.

Chaplin, Sue. "Female Gothic and the Law." In *Women and the Gothic: An Edinburgh Companion*, edited by Avril Horner and Sue Zlosnik, 135–149. Edinburgh: Edinburgh University Press, 2016.

Cohen, Jeffrey Jerome. *Monster Theory: Reading Culture*. Minneapolis/London: University of Minnesota Press, 1996.

Collins, Wilkie. *The Woman in White*. Paris: Leipzig Bernard Tauchnitz, 1861.

Coogan, Michael D. *The New Oxford Annotated Bible. New Revised Standard Version with the Apocrypha*. Oxford/New York: Oxford University Press, 2010.

Cott, Nancy F. "Passionlessness: An Interpretation of Victorian Sexual Ideology, 1790–1850." *Signs* no. 4.2 (Winter 1978): 219–236. JSTOR.

Crawford, Joseph. "'No more than a brute or a wild beast': *Wagner the Wehr-Wolf*, *Sweeney Todd* and the Limits of Human Responsibility." In *In the Company of Wolves: Werewolves, Wolves, and Wild Children*, edited by Sam George and William Hughes, 101–112. Manchester: Manchester University Press, 2020.

Creed, Barbara. "*Ginger Snaps*: the monstrous feminine as femme animale." In *She-wolf: A Cultural History of Female Werewolves* edited by Hannah Priest, 180–195. Manchester: Manchester University Press, 2015.

———. *The Monstrous-Feminine: Film, Feminism, Psychoanalysis*. London/New York: Routledge, 1993.

Daggers, Jenny. "The Victorian Female Civilising Mission and Women's Aspirations Towards Priesthood in the Church of England." *Women's History Review* 10.4, 651–670 (2001).

Darwin, Charles. *The Descent of Man, and Selection in Relation to Sex*. Princeton: Princeton University Press, 1871/1981.

Davidoff, Leonore. *The Best Circles: Women and Society in Victorian England*. London: Rowman and Littlefield, 1973.

Davison, Carol Margaret. *History of the Gothic: Gothic Literature, 1764–1824*. Cardiff: University of Wales Press, 2009.

———. "The Victorian Gothic and Gender." In *Victorian Gothic: An Edinburgh Companion*, edited by Andrew Smith and William Hughes, 124–141. Edinburgh: Edinburgh University Press, 2012.

Del Principe, David. "Introduction: The EcoGothic in the Long Nineteenth Century." *Gothic Studies* no. 16.1 (May 2014): 1–8.

DeLamotte, Eugenia C. *Perils of the Nights: A Feminist Study of Nineteenth-Century Gothic*. Oxford/New York: Oxford University Press, 1990.

Deleuze, Giles, and Felix Guattari. *Kafka: Toward a Minor Literature*. Minneapolis: University of Minneapolis Press, 1986.

Dickens, Charles. *Oliver Twist; or the Parish Boy's Progress*. London/Toronto: J. M. Dent and Sons, 1838.

Doane, Mary Ann. *Femmes Fatales: Feminism, Film Theory, and Psychoanalysis*. London: Routledge, 1991.

Drysdale, George R., and Thomas Robert Malthus. *The Elements of Social Science; or Physical, Sexual, and Natural Religion: An Exposition of the True Cause and Only Cure of The Three Primary Social Evils: Poverty, Prostitution, and Celibacy*. London: E. Truelove, 1854.

Dyer, Richard. *White*. London/New York: Routledge, 1997.

Easley, Alexis, and Shannon Scott. *Terrifying Transformations: An Anthology of Victorian Werewolf Fiction*, edited by Alexis Easley and Shannon Scott. Valancourt Books, 2013.

Edelman, Gerald. *Neural Darwinism: The Theory of Neuronal Group Selection*. New York: Basic Books, 1987.

———. *The Remembered Present: A Biological Theory of Consciousness*. New York: Basic Books, 1989.

Edelman, Gerald M., Joseph A. Gally, and Bernard J. Baars. "Biology of Consciousness." *Frontiers in Psychology* no. 2.4 (Winter 2011): 1–19.

Elliotson, John. *The Principles and Practice of Medicine: Founded on the Most Extensive Experience in Public Hospitals and Private Practice; And Developed in a Course of Lectures*. London: Joseph Butler, 1839.

Errym, Malcolm J. *The Dark Woman; or Days of the Prince Regent*. London: John Dicks Publishing, 1861.

Esquirol, Jean-Étienne Dominique. *Mental Maladies: A Treatise on Insanity*, translated by E. K. Hunt. Philadelphia: Lea and Blanchard, 1838/1845.

Estok, Simon. "Theorising the EcoGothic," *Gothic Nature* no. 1 (September 2019): 34–53.

Fincher, Max. "Werewolves." In *The Encyclopedia of the Gothic*, edited by William Hughes, David Punter, and Andrew Smith, 733–734. West Sussex/Hoboken: Wiley-Blackwell, 2016.

Flanders, Judith. *Inside the Victorian Home: A Portrait of Domestic Life in Victorian England*. New York/London: W. W. Norton & Company, Inc, 2003.

Fleenor, Juliann E. *The Female Gothic*. Michigan: Eden Publishing, 1983.

Foucault, Michel, *The History of Sexuality, Vol 1: An Introduction*. Toronto: Vintage Books Reprint, 1976/1990.

Franck, Kaja, and Janine Hatter. "Werewolves: Studies in Transformation." *Revenant* no. 2 (December 2016): 1–5. http://www.revenantjournal.com/issues/werewolves-studies-in-transformation-guest-editors-kaja-franck-and-janine-hatter/.

Freud, Sigmund. *The Standard Edition of the Complete Psychological Works of Sigmund Freud Vol. 1–24*, translated by James Strachey. London: Hogarth Press, 1893–1974.

———. *Dora: An Analysis of a Case Study of Hysteria*, edited by Philip Reiff. New York: Touchstone, 1997.

Frost, Brian J. *The Essential Guide to Werewolf Literature*. Madison/London: The University of Wisconsin Press, 2003.

George, Sam, and William Hughes. *In the Company of Wolves: Werewolves, Wolves, and Wild Children*. Manchester: Manchester University Press, 2020.

Gibbs, Anna. "After Affect: Sympathy, Synchrony, and Mimetic Communication." In *The Affect Theory Reader*, edited by Melissa Gregg and Gregory J. Seigworth, 186–205. Durham/London: Duke University Press, 2010.

Gilbert, Pamela K. *Mapping the Victorian Social Body*. Albany: State University of New York Press, 2004.

Gilbert, Sandra M. "*Jane Eyre* and the Secrets of Furious Lovemaking." *NOVEL: A Forum on Fiction no. 31.3 Thirtieth Anniversary Issue* (Summer 1998): 351–372.

Gilbert, Sandra M., and Susan Gubar. *The Madwoman in the Attic: The Woman Writer and the Nineteenth-Century Literary Imagination*. Boston: Yale University Press, 1979/2000.

Girdwood, G.F. "On the Theory of Menstruation." In *The London Lancet: A Journal of British and Foreign Medical and Chemical Science, Criticism, Literature and News* no. 39.1018 (March 1843): 809–848.

Greg, William Rathbone. "Prostitution." *Westminster Review* no. 53 (July 1850): 448–506.

Gregg, Melissa, and Gregory J. Seigworth. *The Affect Theory Reader*. Durham/London: Duke University Press, 2010.

Grosz, Elizabeth. "Darwin and Feminism: Preliminary Investigations for a Possible Alliance." *Australian Feminist Studies* no. 14.29 (1999): 31–45.

———. *Volatile Bodies: Toward a Corporeal Feminism*. Bloomington: Indiana University Press, 1994.

———. "Women, *Chora*, Dwelling." *Space, Time, and Perversion: Essays on the Politics of Bodies*, 111–124. London/New York: Routledge, 1995.

Halberstam, J. *Skin Shows: Gothic Horror and the Technology of Monsters.* Durham/London: Duke University Press, 1995.

Hatter, Janine. "Lycanthropic Landscapes: An Ecogothic Reading of Nineteenth-Century Werewolf Short Stories." *Revenant* no. 2 (December 2016): 6–21. http://www.revenantjournal.com/issues/werewolves-studies-in-transformation-guest-editors-kaja-franck-and-janine-hatter/.

Heiland, Donna. *Gothic and Gender: An Introduction.* Malden/Oxford/Victoria: Blackwell Publishing, 2004.

Highmore, Ben. "Bitter After Taste: Affect, Food, and Social Aesthetic." In *The Affect Theory Reader*, edited by Melissa Gregg and Gregory J. Seigworth, 118–137. Durham/London: Duke University Press, 2010.

Hoeveler, Diane Long. *Gothic Feminism: The Professionalization of Gender from Charlotte Smith to the Brontës.* University Park: Penn State University Press, 1998.

Hogg, Michael A., Deborah J. Terry, and Katherine M. White. "A Tale of Two Theories: A Critical Comparison of Identity Theory with Social Identity Theory." *Social Psychology Quarterly* no. 58.4 (1995): 255–269.

Horner, Avril, and Sue Zlosnik. "No Country for Old Women: Gender, Age and the Gothic." In *Women and the Gothic: An Edinburgh Companion*, edited by Avril Horner and Sue Zlosnik, 184–198. Edinburgh: Edinburgh University Press, 2016.

———. *Women and the Gothic: An Edinburgh Companion.* Edinburgh: Edinburgh University Press, 2016.

Hurley, Kelly. *The Gothic Body: Sexuality, Materialism, and Degeneration at the Fin de Siècle.* Cambridge: Cambridge University Press, 1996.

Irigaray, Luce. *This Sex Which is Not One*, translated by Catherine Porter with Carolyn Burke. Utica: Cornell University Press, 1985.

———. *Speculum of the Other Woman*, translated by Gillian C. Gill. Utica: Cornell University Press, 1985.

Keetley, Dawn, and Matthew Wynn Sivils. *EcoGothic in Nineteenth-Century American Literature.* London/New York: Routledge, 2017.

Kingsley Kent, Susan. *Sex and Suffrage in Britain, 1860–1914.* London: Taylor & Francis Reprint, 1987/2005.

Klein, Herbert G. "Strong Women and Feeble Men: Upsetting Gender Stereotypes in Mary Elizabeth Braddon"s *Lady Audley's Secret*." *ATEENEA* no. 28.1 (June 2008): 161–174.

Knelman, Judith. *Twisting in the Wind: The Murderess and the English Press.* Toronto: University of Toronto Press, 1998.

Kramer, Heinrich, and James Sprenger. *The Malleus Maleficarum*, trans. Reverend Montague Summers. New York: Dover, 1978.

Kranidis, Rita S. *The Victorian Spinster and Colonial Emigration: Contested Subjects.* New York: St. Martin's Press, 1999.

Kröger, Lisa. "Panic, Paranoia and Pathos: Ecocriticism in the Eighteenth-Century Gothic Novel." In *Ecogothic*, edited by Andrew Smith and Williams Hughes, 15–27. Manchester: Manchester University Press, 2013.

Lamarck, Jean-Baptiste de Monet de. *Système Des Animaux Sans Vertèbres.* Charleston: Nabu Press, 1801/2011.

Latour, Bruno. *We Have Never Been Modern*. Cambridge: Harvard University Press, 1993.

Laycock, Thomas. *A Treatise on the Nervous Diseases of Women: Comprising an Inquiry into the Nature, Causes, and Treatment of Spinal and Hysterical Disorders*. London: Longman, Orme, Brown, Green, and Longmans, 1840.

Liggins, Emma. "The 'Evil Days' of the Female Murderer: subverted marriage plots and the avoidance of scandal in the Victorian sensation novel." *Journal of Victorian Culture* no. 1 (March 1997): 27–41.

Lombroso, Cesare. *L'uomo delinquente*. Milan: Ulrico Hoepli, 1876.

———. *Ricerche sul cretinismo in Lombardia* (1859). https://www.corriere.it/cultura/09_aprile_28/stella_lombroso_catalogo_assurdita_8bd638b2-33c2-11de-8558-00144f02aabc.shtml.

Lombroso, Cesare, and William Ferrero. *The Female Offender*. New York: D. Appleton and Company, 1895.

Lord, Beth. *Spinoza's Ethics*. Edinburgh: Edinburgh University Press, 2010.

MacDonald, George. "The Gray Wolf." In *Terrifying Transformations: An Anthology of Victorian Werewolf Fiction*, edited by Alexis Easley and Shannon Scott, 112–120. Kansas City: Valancourt Books, 2013.

Mack, Robert. *The Wonderful and Surprising History of Sweeney Todd: The Life and Times of an Urban Legend*. London/New York: Continuum, 2007.

Mangham, Andrew. *Violent Women and Sensation Fiction: Crime, Medicine, and Victorian Popular Culture*. New York/Hampshire: Palgrave Macmillan, 2007.

Margree, Victoria, and Bryony Randall. "Fin-de-Siècle." In *Victorian Gothic: An Edinburgh Companion*, edited by Andrew Smith and William Hughes, 217–233. Edinburgh: Edinburgh University Press, 2012.

Marryat, Frederick. "The White Wolf of the Hartz Mountains." In *Terrifying Transformations: An Anthology of Victorian Werewolf Fiction*, edited by Alexis Easley and Shannon Scott, 23–41. Valancourt Books, 2013.

Mason, Michael. *The Making of Victorian Sexuality*. Oxford/New York: Oxford University Press, 1994.

Mayhew, Henry. *The Criminal Prisons of London and Scenes of Prison Life*. London: Griffin & Bohn, 1862.

Maynard, John. *Charlotte Brontë and Sexuality*. Cambridge: Cambridge University Press, 1984.

McClintock, Anne. *Imperial Leather: Race, Gender and Sexuality in the Colonial Contest*. New York/London: Routledge, 1995.

McWilliam, Rohan. "*The Wonderful and Surprising History of Sweeney Todd: The Life and Times of Urban Legend* (Review)." *Victorian Studies* no. 50.4 (Summer 2008): 731–732.

Merchant, Carolyn. *The Death of Nature: Women, Ecology, and the Scientific Revolution*. New York: Harper Collins Publishing, 1980.

Milbank, Alison. *Daughters of the House: Modes of the Gothic in Victorian Fiction*. London: Macmillan Academic and Professional Ltd, 1992.

Mill, John Stuart. *The Subjection of Women*. London: Longmans, Green and Company, 1869.

Millingen, John Gideon. *The Passions: Or, Mind and Matter.* London: John and Daniel A. Darling, 1848.
Mitchell, Jane. "Reclaiming the Monster: Abjection and Subversion in the Marital Gothic Novel." *Studies in Arts and Humanities* no. 4.1 (2018): 54–72.
Mitchell, Juliet. *Mad Men and Medusas: Reclaiming Hysteria.* New York: Basic Books, 2000.
———. *Psychoanalysis and Feminism: A Radical Reassessment of Freudian Psychoanalysis.* New York: Basic Books, 1974/2000.
Mitchell, Sally. *Daily Life in Victorian England Second Edition.* Westport: Greenwood Press, 2009.
Moi, Toril. *Sexual/Textual Politics: Feminist Literary Theory.* London/New York: Methuen & Co., 1985.
Moore, Jason W. "The Rise of Cheap Nature." In *Sociology Faculty Scholarship* (2016): 78–115. https://orb.binghamton.edu/sociology_fac/2/.
Mulvey-Roberts, Marie. *Dangerous Bodies: Historicising the Gothic Corporeal.* Manchester: Manchester University Press, 2016.
Murdoch, Lydia. *Daily Life of Victorian Women.* Santa Barbara: Greenwood Publishing, 2013.
Nabi, Asmat. "Gender Represented in the Gothic Novel." *IOSR Journal of Humanities and Social Science* no. 22.11 (November 2017): 73–77.
Owen, M. E. "Criminal Women." *Cornhill Magazine* no 14. London: Smith, Elder, & Co., 1866.
Parker, Elizabeth, and Michelle Poland. "Gothic Nature: An Introduction." *Gothic Nature* no. 1 (September 2019): 1–20. https://gothicnaturejournal.com.
Patmore, Coventry. *The Angel in the House.* London: John W. Parker and Son, 1858. https://www.gutenberg.org/files/4099/4099-h/4099-h.htm.
Plumwood, Val. *Feminism and the Mastery of Nature.* London: Routledge, 1993.
Poovey, Mary. *Uneven Developments: The Ideological Work of Gender in Mid-Victorian England.* Chicago: University of Chicago Press, 1988.
Prichard, James Cowles. *A Treatise on Insanity and Other Disorders Affecting the Mind.* London: Sherwood, Gilbert, and Piper, 1835.
Priest, Hannah. *She-wolf: A Cultural History of Female Werewolves.* Manchester: Manchester University Press, 2015.
Punter, David, and Glennis Byron. *The Gothic.* Victoria: Blackwell Publishing, 2004.
Pykett, Lyn. *The "Improper" Feminine: The Women's Sensational Novel and the New Woman Writing.* Abington/London: Routledge, 1992.
———. *Nineteenth Century Sensation Novel.* Devon: Northcote House Publishers, 1994/2011.
Reynolds, George W. *Wagner, the Wehr-Wolf* (1846–1847). Mineola: Dover Publications, 1975.
Ronacher, Bernhard. "Innate Releasing Mechanisms and Fixed Action Patterns: Basic Ethological Concepts as Drivers for Neuroethological Studies on Acoustic Communication in Orthoptera." *Journal of Comparative Physiology* no. 205 (February 2019): 33–50.

Royal, Anna. "Wax Dolls: Shaping a New Identity in Mary Elizabeth Braddon's Lady Audley's Secret." *Nineteenth-Century Gender Studies* no. 9.3 (Winter 2013): 1–24.

Ruskin, John, "Sesame and Lilies. Lecture II-Lilies: Of Queens' Gardens." *Harvard Classic*, Vol. 28 (1865). https://www.bartleby.com/28/7.html.

Russo, Mary. *The Female Grotesque: Risk, Excess, and Modernity*. New York: Routledge, 1994.

Rymer, James Malcolm, or Thomas Peckett Prest. *Sweeney Todd: The String of Pearls* edited by Professor Rohan McWilliam. Mineola: Dover Publications, 1846–47/2015.

Saxby, Jessie. *Shetland Traditional Lore*. Edinburgh: Granted and Murray Limited, 1932.

Scull, Andrew. *Hysteria: The Biography*. Oxford/New York: Oxford University Press, 2009.

Seigworth, Gregory J., and Melissa Gregg. "An Inventory of Shimmers." In *The Affect Theory Reader*, edited by Melissa Gregg and Gregory J. Seigworth, 1–27. Durham/London: Duke University Press, 2010.

Shildrick, Margrit. *Embodying the Monster: Encounters with the Vulnerable Self*. London/Thousand Oaks/New Delhi: Sage Publications, 2002.

Showalter, Elaine. *The Female Malady: Women, Madness, and English Culture 1830–1980*. Michigan: Pantheon Books, 1985.

———. *Hystories: Hysterical Epidemics and Modern Media*. New York: Columbia University Press, 1997.

———. "On Hysterical Narrative." *Narrative* no 1.1 (Winter 1993): 24–35.

Shuttleworth, Sally. *Charlotte Brontë and Victorian Psychology*. Cambridge/New York: Cambridge University, 1994/2004.

Smith, Andrew, and William Hughes, *EcoGothic*. Manchester: Manchester University Press, 2013.

———. *The Victorian Gothic: An Edinburgh Companion*. Edinburgh: Edinburgh University Press, 2012.

Smith, Tyler W. *A Manual of Obstetrics: Theoretical and Practice*. London: Churchill, 1858.

Sparks, Tabitha. "To the Madhouse Born: The Ethics of Exteriority in *Lady Audley's Secret*." In *New Perspectives of Mary Elizabeth Braddon*, edited by Jessica Cox, 19–36. Amsterdam/New York: Rodopi B.V., 2012.

Spinoza, Benedict de. *The Ethics 1–5*, translated by R.H.M. Elwes. London/Scotts Valley: CreateSpace Independent Publishing Platform, 2014.

Spivak, Gayatri Chakravorty. "Three Women's Texts and a Critique of Imperialism." *Critical Inquiry* no. 12.1 (Autumn 1985): 243–261.

Stickney Ellis, Sarah. *The Daughters of England: Their Position in Society, Character and Responsibilities*. New York: D. Appleton and Company, 1842.

———. *The Women of England, Their Social Duties, and Domestic Habits*. New York: D. Appleton and Company, 1839.

Talairach-Vielmas, Laurence. "Madwomen and Attics." In *Women and the Gothic: An Edinburgh Companion*, edited by Avril Horner and Sue Zlosnik, 31–45. Edinburgh: Edinburgh University Press, 2016.

———. "'If I Read Her Right': Textual Secrets in Thou Art the Man (1894)." In *New Perspectives of Mary Elizabeth Braddon*, edited by Jessica Cox, 195–210. Amsterdam/New York: Rodopi B.V., 2012.

Torgerson, Beth. *Reading the Brontë Body: Disease, Desire, and the Constraints of Culture*. Hampshire/New York: Palgrave Macmillan, 2005.

Tylor, Edward Burnett. *Primitive Culture: Researches into the Development of Mythology, Philosophy, Religion, Art, and Custom*. London: John Murray, 1871.

Urban, Septimus R., or James Malcolm Rymer. *The Wronged Wife, or the Heart of Hate*. London/New York: Frank Starr & Co. Publishers, 1870.

Van de Vijver, Gertrudis, and Filip Geerardyn. *The Pre-Psychoanalytic Writings of Sigmund Freud*. Abingdon/New York: Routledge, 2018.

Vicinus, Martha. "'Helpless and Unfriended': Nineteenth-Century Domestic Melodrama." *New Literary History* no. 12.1 (Autumn 1981): 127–143.

Vrettos, Athena. *Somatic Fictions: Imagining Illness in Victorian Culture*. Stanford: Stanford University Press, 1995.

Wallace, Diane, and Andrew Smith. *The Female Gothic: New Directions*. New York: Palgrave Macmillan, 2009.

Ward, Ian. *Sex, Crime, and Literature in Victorian Literature*. Oxford/Portland: Hart Publishing, 2010.

Watkins, Megan. "Desiring Recognition, Accumulating Affect." In *The Affect Theory Reader*, edited by Melissa Gregg and Gregory J. Seigworth, 269–288. Durham/London: Duke University Press, 2010.

Williams, Anne. *Art of Darkness: A Poetics of Gothic*. Chicago/London: University of Chicago Press, 1995.

———. "Wicked Woman." In *Women and the Gothic: An Edinburgh Companion*, edited by Avril Horner and Sue Zlosnik, 91–105. Edinburgh: Edinburgh University Press, 2016.

Willis, Martin. "Victorian Realism and the Gothic: Objects of Terror Transformed." In *Victorian Gothic: An Edinburgh Companion*, edited by Andrew Smith and William Hughes, 15–28. Edinburgh: Edinburgh University Press, 2012.

Wilson, Elizabeth A. *Psychosomatic: Feminism and the Neurological Body*. Durham: Duke University Press, 2004.

Winslow, Forbes. "Woman in Her Psychological Relations." *Journal of Psychological Medicine and Mental Pathology* no. 4.13 (January 1851): 18–50.

Wisker, Gina. "Female Vampirism." In *Women and the Gothic: An Edinburgh Companion*, edited by Avril Horner and Sue Zlosnik, 150–166. Edinburgh: Edinburgh University Press, 2016.

Wood, Jane. *Passion and Pathology in Victorian Fiction*. Oxford/New York: Oxford University Press, 2001.

Yonge, Charlotte Mary. *The Daisy Chain: Or, Aspirations*. Leipzing: Bernhard Tauchnitz, 1856.

Zedner, Lucia. "Women, Crime, and Penal Responses: A Historical Account." *Crime and Justice* no. 14 (1991): 307–362. JSTOR.

Index

"A Woman's Mission," 51
abhuman(ity), 154–55, 157, 174–76, 181n7
Acton, William, 25, 39–40
actor theory, 14
Ada, the Betrayed, 90
affect theory, 18, 138n2
affectio, 108
affective ecocriticism, 18, 106–8
Affective Ecocriticism: Emotion, Embodiment, Environment, 107
affectivity, affective experiences, 100, 106–7, 113–14, 119, 128, 132–33, 137
agency, 1–4, 11, 14–17, 19, 25, 32, 36, 40, 42, 45, 53–54, 58, 66, 69, 73, 78, 80–82, 84, 94–95, 110, 119, 121, 123, 136–37, 145, 151, 153, 160–61, 169, 176, 177–78, 180, 184, 186
Alaimo, Stacy, 16, 17, 19, 60, 68, 70, 100, 107, 119, 125, 132, 133, 144–45
anachronism, 73, 83, 146
Anderson, Vicki, 112
angel, 6–7, 14, 20, 23–24, 33–35, 43–44, 46–49, 51–52, 94, 100–101, 112–13, 124–25, 127, 129–32, 136, 141, 156, 158, 160, 166–67, 171–72, 174–75, 185
"Angel in the House," 44, 100

Anglican Catholicism, 44, 54
animality, 86–87, 111, 143–44, 146, 152, 157, 161, 163, 168, 173, 176
animals, 10, 16, 18, 32, 38, 41, 46, 58–59, 82, 87, 102, 104, 106, 123, 143, 145, 148–50, 152, 161–62, 164–65, 173, 176–77, 181n3
anthropomorphic, anthropomorphism, 17–18
archetype(s), 41
Armitt, Lucie, 67, 185
ars erotica, 27
atavism, 104, 148, 175–76
Atlas, 66
avatar, 81

Barad, Karen, 15, 108
Baring-Gould, Sabine, 141, 150–51, 160, 162, 170, 178
Bartholomew Fair, 149
basilisk, 122
Beard, George, 62
beast within, 150–51, 176
Beer, Gillian, 31
Beeton, Isabella, 101
binaries, 3–4, 7, 14, 16–17, 23, 34, 40, 50, 66, 93, 123, 144, 153, 172, 185
biology, biological, 1–2, 4–7, 10, 16–18, 20, 23–25, 27–28, 30–32, 40, 42–43,

50, 53–54, 56–61, 64–65, 71, 75, 80, 88, 92, 95, 99–105, 122, 132, 138, 144, 146–48, 153–54, 156, 161, 163, 171, 173, 176, 180, 184–86
Biopsychology, 102
Bladow, Kyle and Jennifer Ladino, 18, 107, 132, 159
Bodichon, Barbara Leigh, 45, 54n3
The Book of Werewolves: Being an Account of a Terrible Superstition, 150
born criminal, 103–5, 119, 124–25, 130
Botting, Fred, 2, 8, 9, 147
Boys Own Paper, 49
Braddon, Mary Elizabeth, 2, 127–32, 134, 158
Braidotti, Rosi, 15, 101, 106, 125, 132, 186
Breuer, Josef, and Sigmund Freud, 7–8, 38–39, 97n1
The Bride of Lammermoor, 85, 97n4
Brontë, Charlotte, 2, 61, 74, 80–82, 84–85, 87–90, 93–94, 97n2, 164
Brontë, Emily, 2, 61, 66–68, 70–77, 79, 93
Brown, Isaac Baker, 39, 62
Burkean figure, 82
Butler, Judith, 108
Byronic anti-hero, 66

cannibalism, 114, 118, 150, 162
Chaos, 126
chaotic nature, 9, 101, 141
Carpenter, Mary, 103
Carter, Robert Brudenell, 8, 25, 29–30, 38–39, 65, 102
Cartesian dualism, 3, 5, 10, 12–13, 15, 20n4, 28, 58, 64–65, 85, 102, 109, 145, 152, 169, 183
Chaplin, Sue, 116
Charlotte Brontë and Victorian Psychology, 80
chastity, 30, 33–34, 41–43, 46, 52, 84, 86
Cheyne, George, 55

the Christian Church, 30, 47, 49–50, 54n2, 54n4, 122, 130
Christian morality, 37, 49, 52
Church of England Quarterly Review, 49
clitoridectomy, 39
Cohen, Jeffrey Jerome, 141, 167, 173
Collins, Wilkie, 55
colonialism, 73
conduct manuals, 24, 37, 50–55, 73, 100, 184, 186
conventional femininity, 30, 33–34, 37, 120, 124, 130, 132, 184
conventional roles, 33, 43, 46
Coole, Diana and Samantha Frost, 14
conatus, 3, 5, 106, 157, 161, 167–68
confessions, 25, 27, 57–58, 137
consciousness, 5, 12, 29, 58, 61, 75, 86, 99, 107–10, 115, 132–33, 136, 138n3, 143, 154, 174, 181n5
constructivism, 12, 14
Coogan, Michael, 34
Cornhill Magazine, 103
Cott, Nancy, 40, 41
Coudray, Chantal Bourgault du, 151, 158, 170, 175
Crawford, Joseph, 164
Crazy Jane, 91, 93–94
Creed, Barbara, 168, 170, 176, 178
Creole, 82
criminal, criminality, 2, 4–5, 7–8, 15–16, 18–19, 59, 99–106, 110–22, 124, 130–38, 139n3, 141, 143, 145, 148, 151, 157, 165–66, 175, 180, 184–86
criminology, 102–5, 125, 156, 166

Daggers, Jenny, 47
The Daisy Chain, 49
dark double, 81–82
Darwin, Charles, 10, 30–32, 46, 52–53, 58–59, 63, 73, 83, 102–5, 108–9, 123, 136, 138n3, 146–47, 150–51, 156, 171–72
Davison, Carol Margaret, 6, 95

degeneration, degeneracy, 1, 7–8, 20n2, 33, 38, 72, 74, 77–78, 102–3, 105, 125, 130, 138n3, 139n6, 142–43, 146–47, 150–52, 155, 163–64, 171–72, 175, 184

Del Principe, David, 119

DeLamotte, Eugenia, 3, 9–10, 67–68, 70, 87, 95

Deleuze, Giles, and Felix Guattari, 107

Deleuzian concept, 101

Descartes, René, 12–13

The Descent of Man, and Selection in Relation to Sex, 104

deviance, 99–100, 102, 105, 115, 131, 134–35, 137, 147, 164, 166, 170

dichotomy, 7, 24, 34, 47, 78, 94, 100, 158, 183

Dickens, Charles, 117

dime novel, 93

Doane, Mary Anne, 124

domestication, 26, 33, 37, 43–45, 47–54, 60, 64, 81–82, 112, 128, 160–61, 186

Dora, 60, 97n1

double, doubleness, 9, 41–43, 64, 81–82, 88, 96, 128, 141, 160, 167, 179

double standards, 41–43, 88

Douglas Jerrold's Weekly Newspaper, 66

Drysdale, George R., 30

Dyer, Richard, 42, 160–61

Dynamic Core, 109–10, 123, 133

Easley, Alexis, and Shannon Scott, 151, 159, 163, 176, 179

ecocriticism, 2–3, 18, 106–7

ecofeminism, 90

ecoGothic, 4, 16–17, 70, 91–92, 132, 160, 177, 183

Ecogothic in Nineteenth-Century American Literature, 92

ecology, ecological, 18, 39, 89, 92, 107

ecophobia, 4, 92–93, 107, 183

Edelman, Gerald, 108–10, 114–15, 123, 133, 136, 154

ego, 78, 88, 106, 153–54, 166, 181n5, 181n6

elder women, 95

Ellis, Sarah Stickney, 25, 37, 50–53, 73, 101, 105, 148, 160, 184

embodied wildness, 75

embodiment, 3, 10–11, 15–17, 24, 35–36, 38, 42, 44, 66–7, 69, 81, 96, 102, 107, 110, 112, 120, 123, 126, 131–32, 142–44, 152, 155–59, 161–62, 164–68, 175–77, 180, 183–85

the English malady, 55–56

environment, 4–5, 10, 14, 16–19, 20n2, 35, 37, 48, 53, 54n1, 56–60, 65, 68, 70–71, 89–93, 99–100, 105–10, 112–28, 130, 132–3, 136–37, 138n3, 139n6, 142–43, 147, 154–56, 160–61, 165, 169, 173–74, 176–78, 181n5, 183, 186

ephemeral, 2, 4, 100, 108

epigenetics, 109

Erebus, 126

erotomania, 84–86, 93, 96

Errym, Malcolm J., 117–19, 121–27, 139n7

Esquirol, Jean-Étienne Dominique, 32, 74, 76, 79, 84–85, 97n3

essentialism, 2, 6, 43, 54, 58, 104, 183–84

Estok, Simon, 92

ethology, 58–59

evangelicalism, evangelicals, 47, 49

Eve, 34, 39, 46–47, 122

evolutionary theory, 1, 10, 30, 103, 146–47, 149, 150, 153, 171, 173

excess, 23, 29, 37, 39, 49, 62, 64, 80, 84, 86–89, 96, 105, 129, 135–36, 144, 146, 150–51, 184–85

Faust, 164–65, 181n10

feedback loop, 55, 57, 185

Female Gothic, 9–10, 12, 14, 24, 54, 66, 93–94, 100, 121, 178, 183

The Female Grotesque: Risk, Excess and Modernity, 64
female madness, 2, 39, 55–56, 58, 64–66, 74, 77, 79–80, 84–86, 88–89, 91–92, 94–95, 97n4, 101, 115, 128, 131, 134–35, 150, 163–64, 178
female monstrosity, 1–5, 14–15, 17, 128, 143, 146, 150, 154, 157–58, 167–68, 170, 183, 185
The Female Offender, 103
female sexuality, 5–6, 8, 10–11, 23–26, 28, 30, 35–36, 38–39, 41, 46, 63, 67, 80, 85, 87–88, 90, 94, 122, 141–43, 146, 151–53, 155, 159, 164, 176, 184
female subjugation, 12, 19, 24, 28, 31–32, 38, 40, 46, 50, 66, 87, 94, 101, 180
femininity, 3, 6, 11, 16, 18–19, 23–24, 26, 30–31, 33–34, 36–37, 41–45, 47–54, 54n1, 55–56, 66, 68–69, 72–73, 75, 77–78, 80–83, 93, 99–101, 103–4, 112–13, 115–18, 120–22, 124–25, 127, 129–33, 138, 142, 158, 160–61, 163, 165–68, 178–79, 184–86
femme animale, 178–80
femme fatale, 101, 112, 124
figuration(s), 2–5, 7–17, 19, 24, 33–34, 43–45, 54, 56–61, 64–67, 69–70, 75, 77, 79–80, 82–83, 87–88, 92–93, 95–96, 97n3, 100–101, 105–7, 109–12, 116–21, 124–28, 130–34, 141–45, 150, 152, 154–58, 160–62, 164, 167, 171, 173–75, 178–80, 183, 185–86
fin-de-siècle, 7, 154, 172
Fincher, Max, 155
finite modes, 13
fixed action pattern (FAP), 58
Flanders, Judith, 47
folklore, 150–52, 162, 173, 181n4
Foucault, Michel, 15, 23, 25–27, 42, 57, 153
fragmentation, 7, 11–12, 66–68, 71, 78, 93, 101, 121, 129, 143–44, 186

Franck, Kaja and Janine Hatter, 179
Frank Starr's Fifteen Cent Illustrated Novels, 90
Frankenstein, 89
Freud, Sigmund, 7–8, 38–39, 60–61, 66, 69, 76, 97n1, 97n3, 151, 153–54, 181n5
Frost, Brian J., 14, 158, 168
full moon, 163–65

gender ideologies, 1, 6, 10–11, 64, 115, 161, 184
genetics, 75, 102, 109, 138n3
George, Sam, and William Hughes, 141, 152
George IV, 117–18, 122, 125, 139n8
Gibbs, Anna, 119–20
Gilbert, Panela K., 43
Gilbert, Sandra, and Susan Gubar, 9, 78, 81–82
Gilbert, Sandra M., 88
Girdwood, G. F., 148
Girls Own Paper, 49
The Gothic Body: Sexuality, Materialism, and Degeneration at the Fin de Siècle, 154
gothic fiction, 2, 4–5, 7, 9–10, 12, 56–57, 61, 80, 100, 106, 111, 118, 143, 150, 152, 154, 186
gothic girl child, 67
gothic scholarship, 3
"The Gray Wolf," 142, 146, 172–80
the Great Divide, 144, 180
Greg, W. R., 35
Grosz, Elizabeth, 18, 69, 75, 147, 152–54, 156, 166–68, 181n6, 184, 186
grotesque, 12, 20n5, 64, 94–96, 122, 124
grotesque bodies, 64, 122

Halberstam, Jack, 130, 186
Haraway, Donna, 14–15
Hatter, Janine, 177, 179
Heathcliff, 61, 66–79, 120, 186
heaven, 44, 48, 170

Heiland, Donna, 82
Hekman, Susan, 100
helpmeet, 2, 34, 39, 47, 51
heredity, hereditary, 89, 105, 128, 135, 147, 170
Highmore, Ben, 106
The History of Sexuality, 27
Hoeveler, Diane, 82
Höing, Anja, 16
Horner, Avril and Sue Zlosnik, 36, 95–96
Housman, Clemence, 158, 162
Howard, Jaqueline, 7
Humorist, 155
Hurley, Kelly, 154–55, 157, 174–75, 181n7
hybrid, hybridity, 115, 141, 142, 144, 151, 156–57, 167–68, 172–73, 176–79
hypersexuality, 158–59
hypochondriasis, 56
hysteria, 4–5, 7–8, 29, 36–39, 53, 56–66, 71–72, 74–80, 84–86, 91–96, 148, 157, 186
hysterical conversion disorder, 56–57, 61
hysterical exhibition, 56, 63–66, 70, 77, 79, 84–86, 91, 94

id, 151, 153, 181n5
ideologies, 1, 6, 10–11, 14–15, 20, 23–26, 29, 31, 33–34, 36, 38, 41, 43–45, 47–48, 50–52, 54–55, 57, 64, 74, 79–80, 99, 100, 115, 120, 128, 131, 133, 138, 139n6, 143, 145, 152, 157, 161–62, 171, 184–85
ignis fatuus, 110–11
imitation, 31, 104, 118–21
immaterial-material, 13, 60, 112, 152, 172, 174
immateriality, 13–14, 25, 45–46, 85, 152
imperialism, 82, 156
impersonation, impersonator, 65
In the Company of Wolves: Werewolves, Wolves and Wild Children, 142

Indigenous, 31, 73, 82–83, 105, 144
innocence, 67, 94, 99, 128, 130–31, 133, 167
instincts, 1, 3–6, 8–10, 16, 19, 20n2, 23–25, 31–36, 38–41, 45, 47, 52, 52, 56–61, 63–66, 68–73, 76, 78, 80–89, 91, 94, 96, 99–100, 102, 105, 110, 112, 119–20, 127, 129, 134, 138, 139n6, 141–44, 146, 149, 152–54, 162, 166–69, 171–72, 175–77, 179–80, 181n5, 183–85
institutional rhetoric, 1–3, 7, 9–10, 15, 23–27, 30–31, 33–34, 46, 58–59, 103, 105, 166, 184
intra-action, 15
Irigaray, Luce, 63–64, 66, 68–69, 76–79, 85–86, 88, 118, 120, 134

Jonson, Ben, 149, 181n2

Keetley, Dawn and Matthew Sivils, 17, 92, 183
Kingsley Kent, Susan, 26, 32
Klein, Herbert, 131
Knelman, Judith, 102
Kramer, Heinrich, and Jacob Sprenger, 47
Kröger, Lisa, 17, 169

L'uomo delinquent, 103
Lady "Lucy" Audley, 127–38
language, 7, 9, 11, 14–15, 20n5, 25, 31, 32, 37, 43, 46, 48–49, 55, 63, 73, 89, 104–5, 121, 143, 156, 161
Lamarck, Jean-Baptiste, 10, 102, 109, 138n3, 147, 150, 151
Latour, Bruno, 144
Laycock, Thomas, 8, 25, 29–30, 33, 36–38, 48, 59–60, 102, 147–49, 157, 162
Liggins, Emma, 40
Lombroso, Cesare, and William Ferrero, 1, 2, 31–32, 46, 103–5, 112, 115, 117, 119, 122, 124–25, 130, 134–35, 156, 166, 175

Lord, Beth, 13, 168, 174
lower races, 31, 73, 104, 156
Lucia, Lucy, 85
lycanthrope, lycanthropy, 4, 141, 145, 150–52, 155, 159, 162, 164, 168, 171, 175, 178–79
lype-monomania, 71, 74, 76, 78–79, 97n3

MacDonald, George, 2, 142, 146, 162, 172–80
Mack, Robert L., 111–13, 115–16
madwoman, madwomen, 2, 15–16, 18–19, 53, 56–59, 62, 66–67, 75–77, 79–85, 87–88, 90–94, 96, 97n3, 118, 127, 134–37, 141, 143, 145, 163, 177–78, 180, 185
The Madwoman in the Attic, 81
The Making of Victorian Sexuality, 148–49
maladies, 29, 35, 49, 55–57, 61–62, 72, 74, 96, 137, 178
The Man from Ironbark, 111, 139n5
Mangham, Andrew, 100–101, 115, 131
mapped bodies, 4, 180
mapping, 5, 15, 58–59, 61, 110, 114, 123, 132–33, 136, 154
Margree, Victoria, and Bryony Randall, 147
Marryat, Frederick, 142, 146, 155–64, 167, 171–72, 174–75, 176, 178, 180, 181n8
Mason, Michael, 24, 28, 148–49
material-semiotic, 2–3, 8, 14–15, 19, 20, 65, 77, 80, 101, 106, 111, 132, 138, 143, 145, 152, 155, 160–62, 172, 175, 180, 183, 185
Mayhew, Henry, 103
Maynard, John, 88, 90
McClintock, Anne, 73, 83, 89, 105
McWilliam, Rohan, 111
melancholy, 74, 79
menopause, 29, 101, 150
menstruation, 29, 92, 146, 148–49, 163
Merchant, Carolyn, 16–17, 60

metamorphic, metamorphosis, 16, 33, 106, 124, 152, 154, 175, 184
metaphorical boundaries, 3
middle class, 6, 26, 34, 39, 42, 44, 47–48, 50–52, 72–73, 75, 78, 80, 103, 111–14, 128, 131, 134, 139n6, 151, 179
Milbank, Allison, 86
Mill, John Stuart, 23, 25, 45–46, 54n3
Millingen, John Gideon, 28
mimesis, mimetic, 118–22, 124, 126, 132–34
mimic, 76, 112, 117–18, 121, 123, 127, 133, 137, 166
mind-body, 4–5, 12–15, 18–20, 56–61, 63–65, 72, 78–79, 84, 86, 99–101, 108–10, 132, 141, 143–45, 148, 152–54, 156–57, 162, 167, 169, 174, 176, 178, 180, 183, 185
mirror, 10, 34, 43, 65, 68, 76, 78, 82, 88, 90–95, 158–59, 161, 163, 176
misogyny, 186
Mitchell, Jane, 45, 47, 91
Mitchell, Juliet, 4, 5
Mitchell, Silas Weir, 62
Mitten, Diane, and Chiana D'Amore, 18
modes and attributes, 12–13, 106, 128, 141, 157, 169, 174
Moers, Ellen, 9
monism, 2–3, 5, 12–13, 18–19, 57, 60, 62–63, 65, 70, 80, 95–96, 106–10, 112, 120, 123, 141–45, 152, 156–57, 180, 183, 185
monomania, 38, 71, 74, 76, 78–79, 85, 96, 97n3
monster, 1–3, 6–7, 10–12, 14–15, 17, 19, 24, 32, 35, 81, 84, 87, 93, 100, 112, 126, 143, 152, 156–57, 159–60, 162, 165, 167–68, 172–73, 175–76, 180, 185–86
monstrous body, 12
The Monstrous-Feminine Film, Feminism Psychoanalysis, 168
Moore, Jason, 144–45

morals, morality, 2, 4, 6, 9, 11, 17, 20n2, 23–26, 30–38, 40–41, 43–53, 60, 64–66, 68, 71, 77–78, 80–84, 88–89, 96, 100, 102–3, 105, 117, 126–78, 131, 135–36, 139n6, 147–49, 159–60, 171, 181n5, 184

mother(s), motherhood, 6–7, 23, 33, 36, 39, 42, 45, 47, 50–52, 77–78, 81, 91, 94–96, 97n4, 101, 118, 122, 131, 135, 148, 159, 161, 163, 167, 170, 172, 176, 179

Mulvey-Roberts, Marie, 11, 143

Murdoch, Lydia, 44, 53

myth, 31, 122, 143, 150–51, 166–67, 169–70, 173, 181n3

narrative(s), 2, 4, 9–11, 16, 18–19, 24, 26, 34, 37, 40, 49–50, 57, 59, 66–67, 75, 77, 80, 88, 91–93, 96, 97n1, 103, 110, 126–27, 142, 146, 151–52, 155, 157–58, 164–65, 167–68, 170–71, 175, 177, 180, 185–86

natural selection, 109, 123, 138, 147, 171

nature-culture, 12, 132, 162

nervous system, 29, 37, 38, 59, 61, 63, 72, 85, 86–87, 102, 148, 149, 153

Neural Darwinism, 108–10

Neural Darwinism: The Theory of Neuronal Group Selection, 108–9

neural mapping, 58–59, 114, 132

neurasthenia, 62, 94

neurology, 2–3, 56–57, 109

Neuronal Theory, 61

new materialism, 2

New Monthly Magazine, 155

the New Woman, 147, 158, 163

New York Mercury, 90

Newgate Novel, 111

nympho-erotomania, 84–85

nymphomania, 32, 39, 84–85, 88

occasional offender, 104, 112, 117, 119, 125, 130

Of Queens' Gardens, 48

Oliver Twist, 117

ontology, 11, 17, 19, 44, 107, 113, 119, 122, 125, 130–31, 185

Ophelia, 75–76, 93

Ortner, Sherry, 16, 60

other, otherness, 11, 73, 82–83, 100–101, 105, 107, 131, 133, 144–45, 152, 159, 174–76

Owen, Marianne E., 103

Oxford Movement, 49–50

Parker, Elizabeth, and Michele Poland, 115

pathology, pathologization, 6, 8, 27, 36–37, 40, 61, 64, 74–76, 78–79, 83, 102, 105, 178, 184

Patmore, Coventry, 24, 43–45, 48, 51, 54n2, 83, 112, 130

Patmore, Emily, 54n2

penny bloods, penny dreadfuls, 2, 20n1, 90–91, 93, 97n6, 100, 110–12, 117–18, 127–28, 139n4, 139n8, 109n9, 164, 185–86

The People's Periodical, 110

performativity, 108, 119

Perils of the Night: A Feminist Study of Nineteenth-Century Gothic, 67

phallogocentric, 11, 16, 101, 133, 153

The Phantom Ship, 155

Plumwood, Val, 10, 160

Poovey, Mary, 28, 34

poststructuralism, 15

prescribed roles, 4, 6, 9, 11, 27, 32, 50, 63, 96, 146, 153, 185

Prichard, James Cowle, 84, 135

Priest, Hannah, 151–52, 159

primitivity, 11, 31, 58, 68, 83, 87, 89, 103, 105, 120, 144, 146–50, 153, 156, 158, 162–63, 168, 170–72, 174, 176–77

prostitution, 30, 40, 43

pseudoscience, 6, 10, 55, 57, 96, 122, 163

psyche-soma, 86–87

psychoanalysis, 2–4, 60–61, 168

psychosomatic, 2–5, 8, 29–30, 33, 36, 39, 56–57, 59–65, 72, 74–75, 78–79, 81, 85–86, 88, 91–92, 94–96, 105, 136, 141, 150–51, 154, 174, 176, 183, 186
puberty, 29, 33, 59, 101, 146, 148–49
Punch, 103
pure woman, 27
Pykett, Lyn, 128

race(s), 31–32, 52, 73, 104, 121, 156, 160, 186
radical constructivism, 14
recidivism, 148
reductionism, 2, 4–6, 12, 14–16, 20, 25, 27–28, 30, 40, 54, 60, 64, 109, 144, 153, 174, 183–84
The Religious Tract Society, 49
repression, 1–10, 15, 19, 23–24, 30, 36, 38–39, 46, 54, 56, 58, 61, 63–64, 66–69, 71–81, 83–84, 86, 88–91, 93, 96, 99–100, 132, 141–42, 144–46, 152, 166–67, 174, 175, 183–86
"Repressive Hypothesis," 27
reproductivity, 4, 6, 10, 16, 25, 32, 38–39, 43, 52–53, 58, 92, 143, 148, 158, 162, 170, 180
Reynolds, George W. M., 2, 142, 146, 162, 164–72, 180
Reynolds' Magazine of Romance, General Literature, Science and Art, 164
Richerche sul cretinismo in Lombardia, 103
Roman Catholicism, 44, 54n2
Royal, Anna, 129
Royal Marriage Act, 125
Ruskin, John, 8, 25, 47–49, 73, 83, 112, 130–31, 160
Russo, Mary, 12, 20n5, 64, 95–96, 122
Rymer, James Malcolm, 2, 90–91, 111–22, 114, 116–17, 139n4, 139n7, 162, 164, 181n9

savage(s), 31, 68–69, 71, 73, 82–83, 87, 104–5, 151–52, 156, 160, 162, 168, 170, 173, 176, 178
Saxby, Jessie, 173
scientia sexualis, 27
Scott, Walter, 85, 97n4
Scull, Andrew, 65
Sedgwick, Eve Kosofsky, 9
Seigworth, Gregory J., and Melissa Gregg, 132
semiotic web, 16
Sesames and Lilies, 48
"Seven Theses" of monstrosity, 12, 167
This Sex Which Is Not One, 118
Shaefer, Donovan, 108
Shakespeare, William, 75
shapeshifter(s), 18, 142–43, 145, 150, 155–57, 163, 173–74, 185
she-monster, 2–3, 14
she-wolf, she-wolves, 2, 15–16, 18–19, 125, 141–46, 150–52, 154–63, 166, 170, 172–76, 178–80, 185
She-Wolf: A Cultural History of Female Werewolves, 151
Shildrick, Margrit, 150, 157
Showalter, Elaine, 4, 35, 56, 64–65, 75, 85, 91, 135
Shuttleworth, Sally, 7, 80–81, 84–85
Sixteen-String Jack, 123, 139n9
Smith, Andrew, 11
Smith, Andrew, and William Hughes, 70, 89, 92, 129
Smith, William Tyler, 28
social hierarchies, 146
somatogenesis, 39
somatophobia, 153
Sparks, Tabitha, 130
spatial model, 3, 9
Speculum of the Other Woman, 63, 134
Spinoza, Benedict de, 3, 13, 19, 106, 108, 156–57, 183
spirituality, 28, 33, 38, 40–42, 44, 48, 51, 88, 95, 166
Spivak, Gayatri Chakravorty, 82
status quo, 39, 155

stereotypes and metaphors, 3, 7, 17, 25–27, 30–31, 34–35, 41, 43–45, 48, 56, 62, 65, 67, 73, 74–76, 81, 84–85, 91, 106, 110, 115, 117–18, 120, 122, 125, 127, 137, 143, 167–68
subjectivity, 2, 5, 11, 14–16, 20n4, 24, 34, 44, 66, 80, 82, 101, 110, 119, 125, 133, 152–54, 156, 180, 184, 186
sublimation, 5, 53, 63, 86, 132, 134, 151, 184
substance, 5, 13, 18–19, 69, 106–7, 109, 145, 152, 156–57, 169, 174, 178, 180n1
Summerscale, Kate, 83
Sylph and Hebe, 166
symbolism, 4, 174
symptoms, 56, 60–62, 65, 74, 97n3

Talairach-Vielmas, Laurence, 77, 94, 129
theology, 24, 34, 40–41, 43, 46, 122, 186
theriomorphic, 92
Tomkins, Silvan, 107, 138n2
Torgerson, Beth, 74
Tractarianism, 49
transformation(s), 10, 13, 16, 18, 27, 64, 67, 101, 120–21, 124, 132, 141–42, 145–46, 151, 154, 158, 163–64, 172–75, 177, 179, 184, 186
transgression, 3, 9–10, 65–66, 74–75, 80, 87, 89, 93–96, 115, 117, 126–27, 130, 132, 141–42, 145–47, 154, 161, 170, 175–76
Treatise on Insanity, 84
treatises/journals, 25–26, 37, 57, 148
Tylor, Edward Burnett, 31

undomesticated space, 17, 169
upper class, 6, 20n2, 23–24, 27, 34, 37, 41, 44, 48–50, 52, 54, 54n1, 64, 83, 120, 124, 127, 129–31, 133, 139n6, 142, 166, 185–86
Urban, Septimus R., 61, 90–96, 97nn5–6, 164

uterus, uterine theory, 28–30, 37

vampire, 74, 87
Varney, the Vampire, 90, 164
vendetta, 94, 97n7
The Vendetta: Or a Lesson in Life, 90
Vicinus, Martha, 129
Victorian Gothic, 1, 3–6, 9–10, 12, 14, 56–57, 61, 64, 77, 99–101, 107, 110, 141, 143–46, 183, 185–86
villain, 7, 11, 68, 91, 93, 97n4, 103, 111–12, 115, 119, 121, 124, 127, 168
Violent Women and Sensation Fiction: Crime, Medicine, and Victorian Popular Culture, 100
visibility, 26, 48, 61, 63, 128, 134, 143, 175, 178
Volatile Bodies: Toward a Corporeal Feminism, 152
Voskuil, Lyn M., 127–28

Wallace, Diane, and Andrew Smith, 121
Walsh, Brendan C., 145
Ward, Ian, 49, 126
Watkins, Megan, 108
weaker sex, 32, 51
The Were-Wolf, 158
werewolf, werewolves, 141–6, 150–52, 154–55, 157–60, 162–65, 168–70, 173, 175–77, 180
Western religion, 34, 38, 47, 54n2, 177
White Fell, 158
whiteness, 160–61, 163, 166
whore, 6–7, 14, 20, 23, 25, 34–35, 53–54, 185
wildness, 4, 6, 19, 37, 58, 72, 75–6, 78, 92–93, 122, 162–63, 169, 171
William, William Smith, 84
Williams, Anne, 95
Willis, Martin, 67
Wilson, Elizabeth A., 57, 60–62, 78, 87–88, 94, 154
Winslow, Forbes, 25, 33, 38, 40, 52–53, 148–49, 157, 159–60
Wisker, Gina, 87, 185

witchcraft, 151
womanhood, 6–7, 14, 20n2, 24–26, 31–33, 36, 43–44, 48, 51–54, 60, 73, 75, 79–81, 83, 95, 100, 103, 116, 125, 130–31, 133, 137, 139n6, 142, 148, 150, 152, 161, 164, 184
The Women of England, Their Social Duties, and Domestic Habits, 51
Wood, Jane, 43, 53

working class, 20n2, 54n1, 111–12, 130, 139n6
Works of Fancy and Imagination, 172
wulver, 173

Yonge, Charlotte Mary, 49–50

Zedner, Lucia, 103
zoology, 31, 149

About the Author

Dr. Nicole C. Dittmer is a lecturer at The College of New Jersey and proofreader/editorial board member for *Studies in Gothic Fiction*. Her classes, "The Seduction of Horror and Human Behavior," "Scream Queens and Final Girls: Gender and the Horror Genre," and "Transnationalism and the Global Gothic: Literary Explorations of the Suppressed Voice," address interdisciplinary topics of ecocriticism, medical humanities, and human behavior in Gothic and Horror media. She received her PhD in English and Gothic Studies from Manchester Metropolitan University, UK, in 2021 with a doctoral thesis entitled "Wilderness and Female 'Monstrosity': A Material Ecofeminist Reading of Victorian Gothic Fiction." Some of her published works include "Malignancy of Goneril: Nature's Powerful Warrior," in Krishanu Maiti and Soumyadeep Chakraborty's edited collection, *Global Perspectives on Eco-Aesthetics and Eco-Ethics: A Green Critique* (Lexington, 2020); "Victorian Literature and Ecofeminism," in Douglas A. Vakoch's collection, *The Routledge Handbook of Ecofeminism and Literature* (Routledge, 2022); and is an editor, along with Sophie Raine, and contributor to, the forthcoming collection *Penny Dreadfuls and the Gothic: Investigations of Pernicious Tales of Terror* (University of Wales Press, 2022).

Website: www.nicoledittmer.com
Twitter: @Goth_Prof

www.ingramcontent.com/pod-product-compliance
Lightning Source LLC
Chambersburg PA
CBHW020117010526
44115CB00008B/864